JOSEPH BRODSKY

Joseph Brodsky

The Art of a Poem

Edited by

Lev Loseff

and

Valentina Polukhina

First published in Great Britain 1999 by
MACMILLAN PRESS LTD
Houndmills, Basingstoke, Hampshire RG21 6XS and London
Companies and representatives throughout the world

A catalogue record for this book is available from the British Library.

ISBN 0–333–72040–7

First published in the United States of America 1999 by
ST. MARTIN'S PRESS, INC.,
Scholarly and Reference Division,
175 Fifth Avenue, New York, N.Y. 10010

ISBN 0–312–21834–6

Library of Congress Cataloging-in-Publication Data
Joseph Brodsky : the art of a poem / edited by Lev Loseff and
Valentina Polukhina.
p.   cm.
Includes bibliographical references and index.
ISBN 0–312–21834–6 (cloth)
1. Brodsky, Joseph, 1940–   —Criticism and interpretation.
I. Losev, Lev, 1937–   .   II. Polukhina, Valentina.
PG3479.4.R64Z735   1998
811'.54—dc21
                                                  98–26149
                                                  CIP

This book is printed on paper suitable for recycling and made from fully managed and
sustained forest sources.

10   9   8   7   6   5   4   3   2   1
08   07   06   05   04   03   02   01   00   99

Printed and bound in Great Britain by
Antony Rowe Ltd, Chippenham, Wiltshire

Contents

Preface		vi
Acknowledgements		xii
Notes on the Contributors		xiii
1	**'Singing without Music'** *Gerry Smith*	1
2	**'Odysseus to Telemachus'** *Liudmila Zubova*	26
3	**'On the Death of Zhukov'** *Mikhail Yu. Lotman*	44
4	**'1867'** *Roman Timenchik*	59
5	**'I, Instead of a Wild Beast . . .'** *Valentina Polukhina*	68
6	**'To Urania'** *Barry P. Scherr*	92
7	**'Lithuanian Nocturne'** *Tomas Venclova*	107
8	**'Galatea Encore'** *Leon Burnett*	150
9	**'The Thought of You Is Going Away . . .'** *Willem G. Weststeijn*	177
10	**'Belfast Tune'** *Robert Reid*	191
11	**'Darling, Tonight I Went Out Late . . .'** *Sergey Kuznetsov*	207
12	**'On the Centenary of Anna Akhmatova'** *Lev Loseff*	225
13	**'To My Daughter'** *David M. Bethea*	240

Preface

It was a conscious decision on the part of this book's editors not to strive for methodological uniformity. As a sophisticated literary scholar once said, 'I am really interested in only one thing – an explanation of why the poem gave me such pleasure or shocked me so powerfully, or disturbed me; the rest is just technique.' When our contributors were trying to interpret their relationship with a chosen poem they were guided by an intuition which had evolved over years of reading Joseph Brodsky's poetry, and in some cases they found it useful to refer to facts of the poet's biography and cultural background; in other cases to see how Brodsky's recurrent 'motifs' materialized in one particular text, in still others to hunt for classical and contemporary echoes, or to concentrate on aspects of versification, or, more often than not, to combine some or all of these pursuits. Nevertheless, the reader will find an element of constancy in this motley collection: in almost every article there is a place where the author explains what makes the poem under scrutiny unlike all other poems by Brodsky – an unprecedented metrical pattern, a new treatment of familiar subject matter, heretofore unheard diction, and so forth. This insistence on uniqueness came as a surprise to the editors, who also, in their own respective contributions, enthusiastically proclaimed their chosen poems as unique.

This is also, perhaps, the most significant result yielded by the collective effort: the autonomy of the individual poem within Brodsky's *œuvre*. The result is even more surprising, if one considers how prolific Brodsky was: there are 606 poems in his fullest collection to date,[1] which is probably one half of his total output (a great number of poems, especially early ones, were edited out by the poet). For comparison, the complete poetic works by Fedor Tiutchev (1803–73), whose life was some fifteen years longer than Brodsky's, number 402 (including the preserved juvenilia and incidental verses), and there are 756 pieces (including a significant number of unfinished drafts, some of which are only 3–4 lines long) in the 'complete poetry' of Anna Akhmatova (1889–1966), whose life was twenty years longer.

The autonomous status of an individual poem in Brodsky's world has been corroborated by some earlier observations of the unusual, indeed unsurpassed, diversity of stanzaic forms in Brodsky's poetry[2] and of his vast repertoire of genres, some of which are yet to be named.[3] He experimented with various poetic genres – descriptive poems, odes, elegies and sonnets – by introducing new and provocative elements into their structure, prosody and syntax. Adding to that the fact that Brodsky had little propensity for stylistically unified cycles, let alone 'books', so common in twentieth-century Russian poetry,[4] we realize that his creativity was utterly discrete: with very few exceptions, such as the cycles 'The July Intermezzo' (1961), 'Instruction to an Inmate' (1964), 'The Songs of a Happy Winter' (1964–5), 'From the "School Anthology"' (1968–9) and 'A Part of Speech' (1974–6). The composition of each new poem implied a search for a yet untried stylistic strategy.

This book comprises thirteen analytical studies of individual poems written between 1970 and 1994 when Brodsky reached maturity and the peak of his poetic career (in 1987 he was awarded the Nobel Prize for Literature and in 1991 he was appointed Poet Laureate of the United States). The broad selection of poems draws together those most representative of Brodsky in terms of the sheer variety of poetic means: his use of metre and rhymes, the type of stanza form, syntax and vocabulary, conceits, tropes and figures of speech. The choice of poems reflects Brodsky's diversity of themes, such as those of time, faith and love, loss and grief, meditation on fate and poetry, death and memory. Since Brodsky is a highly referential poet, some contributors have tried to unravel the main hidden allusions to Latin, Russian, English and American poetry, culture and history, in order to promote an understanding of key philosophical ideas which are contained in his poetry. Each essay aims at a balance between detailed structural analysis and commentary upon Brodsky's principal themes.

Among the contributors are two poets, Russian and Lithuanian; some are young, others well-established Brodsky scholars; two of them were witnesses of the events described in the poems. Professor Venclova, a long-standing friend of the poet, the addressee of 'Lithuanian Nocturne', provides a biographical background to the context of a 'Lithuanian cycle' in Brodsky's works. Robert Reid was a Lecturer at Queen's University, Belfast at the time of Brodsky's visit to the city. They are in a unique position to unravel the sphinx-like quality of their respective poems.

Gerry Smith has chosen for his interpretation one of the most Donnean of Brodsky's poems, 'Singing without Music' (1970), which he considers one of the great longer love poems of twentieth-century Russian literature. He shows how Brodsky made the most common Russian metre sound completely original by inventing a rhythm that goes against all the norms. Brodsky's outrageously elaborate conceits evoke two of the best-known love poems by Marvell and Donne. This 'almost excessively original achievement' is a poem about emotional passion being mastered with the aid of intellectual passion.

Two of Brodsky's poems in the genre of mourning are subjects for discussion – 'On the Death of Zhukov' (the Soviet Second World War military commander, 1974), discussed by Mikhail Yu. Lotman, and 'The Thought of You is Going Away...' (1985), discussed by Willem Weststeijn. Professor Lotman provides a careful comparison between Brodsky's poem and Derzhavin's 'Bullfinch' (written on the occasion of Suvorov's death): both poets used a very rare metre and were fond of stylistic conflict and antithesis. While Mikhail Lotman deals with Brodsky's treatment of a national hero, Professor Weststeijn comments on the poem which commemorates the death of the poet's mother. He looks at the development of the lyrical plot which is constructed from a succession of statements, observations, quotations and exclamations, drawing a distinction between the author outside and the speaker inside the text. Liudmila Zubova devotes her attention to a subject always central to Brodsky's concerns: the effects of time on man, 'how it changes him', in the poem 'Odysseus to Telemachus' (1972), which is full of biographical and mythological allusions as well as echoes of Mandelshtam's poetry. Her essay indicates the complexity of the poet's vision of our time. Roman Timenchik focuses his attention on Brodsky's use of musical motifs in the poem '1867'(1975), 'this dance in verse', written after Brodsky's trip to Mexico in 1975. In a short and fascinating study, Professor Timenchik demonstrates how the 'implied music causes words to display double semiotic allegiance' when words become signs of themselves.

Another poem of 'musical genres', 'Lithuanian Nocturne', is discussed by Tomas Venclova, who, being a partner in the dialogue as well as a researcher, finds himself in a most unusual position: 'inside' and 'outside' the text under discussion. His extensive study of the poem, on both formal and thematic levels, shows how it moves as if in a single seamless flow, approaching prose, and comes sharply into conflict with its multi-dimensional articulations 'which go beyond the traditional poetics of the nineteenth and twentieth centuries'. Barry Scherr set himself the task of establishing the relationship between the beginning and the end of the poem 'To Urania' (1982) as well as elucidating the key words and images which resist ready interpretation. Being a renowned expert on Russian versification, he scrutinizes the structural elements showing how 'many semantic features of the poem become emphasized through the rhyme words . . . and create natural thematic groupings', how enjambments are used to summarize the theme and how the metre and rhythm affect the poem's structure, in short, how they all work in harmony. Valentina Polukhina's close reading of Brodsky's 40th birthday poem places it in the context of his whole output. She shows how the poet extends the sphere of the possible, both in experience and in its expression, achieving a strangely moving blend of humility and pride, irony and grief. Following in the footsteps of Horace, Derzhavin and Pushkin, Brodsky has created his own *Exegi monumentum*. Another Horatian 'poem-monument' was written by Brodsky 'On the Centenary of Anna Akhmatova' (1989), his dear older friend and mentor. Professor Lev Loseff offers his interpretation of how Akhmatova's monument was made: by borrowing Akhmatova's metre Brodsky achieved 'great artistic economy and depicted her as a regal and tragic heroine, a new Phaedra or Dido, without using direct comparisons and epithets, which had become cliché'. He also points out the extent to which Brodsky departed from the genre of the 'in memoriam' in this particular poem. Sergei Kuznetsov (1989) takes up Brodsky's last love poem, 'Darling, Tonight I Went Out Late . . .', examining a network of motifs in the context of a large cycle of poems dedicated to M.B. and also brings to his discussion the poet's treatment of time and space which are linked to the history of the relationship between the author and his beloved.

For the first time three of Brodsky's poems written in English become a subject of detailed formal and thematic analysis. Dr Leon Burnett unravels broad cultural references in Brodsky's miniature 'Galatea Encore' (1983) from Ovid's *Metamorphoses* to the poets and writers of the twentieth century. He locates the surprising kinship between Brodsky and Berryman. This poem

facilitates discussion of Brodsky's technical resources as well as
his views on art and language. Robert Reid illuminates semantic
meanings of metre in 'Belfast Tune' (1986) and the function of
monosyllabic words as well as the whole lexical organization of
the poem, pointing out Brodsky's ability to address a politically
charged subject without using a single word of political vocabulary. Leaving out of the poem the political reality of Northern
Ireland, Brodsky has demonstrated an exceptional tact, sympathy and detachment: 'This is an extraordinary penetration into
the nature of the Northern Irish Troubles, all the more remarkable for its being effected via structure and poetic artifice.' Robert
Reid detects an Irish accent in Brodsky's use of such rhymes as
'hurt/short' which reveals the exceptional sensitivity of Brodsky's
ear. He goes as far as to suggest that the whole tragic fabric of
the city is carried by the poem's rhymes: hurting and frowning,
violence and trauma. Mr Reid shows that enjambments, especially across the stanza-break (e.g. 'and her stare stains your retina
like a grey / bulb when you switch / / hemisphere') have a significant semantic function in the poem. Professor David Bethea
establishes a link between Brodsky's English poem 'To My
Daughter' (1994) and Robert Frost and Thomas Hardy: the same
'predominance of the rational over emotional immediacy', the
same 'self-deprecation', sustained detachment and merciless self-
irony. All three were capable of taking 'a full look at the worst'.

These three studies demonstrate that Brodsky's English poems
continue to develop the poetics of his Russian verse: implicitly
'unlyrical' diction; the use of the sources and resources of language;
the semantization of every formal and structural element in a poem,
be it rhyme, enjambment or metre. Metamorphoses of man in
history, time, faith and language are his major concern, whether
he is writing in Russian or in English. In both languages he was
seeking to preserve 'words against the time of cold'.

The task set for the authors of this book precluded generaliza-
tions, and yet there are some fundamental questions concerning
Brodsky's art of a poem as a whole. A learned reader would inevitably ask: what determines the length of any of Brodsky's poems
– the subject matter, the prosody, the desire to exhaust thematic
variations or some combination of the above? What are the major characteristics of his lyrical persona and when are disguises
used? What makes Brodsky's openings and closures so memorable?
What about the diachronic development of our poet's concept of

a poem? What is a 'Brodsky poem' in comparison with established tradition? None of the present book's articles provides answers to these questions alone, but we believe that cumulatively they do, and thus enrich our experience of reading Brodsky.

LEV LOSEFF
VALENTINA POLUKHINA

Notes

1. *Sochineniia Iosifa Brodskogo* [Works of Joseph Brodsky], vols I–IV (St Petersburg: Pushkinskii fond, 1992–5). All the references in the present volume are to this edition of Brodsky's work.
2. See Barry Scherr, 'Strofika Brodskogo' [Brodsky's Stanzaic Forms], in *Poetika Brodskogo. Sbornik Statei* [Brodsky's Poetics], ed. Lev Loseff (Tenafly, N.J.: Hermitage, 1986) pp. 97–120.
3. Valentina Polukhina, 'Zhanrovaia klaviatura Brodskogo' [Brodsky's Keyboard of Genres], *Russian Literature*, vol. XXXVII, no. ii–iii, Special Issue: Joseph Brodsky (1995) pp. 145–56.
4. The majority of poems by Alexandr Blok, Anna Akhmatova, Boris Pasternak and Marina Tsvetaeva appear within thematically and stylistically unified cycles, whereas collections published by Khodasevich, Mandelshtam and Zabolotskii display a distinctly uniform style characteristic of the given period in the poet's life. In Brodsky, on the contrary, even when he presents his travelogues ('Lithuanian Divertimento' [1970], 'The Mexican Divertimento' [1974] and 'In England' [1976]) as cycles, we deal with extremely contrasting components: a lyrical poem followed by a comic pastiche followed by an elegy followed by a ballad, etc. (Try to compare, for example, Pasternak's 'Caucasian Divertimento', 'Waves' [1931], to each of the three travel cycles of Brodsky!)

A NOTE ON THE TEXT

All the articles bear the title of their respective poems and are arranged here in the chronological order of the poems under discussion.

Acknowledgements

Acknowledgement is made to Farrar, Straus & Giroux for permission to quote from Brodsky's *Less than One: Selected Essays* (New York, 1986), *Watermark* (New York, 1992), *On Grief and Reason: Essays* (New York, 1995), as well as for permission to reproduce Brodsky's English poems 'Galatea Encore' and 'Belfast Tune' from *To Urania: Selected Poems, 1965–1985* (New York, 1988), and 'To My Daughter' from his last English collection, *So Forth* (New York, 1996).

We are grateful to Pushkinskii fond (St Petersburg) for permission to use ten Russian texts from *Sochineniia Iosifa Brodskogo* [Works of Joseph Brodsky], vols I–IV.

We would also like to acknowledge our gratitude to Brodsky's estate for allowing us to quote from Brodsky's Russian poems. Interlinear translations of Brodsky's original Russian poems are offered here for reference purposes with respect to these essays only and are not to be regarded as definitive or to be reproduced independently.

Notes on the Contributors

The Editors

Lev Loseff is a poet and Professor of Russian Literature at Dartmouth College (New Hampshire), and has published four collections of poems and *On the Beneficence of Censorship: Aesopian Language in Modern Russian Literature* (1984). He edited *Poetika Brodskogo* (1986), *Brodsky's Poetics and Aesthetics* (with Valentina Polukhina, 1990), *Norwich Symposia on Russian Literature and Culture*, vol. I, *Boris Pasternak* (1991), *A Sense of Place: Tsarskoe Selo and its Poets* (with Barry P. Scherr, 1993) and *Iosif Brodskii: Trudy i dni* (with Petr Vail, 1998).

Valentina Polukhina is Professor of Russian Literature at Keele University (England). She specializes in Modern Russian Poetry and is the author of several major studies of Brodsky: *Joseph Brodsky: A Poet for Our Time* (1989), and *Brodsky through the Eyes of his Contemporaries* (1992). She is also the editor of *Brodsky's Genres* (1995) and co-editor, with Lev Loseff, of *Brodsky's Poetics and Aesthetics* (1990) and a principal compiler, with Ülle Pärli, of *The Dictionary of Brodsky's Tropes* (1995).

The Other Contributors

David M. Bethea is Vilas Research Professor of Russian Literature at the University of Wisconsin–Madison (USA). He is the author of various books on modern Russian literature and culture, including *Khodasevich: His Life and Art* (1983), *The Shape of Apocalypse in Modern Russian Fiction* (1989), *Joseph Brodsky and the Creation of Exile* (1994), *Realizing Metaphors: Alexander Pushkin and the Life of the Poet* (Wisconsin, 1998).

Leon Burnett is Reader in Literature at the University of Essex, Colchester. His research interests and publications cover modern Russian poetry, literary translation theory, the revival of myth in

modern culture and Russian fiction before the Soviet era. He edits
New Comparison: A Journal of Comparative and General Literary Studies
and is currently working on a book, *Faces of the Sphinx: Literary
Encounters between Russia and the West.*

Sergey Kuznetsov is a freelance literary and film critic. He has
published numerous articles in *Iskusstvo kino, Inostrannaia literatura,
Znamia, Znakolog, Pynchon Notes* and many other magazines. He
lives in Moscow.

Mikhail Lotman is Professor in the Department of Semiotics and
Literary Theory at the Estonian Institute of Humanities (Tallin).
His publications include numerous articles on semiotics, linguis-
tics, theory of versification and Russian poetry. He is co-editor of
Pushkin's Metrics and Strophics (1979) and *A Collection of Articles
on Russian and Soviet Poetry* (with Z. G. Mints, 1989) and the author
of *Mandelshtam i Pasternak* (1996).

Robert Reid is Reader in Russian Studies at Keele University. He
has translated a number of modern Russian poets, including
Sedakova, Prigov and Prokofiev, as well as lesser-known names
for *Essays in Poetics.* His major research interest is nineteenth-
century Russian romanticism, and publications in this area include *Problems of Russian Romanticism* (1986) and *Pushkin's 'Mozart
and Salieri'* (1995) and *Lermontov's 'A Hero of Our Time'* (1997). He
is currently preparing a monograph on Lermontov.

Barry P. Scherr is Mandel Family Professor of Russian and Associate Dean for the Humanities at Dartmouth College (New Hampshire). His research interests include Russian verse theory,
twentieth-century Russian poetry, and Russian prose from the
late nineteenth and early twentieth centuries; he has published
several articles on Brodsky, *Russian Poetry: Meter, Rhythm and Rhyme*
(1986) and *Maxim Gorky* (1988); his most recent book is *Maksim
Gorky: Selected Letters* (co-editor and co-translator with Andrew
Barratt).

Gerry Smith has been Professor of Russian at the University of
Oxford, and a Fellow of New College since 1986. His recent books
include *Contemporary Russian Poetry: A Bilingual Anthology* (1993),
The Cambridge Encyclopedia of Russian and the Former Soviet Union

(edited with Archie Brown and Michael Kaser, 1994); *The Letters of D. S. Mirsky to P. P. Suvchinsky, 1922–1931* (1995), and (as co-translator and co-editor) M. L. Gasparov, *A History of European Versification* (1996). His translation of Boris Slutsky's poems and prose, *Things that Happened*, will appear in 1998.

Roman Timenchik is Professor of Russian at the Hebrew University of Jerusalem. He has published extensively on Silver Age, especially on Akhmatova, including *Akhmatova i muzyka* (with B. Kats, 1989); he has also compiled and edited an annotated 4-volume edition of Akhmatova's poetry with critical responses and memoirs of her contemporaries (1989).

Tomas Venclova is a poet and Professor of Slavic Literature at Yale University. He has published more than twenty books of poetry and prose in Lithuanian, English and Russian. Among his recent publications are *Winter Dialogue* (1997) and *Sobesedniki na piru: stat'i o russkoi literature* (1997). He is also the author of *Unstable Equilibrium: Eight Russian Poetic Texts* (1986) and *Aleksandr Wat: Life and Art of an Iconoclast* (1996).

Willem G. Weststeijn is Professor of Slavic Literature at the University of Amsterdam (The Netherlands). He is the editor of the international journal *Russian Literature* (Elsevier, Amsterdam) and one of the editors of the series 'Studies in Slavic Literature and Poetics' (Rodopi, Amsterdam). He is also the author of a monograph on Velimir Khlebnikov (1983), and co-author of two introductory books on literary theory and co-editor of a number of books. The most recent is *Vtoraia proza: russkaia proza 20-kh–30-kh godov XX veka* (1995).

Liudmila Zubova is Professor of Russian at St Petersburg University. Her main research interest is the language of post-modernism, and she has published numerous articles on modern Russian poetry, and two monographs, *Poeziia Mariny Tsvetaevoi: lingvisticheskii aspekt* (1989) and *Iazyk Mariny Tsvetaevoi* (1998).

1

'Singing without Music'
Pen'e bez muzyki

GERRY SMITH

———————————————————————

F.W.

Когда ты вспомнишь обо мне
в краю чужом – хоть эта фраза
всего лишь вымысел, а не
пророчество, о чем для глаза,

вооруженного слезой,   5
не может быть и речи: даты
из омута такой лесой
не вытащишь – итак, когда ты

за тридевять земель и за
морями, в форме эпилога   10
(хоть повторяю, что слеза,
за исключением былого,

все уменьшает) обо мне
вспомянешь все-таки в то Лето
Господне и вздохнешь – о не   15
вздыхай! – обозревая это

количество морей, полей,
разбросанных меж нами, ты не
заметишь, что толпу нулей
возглавила сама.   20
            В гордыне

твоей иль в слепоте моей
все дело, или в том, что рано

1

об этом говорить, но ей-
же Богу, мне сегодня странно,　　　　　　　25

что, будучи кругом в долгу,
поскольку ограждал так плохо
тебя от худших бед, могу
от этого избавить вздоха.

Грядущее есть форма тьмы,
сравнимая с ночным покоем.　　　　　　　30
В том будущем, о коем мы
не знаем ничего, о коем,

по крайности, сказать одно
сейчас я в состояньи точно:
что порознь нам суждено　　　　　　　35
с тобой в нем пребывать, и то, что

оно уже настало – рёв
метели, превращенье крика
в глухое толковище слов
есть первая его улика –　　　　　　　40

в том будущем есть нечто, вещь,
способная утешить или
– настолько-то мой голос вещ!
занять воображенье в стиле

рассказов Шахразады, с той　　　　　　　45
лишь разницей, что это больше
посмертный, чем весьма простой
страх смерти у нее – позволь же

сейчас, на языке родных
осин, тебя утешить; и да　　　　　　　50
пусть тени на снегу от них
толпятся как триумф Эвклида.

*　　　*　　　*

Когда ты вспомнишь обо мне,
дня, месяца, Господня Лета
такого-то, в чужой стране,   55
за тридевять земель – а это

гласит о двадцати восьми
возможностях – и каплей влаги
зрачок вооружишь, возьми
перо и чистый лист бумаги   60

и перпендикуляр стоймя
восставь, как небесам опору,
меж нашими с тобой двумя
– да, точками: ведь мы в ту пору

уменьшимся и там, Бог весть,   65
невидимые друг для друга,
почтем еще с тобой за честь
слыть точками; итак, разлука

есть проведение прямой,
и жаждущая встречи пара   70
любовников – твой взгляд и мой –
к вершине перпендикуляра

поднимется, не отыскав
убежища, помимо горних
высот, до ломоты в висках;   75
и это ли не треугольник!

Рассмотрим же фигуру ту,
которая в другую пору
заставила бы нас в поту
холодном пробуждаться, полу-   80

безумных лезть под кран, дабы
рассудок не спалила злоба;
и если от такой судьбы
избавлены мы были оба –

от ревности, примет, комет,   85
от при́воротов, порч, снадобья
– то, видимо, лишь на предмет
черчения его подобья.

Рассмотрим же. Всему свой срок,
поскольку теснота, незрячесть   90
объятия – сама залог
незримости в разлуке – прячась

друг в друге, мы скрывались от
пространства, положив границей
ему свои лопатки, – вот   95
оно и воздает сторицей

предательству; возьми перо
и чистую бумагу – символ
пространства – и, представив пропорцию – а нам по силам   100

представить все пространство: наш
мир все же ограничен властью
Творца: пусть не наличьем страж
заоблачных, так чьей-то страстью

заоблачной – представь же ту   105
пропорцию прямой, лежащей
меж нами – ко всему листу
и, карту подстелив для вящей

подробности, разбей чертеж
на градусы, и в сетку втисни   110
длину ее – и ты найдешь
зависимость любви от жизни.

Итак, пускай длина черты
известна нам, а нам известно,
что это – как бы вид четы,   115
пределов тех, верней, где места

свиданья лишена она,
и ежели сия оценка
верна (она, увы, верна),
то перпендикуляр, из центра   120

восставленный, есть сумма сих
пронзительных двух взглядов; и на
основе этой силы их
находится его вершина

в пределах стратосферы – вряд   125
ли суммы наших взглядов хватит
на большее; а каждый взгляд,
к вершине обращенный, – катет.

Так двух прожекторов лучи,
исследуя враждебный хаос,   130
находят свою цель в ночи,
за облаком пересекаясь;

но цель их – не мишень солдат:
она для них – сама услуга,
как зеркало, куда глядят   135
не смеющие друг на друга

взглянуть; итак, кому ж, как не
мне, катету, незриму, нему,
доказывать тебе вполне
обыденную теорему   140

обратную, где, муча глаз
доказанных обильем пугал,
жизнь требует найти от нас
то, чем располагаем: угол.

Вот то, что нам с тобой ДАНО.   145
Надолго. Навсегда. И даже
пускай в неощутимой, но
в материи. Почти в пейзаже.

Вот место нашей встречи. Грот
заоблачный. Беседка в тучах.   150
Приют гостеприимный. Род
угла; притом, один из лучших

хотя бы уже тем, что нас
никто там не достигнет. Это
лишь наших достоянье глаз,   155
верх собственности для предмета.

За годы, ибо негде до –
до смерти нам встречаться боле,
мы это обживем гнездо,
таща туда по равной доле   160

скарб мыслей одиноких, хлам
невысказанных слов – все то, что
мы скопим по своим углам;
и рано или поздно точка

указанная обретет   165
почти материальный облик,
достоинство звезды и тот
свет внутренний, который облак

не застит – ибо сам Эвклид
при сумме двух углов и мрака   170
вокруг еще один сулит;
и это как бы форма брака.

Вот то, что нам с тобой дано.
Надолго. Навсегда. До гроба.
Невидимым друг другу. Но   175
оттуда обозримы оба

так будем и в ночи и днем,
от Запада и до Востока,
что мы, в конце концов, начнем
от этого зависеть ока   180

всевидящего. Как бы явь
на тьму ни налагала а́рест,

возьми его сейчас и вставь
в свой новый гороскоп, покамест

всевидящее око слов   185
не стало разбирать. Разлука
есть сумма наших трех углов,
а вызванная ею мука

есть форма тяготенья их
друг к другу; и она намного   190
сильней подобных форм других.
Уж точно, что сильней земного.

*   *   *

Схоластика, ты скажешь. Да,
схоластика и в прятки с горем
лишенная примет стыда   195
игра. Но и звезда над морем –

что есть она как не (позволь
так молвить, чтоб высокий в этом
не узрила ты штиль) мозоль,
натертая в пространстве светом?   200

Схоластика. Почти. Бог весть.
Возможно. Усмотри в ответе
согласие. А что не есть
схоластика на этом свете?

Бог ведает. Клонясь ко сну,   205
я вижу за окном кончину
зимы; и не найти весну:
ночь хочет удержать причину

от следствия. В моем мозгу
какие-то квадраты, даты,   210
твоя или моя к виску
прижатая ладонь . . .
                          Когда ты

однажды вспомнишь обо мне,
окутанную вспомни мраком,

висящую вверху, вовне,   215
там где-нибудь, над Скагерраком,

в компании других планет,
мерцающую слабо, тускло,
звезду, которой, в общем, нет.
Но в том и состоит искусство   220

любви, вернее, жизни – в том,
чтоб видеть, чего нет в природе,
и в месте прозревать пустом
сокровища, чудовищ – вроде

крылатых женогрудых львов,   225
божков невероятной мощи,
вещающих судьбу орлов.
Подумай же, насколько проще

творения подобных дел,
плетения их оболочки   230
и прочих кропотливых дел –
вселение в пространство точки!

Ткни пальцем в темноту. Невесть
куда. Куда укажет ноготь.
Не в том суть жизни, что в ней есть,   235
но в вере в то, что в ней должно быть.

Ткни пальцем в темноту – туда,
где в качестве высокой ноты
должна была бы быть звезда;
и, если ее нет, длинноты,   240

затасканных сравнений лоск
прости: как запоздалый кочет,
униженный разлукой мозг
возвыситься невольно хочет.

                                                (II: 232–9)

*   *   *

'Singing without Music'[1]

When you remember me / in an alien land – though this phrase
/ is no more than a flight of fancy, and not / a prophecy, about
which for an eye / / (5) armed with a tear, / cannot even be
spoken of, for a date / out of the depths with such a rod /
cannot be fished, – anyway, when you / / are thrice nine lands
away and across / (10) the seas, in the form of an epilogue /
(although I repeat that a tear, / with the exception of what has
been, / diminishes everything) about me / you'll remember in
any case in that Year / (15) of Our Lord and you'll sigh – O do
not / sigh! – surveying this / / quantity of seas, fields, / scattered between us, you will not / notice, that the crowd of noughts
/ (20) you yourself have headed. Whether in pride / / of yours
or blindness of mine / is the whole thing, or in that it's too
soon / to talk about this, but hon- / est to God, I feel strange
today, / / (25) that, being all entirely indebted, / in so far as I
guarded so badly / you from worse disasters, I can / spare my
sigh from this. / / Time to come is a form of darkness, / (30)
comparable with nocturnal peace. / In that future about which
we / know nothing, about which, / / at the extreme to say one
thing / right now I am able exactly, / (35) that apart are you
and I fated / to be in it, and that / / it is already upon us – the
roar / of the snowstorm, the turning of [my] cry / into an
obscure scrum of words / (40) is the first clue to it – / in that
future there is something, a thing / able to console or / – so
prophetic is my voice! – / to occupy the imagination in the
style / / (45) of the stories of Scheherazade, with the / difference only that this is more / a posthumous than that exceed-
ingly ordinary / fear of death of hers – so permit me / / right
now in the language of my native / (50) aspens to console you;
and indeed / may the shadows on the snow of them / crowd
together like a triumph of Euclid. / / *** When you remember
me, / on one day, month, of Our Lord the Year / (55) such-
and-such, in an alien land, / thrice nine away – and this / /
speaks of [twenty-six] / possibilities – and with a drop of mois-
ture / your pupil you arm, take / (60) a pen and a clean sheet
of paper / and a perpendicular standing upright / set up, like
for the heavens a support, / twixt our two / – yes, points, for
after all we at that time / / (65) will diminish and there, God
knows, / invisible to each other, / you and I will consider it an

honour / to be known as points; well then, being apart / / is
drawing a straight line, / (70) and the thirsting-for-a-meeting
pair / of lovers – your gaze and mine – / towards the summit
of this perpendicular / / will rise, not having found / a refuge,
further than heavenly / (75) heights, till one's temples crack; /
and is this not a triangle! / / Let us then examine that figure /
which at another time / would make us in a cold / (80) sweat
wake up, like half- / / mad people rush under the tap, that /
reason be not set fire to by ill-feeling; / and if from such a fate
/ delivered we both have been – / / (85) from jealousy, omens,
comets, / spells, spoilings, potions / – then apparently it's only
in order / to map out its likeness. / / Let's examine it, then.
Everything has its term, / (90) for as much as the closeness
and unseeability / of an embrace – itself a token / of the invisibility of being apart – hiding / / in each other, we concealed
ourselves from / space, placing as a limit / (95) to it our shoul-
der-blades – so there / it is and it renders one hundred fold /
/ to treason; take a pen / and a clean sheet of paper – a symbol
/ of space – and, displaying the pro- / (100) -portion – and we
are strong enough / to display the entire space, for our / world
is limited after all, by the power / of the Creator, if not by the
presence of guards / beyond the clouds, then by someone's
passion / / (105) that is beyond the clouds – display, then, that
/ proportion as a straight line lying / between us – over the
entire sheet / and, having spread out a map for greater / detailing,
split the sketch / (110) into degrees, and into the squaring force
in / its length – and you will find / the dependence of love on
life. / / So, suppose the length of the line / is known to us, and
we know / (115) that this is as it were a kind of pair, / or of
those bounds, more truly, where of a place / / to meet it is
deprived, / and if this estimate / is true (it, alas, is true), / (120)
then the perpendicular, from the centre / / set up, is the sum
of these / two penetrating gazes; and at / the basis of this power
of theirs / is found its summit / / (125) within the stratosphere
– hardly / can the sum of our gazes suffice / for more; and
every gaze, / directed at the summit, is a cathetus. / / Thus the
beams of two searchlights, / (130) exploring hostile chaos, / find
their goal in the night, / as they intersect behind a cloud; / but
their goal is not a target for soldiers / but for them is the service itself, / (135) like a mirror into which gaze / people who
do not dare at each other / / to look; so, who, if not / I, a

cathetus, invisible, unspeaking, / should prove to you this completely / (140) ordinary theorem / which is in reverse, where,
torturing the eye / with a multitude of proven scarecrows, /
life demands from us that we find / that which we have available, – an angle. / / (145) This is what to us two is GIVEN. / For
a long time. For ever. And even / albeit imperceptibly, but still
/ in matter. Almost in the landscape. / / Here is the place of
our meeting. A grotto / (150) beyond the clouds. A summer-
house in the clouds. / An hospitable sanctuary. A kind / of
angle; and to boot, one of the best / / if only because of the
fact that no-one / will get to us there. This / (155) is merely a
property of our eyes / the height of ownership for a thing. / /
After years pass, for there is nowhere before that – / before
death we will meet no more, / we will make habitable the nest,
/ (160) dragging into it in equal share / / the chattels of lonely
thoughts, the clutter / of unsaid words – all those things that /
we amass in our corners; / and sooner or later the point / /
(165) indicated acquires / an almost material aspect, / the dignity
of a star and that / light internal, which will not hide / / the
clouds – for Euclid himself / (170) with his sum of two angles
and the gloom / around predicts one more / and this is as it
were a form of marriage. / / That's what is given to the two of
us. / For a long time. For ever. To the grave. / (175) [To be]
invisible to each other. But / thence visible both / / to such an
extent will we be both night and day, / from the West unto
the East, / that we in the end will begin / (180) to depend on
this eye / / all-seeing. No matter how reality / on darkness might
impose arrest, / take it right now and put it in / your new
horoscope, until / / (185) the all-seeing eye of words / begins
to sort it out. Being apart / is the sum of our three angles, /
and the torment summoned by it / / is the form of their gravitation / (190) towards each other; and it by far / is stronger
than the similar forms that other people have. / It's certainly
stronger than the earth's. / / *** Scholasticism, you'll say. Yes,
/ it is scholasticism and hide-and-seek with grief / (195) deprived
of marks of shame / a game. But that star too above the sea –
/ / what is it if not (permit [me] / to utter thus, that no lofty
style in this / you discern) a callus / (200) rubbed up on space
by the light? / / Scholasticism. Almost. God knows. / Possibly.
Discern in [my] answer / agreement. But what is not / scholasticism in this world? / / (205) God knoweth. Slipping into sleep,

/ I see outside the demise / of winter; and spring's not to be found, / for night wishes to hold back the cause / / from the consequence. In my brain / (210) are some squares, dates, / your or my to temple / pressed palm . . . When you / / some day remember me, / remember a – wreathed in gloom, / (215) hanging above, outside, / somewhere out there, above the Skagerrak, / / in the company of other planets, / and twinkling weakly, dimly, – / star, which in general does not exist. / (220) But the thing that defines the art / of love, or rather of life, is / to see what is not in nature, / and to discern in an empty place / a treasure, monsters, – such as / / (225) the winged female-breasted lions, / those little gods of improbable might, / which solemnly proclaim the fate of eagles. / Just think how much more simple / / than creating such things, / (230) than weaving their covering / and other fussy matters / is installing a point in space! / / Poke your finger at the darkness. Goodness knows / where. Where your fingernail points. / (235) The essence of life is not in what exists in it, / but in having faith in what ought to be in it. / / Poke your finger at the darkness, towards / where acting as a high note / there ought to be a star; / (240) and if it's not there, then these longueurs, / / the gloss of these trite comparisons / forgive, for like a belated rooster / humiliated by separation the brain / cannot help but wish to rise up.

*   *   *

Joseph Brodsky's *Pen'e bez muzyki* (hereafter *Pbm*) is one of the outstanding longer love poems in twentieth-century Russian literature, meriting a place alongside Mayakovsky's *Pro eto* and Tsvetaeva's *Poema kontsa*. Both these poems were written in the early 1920s, and after them, no major Russian poet had attempted a love poem on this sort of scale. Like all Brodsky's love poetry, *Pbm* is much more than a testimony to private experience. It engages such topics as the function of art and the relationship between art and life, arguing throughout for the superiority of the metaphysical over the physical, and it culminates in the most concise and unambiguous formulation in all Brodsky's writing of an idealist philosophical standpoint (ll. 235–6): 'Ne v tom sut''

zhizni, chto v nei est', / no v vere v to, chto v nei dolzhno byt''
[The essence of life is not in what exists in it, / but in having
faith in what ought to be in it].

Considering that *Pbm* can be read in most of its principal aspects
– as can all Brodsky's work, if one cared to be so perverse – as a
direct counter to the official literature being written inside Russia
at the time of its conception, it is richly ironic that this formula
also perfectly captures the spirit of Soviet Socialist Realism.

Pbm was apparently finished in 1970; it appeared the following year in the very first issue of the journal founded by Carl
and Ellendea Proffer shortly before the poet himself arrived in
the USA through their good offices.[2] This first publication has a
dedication, 'To Faith Wigzell', which was contracted to 'F.W.' when
Brodsky included the poem in the collection that brings together
the work of his last years in Russia, *Konets prekrasnoi epokhi* (Ann
Arbor: Ardis, 1977, pp. 75–82). This text will be taken as definitive for the purposes of the present analysis.[3] *Pbm* was not
included in Brodsky's own selection of his love poetry, *Novye
stansy k Avguste* (Ann Arbor, 1983), no doubt because the dedicatee
was someone other than 'M.B.' The poem has been collected several
times since then.[4]

The poem has been little discussed; not a single article has yet
been specifically devoted to it. The most significant existing commentary on *Pbm* consists of some remarks made in passing by
David Bethea.[5]

Even if it were nothing else, *Pbm* would merit careful study as
a technical achievement. It is one of the most remarkable *tours
de force* in Brodsky's œuvre; he takes some of the most hackneyed formal elements in the Russian metrical repertoire, and
radically refashions them. *Pbm* is a monometric stanzaic *poema*,
which is normal for Brodsky but unusual in Russian poetry of
the modern period; after Blok's *Dvenadtsat'*, the significant long
poems that have been written in Russian are almost all polymetric.
The form of *Pbm* is extremely unusual within Brodsky's work in
two respects. The first is the use of iambic tetrameter (I4) instead
of the pentameter that the poet employed almost invariably when
he still used the so-called classical metres for the bulk of his poetry,
that is, broadly speaking, until he emigrated. The second unusual
formal feature is the use of the quatrain which, no doubt because
it is by far the most common stanza length in Russian poetry,
Brodsky always tended to avoid, preferring either stanzas longer

than the quatrain or non-stanzaic structures.[6] By far the most
common rhyme scheme used in Russian quatrains, four or five
times more common than the next most frequently used form, is
AbAb, with feminine rhymes in the first and third lines and
masculine in the second and fourth lines; the masculine endings
are strongly associated with syntactic and intonational closure.
For *Pbm*, however, Brodsky chooses the second most common
form of quatrain, with masculine–feminine alternation (aBaB),
reversing the scheme just mentioned. The consequences of this
for the poem's intonation are very important. Feminine endings
are located in the positions where closure would normally be
found.

The 244-line text of *Pbm* is segmented, characteristically for
Brodsky, at a higher level than the stanza:[7] it is divided typographically (by asterisks) into three sections. The sections comprise: ll. 1–52; 53–192; and 193 to the end, l. 244. That is, two
sections each of 52 lines frame a section more than twice that
length, in fact of 140 lines. The long inner section contains the
poem's central image, or 'conceit' ('a figure of speech that employs
unusual and paradoxical images'); and the outer sections present
an introduction and coda to this conceit.

The most remarkable formal aspect of this text is its verse rhythm.
Brodsky has here taken the most humdrum of all measures in
Russian poetry, I4, and fashioned a rhythmical profile for it that
is startlingly original and fresh. The characteristics of this rhythm
can best be discussed on the basis of the statistical analysis that
has long been part of the standard practice of Russian metrists.
Table 1 spells out the percentages for the stressing of each ictus
(metrically strong syllable) in Brodsky's poem, and the average
stressing for the poem as a whole. The 'Average' figure of 74.1%
means that this proportion of all the 976 metrically strong syllables is stressed. To permit a comparative evaluation, in Table 1
the corresponding figures have been supplied for *Evgenii Onegin*,
for four different periods in the history of Russian poetry, and
for a renowned experimenter with Russian verse form, Andrei
Belyi.

It is clear from these figures that the 'normal' rhythm of Russian I4 in the periods set out here has certain constants, domi-
nants and tendencies: there is always a stress on the eighth syllable
of the line (ictus IV, where the rhyme is located); the next strongest
is the second ictus, next is the first, and weakest is the third.

TABLE 1   *Rhythmical Structure of* Pbm *and other Russian I4 (per cent)*[8]

	I	II	III	IV	Lines	Average
Pbm	96.7	16.0	87.7	95.9	244	74.1
EO	84.4	89.9	43.1	100.0	5320	79.4
Older 19c	84.4	92.2	46.0	100.0	?	80.7
Younger 19c	82.1	96.8	34.6	100.0	?	78.4
Early 20c	83.5	87.4	49.1	100.0	?	80.0
Soviet	82.2	87.2	46.8	100.0	?	79.1
Belyi 1908–9	78.0	62.5	52.7	100.0	851	73.3

Here we observe the phenomenon known as 'regressive accentual dissimilation', which is a formulation of what tends to happen when the Russian language is shaped to comply with the conventional matrix of the iambic tetrameter. We also note that the overall average stressing for I4 has hovered around 80% since the beginning of the nineteenth century.

Brodsky, however, has invented something very strange. He has managed to produce a rhythm that goes against these norms. In the rhythmical profile of *Pbm*, the fourth ictus is not always stressed (95.9%), and is in fact weaker than the first, which stands at 96.7%. At 87.7% the third ictus is vastly stronger than the 16.0% of the second; in fact, the latter is weaker than the *third* ictus ever gets in normal I4. The result is a completely original rhythm whose structure contradicts the law of regressive accentual dissimilation.

The oddest rhythm in I4 ever discerned before this was produced by Andrei Belyi in the years 1908–9, when, at the same time as he was working on his pioneering theoretical studies of Russian verse rhythm, he deliberately set out to make his own poetry rhythmically distinctive. It is clear, though, that in *Pbm* Brodsky has done something even more peculiar. In addition, the average stressing in Brodsky's poem has come down from the norm by about 6%, which is a marked fall.

One clue to a possible stimulus for the creation of this rhythm is suggested by James Bailey's pioneering analysis of the iambic tetrameter of English poetry using the Russian statistical method[9] (see Table 2). It is clear that in some respects, most significant of which is the treatment of the final ictus, Brodsky's verse in *Pbm* is nearer the English model than the Russian.

Besides the overall rhythmical characteristics that were pointed

TABLE 2   *Rhythmical Profile of English I4 (per cent)*

	I	II	III	IV	Lines	Average
Milton	74.5	77.0	82.4	93.9	165	81.9
Wordsworth	78.3	74.9	81.0	91.5	295	81.4
Auden	77.7	68.9	61.7	84.0	206	73.1

TABLE 3   *Stanza Rhythm in* Pbm (%)

	I	II	III	IV	Total	Average
Line 1	93.4	27.9	83.6	91.8	61	74.2
Line 2	100.0	16.4	93.4	96.7	61	76.6
Line 3	98.4	24.6	88.5	95.1	61	76.3
Line 4	95.1	11.5	85.2	100.0	61	72.9

out above, metrists have also observed that when I4 is written in quatrains, there is a tendency for the average stressing of the lines to fall over the four lines, sometimes progressively through the four lines, sometimes in two groups of two lines.[10] Table 3 gives the data for the stanza rhythm of *Pbm*.

In the stanza rhythm of *Pbm*, the fourth line is indeed the most weakly stressed, but the stanza is weighted in the middle instead of the beginning. It is also clear from Table 3 that the four lines of the stanza express the poem's overall rhythm to different degrees. The fourth line at least has a normal final ictus. But the second line is altogether a monster: it is as if Brodsky had set out to reverse the normal stress profile of the Russian I4 before Pushkin, and establish progressive rather than regressive accentual dissimilation.

Another respect in which Brodsky has made some technical innovations in *Pbm* is the treatment of rhyme, with regard to both phonology[11] and grammar.[12] The most consistent tendency in the development of modern Russian rhyme is degrammaticization. In *Pbm* there are few examples of grammatical rhyme. The first of them is *slezói/lesói* (ll. 5–7); here, both members of the pair are feminine nouns in the instrumental singular. However, this rhyme is somewhat deviant in phonetic terms. The minimum requirement for constructing a rhyme in Russian poetry since the mid-eighteenth century has been one vowel and one consonant. This means that in open masculine rhyme, the consonants preceding the stressed vowel must be identical. This is not the case with *slezói/lesói*; these consonants contrast – in a minimal way, admittedly, in terms of voiced versus unvoiced. Instead, Brodsky has enriched the rhyme, that is, added an extra identical consonant (here, *l*) to the left of the rhyming vowel. Similarly enriched are the feminine pairs *opóru/v tu póru* (62–4); *nadób'ia–podób'ia* (86–8); *mráka-bráka* (170–2); *v otvéte–(na etom) svéte* (202–4); *konchínu–prichínu* (206–8); *mrákom–Skagerrákom* (214–16). Also enriched are the masculines *polei–nulei* (17–19), *cherty–chety* (113–5); *grot-rod* (149–51), and the tautologous *del–del* (229–31). In this context, the grammatical rhymes without enrichment seem almost perfunctory: the masculines *srok-zalog* (89–91); *l'vov–orlov* (224–6); *losk–mozg* (240–2), and the feminines *vlági–bumági* (58–60); the only really hackneyed rhyme in the poem, the venerable *vlást'iu–strást'iu* (102–4); and *s górem–nad mórem* (194–6).

The next stage in Brodsky's treatment of rhyme may illustrated from ll. 37–40, where we find the sequence *rëv–kríka–slov–ulíka*; here, both pairs consist of nouns, but none of them share the same gender, case and number. These rhymes are exact and, perhaps because of this and the grammatical differentiation, there is no need for enrichment. The next stage of sophistication may be observed in lls. 109–12, where we find *chertëzh–vtísni–naidësh'–zhízni*. Both pairs here rhyme a verb with a noun, but the verbs and nouns concerned have different grammatical forms. The masculine rhymes are exact, and the feminines have one deviation from exactitude, again minimal, involving a voiced/unvoiced pair: -s- in *vtisni* versus -z- in *zhizni*. There is no enrichment. Elsewhere in the text we can find many examples of rhymes, especially feminines, that are less exact than those we have mentioned so far: *górnikh–treugól'nik* (74–6); *símvol–sílam* (98–100); *otsénka–tséntra* (118–20).

But Brodsky goes further still. He systematically rhymes stressed with what would be unstressed vowels in the performance of normal spoken Russian. The very first rhyme in the poem is of this kind: *obo mné–a ne [proróchestvo]* (1–3); we then find *i za–slezá* (9–11); *obo mné–o ne* (13–15); *ty ne–gordyne*, 18–20; the outrageous *moéi–ei/[zhe Bógu]* (21–2/3); *i da–Evklída* (50–2), *peró–pro/ [pórtsiiu]* (97–99), and others.[13] Nobody has ever habitually rhymed prepositions and particles with fully stressed words in this way in serious Russian poetry. The adoption of this technique constitutes the main reason why Brodsky has been able to liberate himself from the tyranny of I4's usual alternating rhythm, which is determined by the fact that the fourth ictus (the rhyme) is always stressed. Again, it would seem that Brodsky introduced this feature under the influence of English rhyme, where it is perfectly normal and has been so for ages.

As an example of these procedures, we may cite ll. 120–7, where the poet is constructing his conceit:

[. . .] то перпендикуляр, из центра   120

восставленный, есть сумма сих
пронзительных двух взглядов; и на
основе этой силы их
находится его вершина

в пределах стратосферы – вряд   125
ли суммы наших взглядов хватит
на большее;

[. . . then the perpendicular, from the centre / / set up, is the sum of these / two penetrating gazes; and at / the basis of this power of theirs / is found its summit / / within the stratosphere – hardly / can the sum of our gazes suffice / for more]. We can sense clearly here how in the complete stanza (121–4), which is enjambed at both the beginning and the end, the semantic weight has been shifted away from the normally strong fourth and eighth syllables and redistributed on to the second and sixth. Of the rhyming syllables in this stanza, only one (*vershína*) would normally be considered to carry an obligatory full stress in whatever syllable of an iambic line it is located.

Table 4 shows the elementary mechanics of this situation by plotting how many times stops occur after each of the 34 syllables in the stanza matrix of the poem. We see that the last syllable in the stanza (no. 34) remains by far the most likely to be followed by full syntactic closure; this happens 16 times. Predictably again, the stanza's half-way point, syllable 17, is the next most likely place for syntactic closure to occur; but this happens only four times. Just as many stops appear after syllable 4, which has no particular metrical marking. And the number of stops towards the end of the first line of the stanza is remarkable. To

TABLE 4   Syntactic and Metrical Boundaries in Pbm

After syllable:	1	2	3	4	5	6	7	8		Total
No. stops:	0	0	0	4	1	2	2	3		12
After syllable:	9	10	11	12	13	14	15	16	17	
No. stops:	0	1	3	1	0	3	1	0	4	13
After syllable:	18	19	20	21	22	23	24	25		
No. stops:	0	0	0	1	0	0	2	3		6
After syllable:	26	27	28	29	30	31	32	33	34	
No. stops:	0	1	0	1	0	1	1	0	16	20

understand the significance of this distribution, we should remember that the poem is made up of 61 stanzas; the fact that only 16 of them end with full syntactic closure, and that only four of the second lines in the stanza do so, is altogether extraordinary.

The total number of stops tells us that this text is made up of 51 sentences. This feature too is idiosyncratic: in conventional Russian stanzaic poetry, especially in quatrains, there are always more sentences than stanzas. Obviously, Brodsky must have used some long, complex sentences. In fact, four of them are 20 or more lines long: the poem demonstratively opens with the first of them, which eventually terminates half-way through l. 20; this is followed by the sentences occupying ll. 31–52, 53–76 and – the longest of them all – 89–112.[14] But in addition, Brodsky has subverted the usual symmetry of the relationship between syntax and metre by using not just some very long sentences, but some very short ones as well. They occur in four particular segments of the poem, and several of them are only one word long: ll. 145–54, 173–5, 201–5, 233–4. There is thus a large-scale pattern: the longer, more complex sentences occur in the first half of the poem, as if the poet were winding up before getting going, and then come the shorter ones, as if he were running out of breath under the pressure of emotion as he approaches the end.

This peculiar use of sentence lengths serves two ends. One is, clearly, to give the impression of stream of consciousness, of an unpremeditated outpouring of thoughts that spills over the formal restraints of the stanza boundaries. The other is surely to cock a snook at earlier models of this form, just as Brodsky has done here with his rhythm, as if to suggest that it is not necessary,

if one can find the technical resources to avoid it, to accept the
conventional deformations other poets have imposed on themselves when forcing their language into syntactically self-contained
34-syllable boxes.[15] This text contains two classic Brodsky inversions, where a noun
is placed last in a sentence, its appearance delayed by a syntactically complex antecedent. The first occupies ll. 193–5: 'Da, /
skholastika i v priatki s gorem / lishennaia primet styda / igra.'
[Yes, / it is scholasticism and hide-and-seek with grief / deprived
of marks of shame / a game.] The second is found in ll. 214–18:
'. . . okutannuiu vspomni mrakom, / visiashchuiu vverkhu, vovne, /
tam gde-nibud', nad Skagerrakom, / v kompanii drugikh planet,
/ mertsaiushchuiu slabo, tusklo, / zvezdu . . . [wreathed in gloom,
/ hanging above, outside, / somewhere out there, above the
Skagerrak, / / in the company of other planets, and twinkling
weakly, dimly, – star].

Besides tantalizing his readers in this way, though, Brodsky
also helps us by punctuating the text with a few repetitions. Line
1 ('Kogda ty vspomnish' obo mne') is recapitulated at l. 53 and
again, with a slight variation, at l. 212. Part of ll. 59–60 ('zrachok
vooruzhish', voz'mi / pero i chistyi list bumagi') reappear at ll.
97–8; and the first two words of l. 146 ('Nadolgo. Navsegda. I
dazhe') reappear at l. 173, this time followed by 'Do groba'.

As we said earlier, at the highest level of structure, *Pbm* consists of a central conceit framed by an introduction and coda.
The vehicle of the conceit is a geometrical figure, in fact a triangle that the poet asks his addressee, the woman who has left for
another country, to put down on paper to symbolize the connections between them: they will be at the bases, separated by
distance and invisible to each other; but the apex will be a star
that they both can see.

For English readers, this use of a geometrical conceit inevitably
evokes two of the best-known love poems by the metaphysicals,
both of them, incidentally, composed in 14 quatrains with
alternating rhyme. The first of them is Marvell's 'The Definition
of Love':

> My Love is of a birth so rare
> As 'tis, for object, strange and high;
> It was begotten by Despair
> Upon Impossibility.

Magnanimous Despair alone
Could show me so divine a thing,
Where feeble Hope could ne'er have flown
But vainly flapped his tinsel wing.

For Fate with jealous eye does see
Two perfect loves, nor lets them close;
Their union would her ruin be,
And her tyrannic power depose.

And therefore her decrees of steel
Us as the distant poles have placed,
(Though Love's whole world on us doth wheel)
Not by themselves to be embraced,

Unless the giddy heaven fall,
And earth some new convention tear,
And, us to join, the world should all
Be cramped into a planisphere.[16]

As lines, so loves, oblique may well
Themselves in every angle greet;
But ours, so truly parallel,
Though infinite, can never meet.

Therefore the love which us doth bind,
But Fate so enviously debars,
Is the conjunction of the mind,
And opposition of the stars.

The second poem was translated into Russian by Brodsky at about
the time he created *Pbm*; it is, of course, Donne's 'Valediction, Forbidding Mourning',[17] which includes the famous image of the compasses:

Our two souls, therefore, which are one,
    Though I must go, endure not yet,
A breach, but an expansion,
    Like gold to airy thinness beat.

If they be two, they are two so
    As stiff twin compasses are two;

Thy soul, the fixed foot, makes no show
To move, but doth if the other do.

And though it in the centre sit,
    Yet when the other far doth roam,
It leans, and hearkens after it,
    And grows erect as that comes home.

Such wilt thou be to me, who must,
    Like the other foot, obliquely run;
They firmness makes my circle just,
    And makes me end where I begun.

Manifestly, we have here the literary sources of Brodsky's conceit. In turning to these sources, Brodsky was re-orienting Russian literary conventions. In terms of its conceptual world, the result has no real antecedents in Russian poetry. Like many of Brodsky's pieces, the text of *Pbm* contains hardly any descriptive adjectives, and very few indeed that pertain to sense perception (colour, heat, taste, smell, sound). Brodsky, of course, is fully aware of this peculiarity; that is partly why he says in l. 193, where the coda begins, 'Skholastika, ty skazhesh' [Scholasticism, you'll say]. The poem is completely abstract in the sense of not giving us any information about who the lovers actually are or anything about the story of their relationship; there is no geography (except for the Skagerrak in l. 215) and no history. The similarity to the ratiocinative mentality of the metaphysicals is very striking.

Notwithstanding this alien atmosphere, *Pbm* articulates the most canonical attitude to male–female relationships by male Russian poets. The poem is elegaic; that is, the relationship is celebrated after it is over. Pushkin's 'Ia vas liubil . . .' is the quintessential statement of the theme of lost love, after which any other treatment of it seems indecorous. To this day it seems to be unthinkable for a male Russian to write love poetry about an enduring, requited relationship – especially if it is legally registered. Pushkin's suave surrender of the woman to another man, though, finds no echo in this or any other poem by Brodsky. At the same time, Brodsky's poem is much more about emotional and physical passion being mastered with the aid of intellectual passion. Emotion has been restrained or fettered by the mind, instead of paralysing it and rendering it inarticulate, as is conventionally the case.

The poem's title hints at this situation: it is poetry (singing) without the wordless element of melody. The poem argues in a complex way, using many abstract terms; and at the same time, its structure mimics stream-of-consciousness: it stops and starts, goes back on itself, hesitates. In this respect, *Pbm* is absolutely typical of Brodsky, and it is an almost excessively original achievement.

Pbm, then, is an elegaic love poem; perhaps it should rather be called, following Donne, a valediction forbidding mourning. The lovers have parted, the poet is left alone, the woman has left for another country. The poem acts out the thought processes of the poet 'one day' when he thinks of her possibly remembering him with sadness; he has the strange sensation that he can console her, dry her tears, exorcise her pain and his own grief (like Scheherazade) by 'telling stories', inventing an absorbing and diverting fiction. He works out an elaborate figure, the triangle conceit, as something that will at least intellectually overcome the pain of their physical separation. He does not tell the reader about who made the decision to end the affair, and for what reasons, stating instead – repeatedly, and with great emphasis in l. 145 – that separation is somehow 'given'; but there is a sense in which the figure is a dubious gesture, perhaps masking the man's cruelty and immaturity in declining the fidelity, responsibilities and sacrifices entailed in actually living together. After all, it may be more difficult and more meritorious to build a sustained, ethically elegant marriage in life than to weave the aesthetically elegant, metaphorical 'sort of marriage' represented by the nest in the sky of ll. 157–70. But it seems that the poet knows he is deceiving himself and, as it were, fighting a lost battle. The outrageously elaborate, over-extended nature of the central conceit suggests how preposterous the poet feels his enterprise to be in actual fact. At the end, he admits as much, but goes on to argue that what matters most consists not in what *is* in actuality, but in having faith (which for Brodsky implies creative ability) that a better world exists beyond the real one. This is the consolatory purpose of that defiant couplet (ll. 235–6) with which, as we said earlier, the poem culminates. It is a consolation available, surely, only to very few.

24 *Joseph Brodsky*

Notes

1. The translation that follows attempts to retain as far as possible the word order of the original, and in many places distorts normal English word order in order to do so.
2. *Russian Literary Triquarterly*, vol. I (1971) pp. 414–19.
3. The collected version differs from the first publication mainly in details of punctuation, which do not affect the analysis below (Table 4).
4. Subsequent publications include: Iosif Brodskii, *Chast' rechi. Izbrannye stikhi 1962–1989* (Moscow, 1990) pp. 151–9, with the dedication 'F.W.'; Iosif Brodskii, *Kholmy* (St Petersburg, 1991) pp. 201–8 (dedication deleted); Iosif Brodskii, *Sochineniia Iosifa Brodskogo* vol. II (4 vols, St Petersburg: Pushkinskii fond 1992) pp. 232–8 ('F.W.'). There is a translation of the poem into English by David Rigsbee and the author, 'A Song to No Music', in Joseph Brodsky, *A Part of Speech* (Oxford-Melbourne, 1980) pp. 26–33 '[For Faith Wigzell]'.
5. David Bethea, *Joseph Brodsky and the Creation of Exile* (Princeton University Press, 1994), especially pp. 110–19. *Pbm* is not even mentioned in Elena Chizhova, '"Evterpa, ty?" Liubovnaia lirika Brodskogo', *Russian Literature*, vol. XXXVII (1995) pp. 393–404. The present analysis of *Pbm* was written in 1979, presented several times as a lecture, and revised for publication here in certain minor respects.
6. See Barry Scherr, 'Strofika Brodskogo', in *Poetika Brodskogo. Sbornik statei*, ed. L. Loseff (Tenafly, NJ: Hermitage 1986) pp. 97–120.
7. On the various metricized forms of this device, see M. Iu. Lotman, 'Giperstrofika Brodskogo', *Russian Literature*, vol. XXXVII (1995) pp. 303–32.
8. The data for *Evgenii Onegin* are taken from K. F. Taranovsky, *Ruski dvodelni ritmove* (Belgrade, 1953); those for the four broad historical groups from M. L. Gasparov, *Ocherk istorii russkogo stikha. Metrika, ritmika, rifma, strofika* (Moscow: Nanka, 1984), where the calculations are made in terms of total numbers of poems rather than lines, and have been omitted here from Table 1; and for Belyi, from K. F. Taranovsky, 'Chetyrekhstopnyi iamb A. Belogo', *IJSLP*, vol. X (1966) pp. 127–47.
9. James Bailey, *Toward a Statistical Analysis of English Verse* (Lisse, 1975).
10. G. S. Smith, 'Stanza Rhythm and Stress Load in the Iambic Tetrameter of V. F. Khodasevich', *Slavic and East European Journal*, vol. XXIV (1980) no. 1, pp. 25–36; id., 'Stanza Rhythm in the Iambic Tetrameter of Three Modern Russian Poets', *IJSLP*, vol. XXIV (1981) pp. 135–52. The latter article includes an appendix (pp. 150–2) by M. L. Gasparov giving statistics for the stanza rhythm of 14 quatrains by a number of Russian poets; his studies of this subject, which began to appear in 1974, culminate in 'Stroficheskii ritm v russkom chetyrekhstopnom iambe i khoree', reprinted in his *Izbrannye stat'i* (Moscow, 1995) pp. 48–59.
11. See M. L. Gasparov, 'Rifma Brodskogo', *Russian Literature*, vol. XXXVII (1995) no. ii–iii, pp. 189–201.
12. See Kari Egerton, 'Grammatical Contrast in the Rhyme of Joseph Brodsky', *Essays in Poetics*, vol. XIX (1994) no. i, 7–24.

13. Obviously, I am leaving aside here the vexed question of the relationship between text and performance; in reading his poetry, Brodsky habitually made a pause to emphasize the ends of metrical lines, thereby pointing up the rhyme, whatever stressing might be stipulated by normal Russian syntax and intonation. Gasparov (see n. 11 above) appears not to treat these stressed/non-stressed pairs as an exceptional case. Incidentally, l. 100 of Pbm, whose first syllable is occupied by the stressed syllable of the noun *pro/pórtsiiu*, is one syllable short, and is strictly speaking a trochaic tetrameter.

14. A possible source for Brodsky's practice is suggested by a remark by D. S. Mirsky on Baratynsky's later poetry in an article that was originally published as the introduction to the *Biblioteka poeta* edition of 1935: 'Szhatost' dostigaetsia v ushcherb iasnosti. On vyrabatyvaet sebe kraine zatrudnennyi sintaksis, obrashchaias' s russkim iazykom kak s latinskim, ispol'zuia sverkh vsiacheskoi priniatoi mery soglasovanie i podchinenie grammaticheskikh form.' ['Conciseness is achieved at the expense of clarity. He develops an extremely difficult syntax, treating the Russian language like Latin, and using beyond any accepted degree the agreement and subordination of grammatical forms.'] D. S. Mirsky, 'Baratynsky', reprinted in *Stikhotvoreniia i stat'i o russkoi poezii* (Berkeley, 1996) p. 131.

15. Our understanding of syntactic and grammatical norms in Russian I4 is less advanced than is the case with its rhythm, but there is considerable evidence to support the subjective view expressed here that Brodsky's practice here is consciously counter-traditional; for the conventional patterning of grammar and syntax in Russian I4, see M. L. Gasparov, 'Lingvistika stikha', in *Slavyanskii stikh*, eds M. L. Gasparov and T. V. Skulacheva (Moscow, 1996) pp. 5–17, especially pp. 7–11; T. V. Skulacheva, 'Lingvistika stikha: struktura stikhotvornoi stroki', ibid., pp. 18–23, S. E. Liapin, 'O raspredelenii slov v stikhotvornoi stroke', ibid., pp. 24–33, and especially M. L. Gasparov, 'Ritm, sintaksis i semantika: smyslovye uzly v 4-stopnom iambe', in *Istoriko-literaturnyi sbornik k 60-letiiu Leonida Genrikhovicha Frizmana* (Khar'kov, 1995) pp. 14–22.

16. Planisphere: a map of the world projected on a flat surface.

17. 'Proshchan'e, zapreshchaiushchee grust'', in Iosif Brodsky, *Ostanovka v pustyne* (New York, 1970) pp. 224–5. The translation has been reprinted twice in Russia: see *Inostrannaia literatura*, IX (1988) p. 179, and Iosif Brodsky, *Bog sokhraniaet vse* (Moscow, 1992) pp. 271–2. Alas, the connection between Donne and Pbm is not mentioned by Viktor Kulle in his extremely useful essay '"Tam, gde on konchil, ty nachinaesh' . . ." (O perevodakh Iosifa Brodskogo)', *Russian Literature*, vol. XXVII (1995) pp. 267–88.

2

'Odysseus to Telemachus'*

Odissei Telemaku

LIUDMILA ZUBOVA

Мой Телемах,
            Троянская война
окончена. Кто победил – не помню.
Должно быть, греки: столько мертвецов
вне дома бросить могут только греки . . .
И все-таки ведущая домой
дорога оказалась слишком длинной,
как будто Посейдон, пока мы там
теряли время, растянул простанство.
Мне неизвестно, где я нахожусь,
что предо мной. Какой-то грязный остров,
кусты, постройки, хрюканье свиней,
заросший сад, какая-то царица,
трава да камни . . . Милый Телемак,
все острова похожи друг на друга,
когда так долго странствуешь, и мозг
уже сбивается, считая волны,
глаз, засоренный горизонтом, плачет,
и водяное мясо застит слух.
Не помню я, чем кончилась война,
и сколько тебе лет сейчас, не помню.

Расти большой, мой Телемак, расти.
Лишь боги знают, свидимся ли снова.
Ты и сейчас уже не тот младенец,
перед которым я сдержал быков.
Когда б не Паламед, мы жили вместе.

* Translated from the Russian by Chris Jones.

Но, может быть, и прав он: без меня
ты от страстей Эдиповых избавлен,
и сны твои, мой Телемак, безгрешны.

(II: 301)

*   *   *

'Odysseus to Telemachus'

My Telemachus, the Trojan War / is over. Who was victorious –
I do not remember. / It must have been the Greeks: / only the
Greeks could have forsaken so many corpses / abroad . . . / And,
nevertheless the way leading / home turned out to be too long,
/ as if Poseidon had, while we were there / wasting time,
stretched out space. / It is not known to me where I am, /
what is in front of me. Some sort of filthy island, / bushes,
buildings, snorting swine, / an overgrown garden, some sort
of queen, / grass and stones . . . Dear Telemachus, / all islands
resemble one another / when you have been wandering for so
long, and your brain / is already confused, trying to count the
waves, / your eye, soiled by the horizon, weeps, / and the watery
meat obstructs the hearing, / I don't remember how the war
finished, / and how old you are now, I don't remember. / /
Grow tall, my Telemachus, grow. / Only the gods know whether
we'll see each other again. / Even now you're not the young
boy you were / the one I held the bullocks back from. / If it
were not for Palamedes we would have lived together. / But,
perhaps, he was right: without me / you are spared the Oedipus complex, / and your dreams, my Telemachus, are sinless.

*   *   *

The poem deals with a subject always central to Brodsky's concern:
'What interests me most of all, has always interested me, on this
earth [. . .] is time and that effect it has on man, how it changes
him, grinds away at him [. . .]. On the other hand its just a metaphor for what time generally does to space, to the world.'[1]

In 'I, like Ulysses' (1961) one can glimpse an urtext, a premonition of 'Odysseus to Telemachus': '. . . гони меня, несчастье по земле, / хотя бы вспять, гони меня по жизни. / [. . .] гони меня, как новый Ганимед / хлебну зимой изгнаннической чаши / / и не пойму, откуда и куда / я двигаюсь, как много я теряю / во времени, в дороге повторяя: / ох, Боже мой, какая ерунда. / [. . .] Мелькай, мелькай по сторонам, народ, / я двигаюсь, и, кажется, отрадно, / что, как Улисс, гоню себя вперед, / но двигаюсь по-прежнему обратно' (I: 152). [Chase me, misfortune, over the earth, / though it be backwards, chase me through life. [. . .] chase me, like a new Ganymedes / I will drink this winter cup of exile / and not grasp whence or wither / I go, how much I lose / in time, repeating on my way, over and over again: / Oh! my God, what rubbish. / [. . .] people, pass by, pass by / I move and, it seems, with joy, / that, like Ulysses, I drive myself forward, / but move, as before, backward.]

Ulysses appears in the poem 'Letter in a Bottle', written in 1964, in Norenskaia, as an exaggeratedly romantic character.[2] 'The Sirens do not conceal their beauteous faces / and loudly from the cliffs they sing in unison, / while the jovial captain Ulysses / cleans his Smith and Wesson on the bridge' (I: 362). This poem's tone contrasts sharply with that of the testamentary epistle genre to which, as we read on, we realize it belongs: 'I sailed fair and square but hit a reef, / and it tore through my side, / [. . .] But despite the binoculars, I / couldn't make out the Young Pioneer beach. / [. . .] I saw that I had lost the case' (I: 363). However, there is also this: 'The water sprite at the bowsprit is shedding tears / from her eyes, counting the billions of waves [. . .] I lost count of the clouds and the days' (I: 364).

The image of Ulysses reappears – cast in quite a different tonality – in the poem 'Adieu, Mademoiselle Véronique' (1967), where the theme of the son makes its appearance: '. . . in twenty years from now when my offspring, / not being able to bask in the laurel reflection, / can earn a living, I will dare . . .' (II: 50) as well as the words, 'The Greek principle of masks / is again in fashion' (II: 51); 'with the anguish of Ulysses' (II: 53).

The obvious biographical relevance of its mythological references and characters sometimes leads to simplistic interpretations of Brodsky's poetry: 'Almost every poem of Joseph Brodsky's after 1965, when carefully analyzed, turns out to be a sort of meditation upon some actual personal situation which gains in significance by its being embedded in a plot line taken from classical mythology'.[3] That might well be said of 'Odysseus to Telemachus' if the Odysseus/Brodsky character, could be interpreted as the Odysseus of the literary tradition,[4] the romantic wanderer and conqueror surmounting his trials and tribulations – and if Brodsky were a poseur rather than a poet. But Brodsky's text is emotionally detached, and the picture he paints is more of a deflation of the literary Odysseus figure than an aggrandizement of his own. His concept of the character undervalues or excises any hint of the heroic:[5] the only romantic aspect that remains is the name as sign of cultural allegiance. Clearly its personal aspect lies in the poet's quest for salvation from his own desolation at a time when everything in the outside world lies in ruins. The poem conforms to the basic rules: 'The classical motifs in Brodsky's work are organically related to one of the main recurring themes of his poetry – the catastrophic decay of our culture and its traditional moral and spiritual roots. On the lyrical level this is paralleled by the equally persistent theme of the tragic instability and the disintegration of personal relationships, resulting in separation, betrayal, departures'.[6] 'Odysseus to Telemachus' contains no declarations concerning the state of culture. The concern can, nevertheless, be felt and is of the utmost importance. In his search for salvation, Brodsky turns to his own spiritual experience and to that of his mentors', primarily Mandelshtam, Akhmatova and Tsvetaeva. Through them he learns how to combat the destructive forces of time and space. However, Brodsky digests the teachings of his mentors critically, searching continually for his own means of carrying on the fight.

Firstly, let us define the precise relationship between the text under analysis with the myth and Homer's epic poem, which is something which has been examined by both M. Kreps[7] and Shtal'.[8] I would add to what Kreps has to say, that Brodsky blends together two separate episodes. In the first, Odysseus is detained for a year on the island of Aeaea by Circe, who transforms his men into swine. In the second – which occupies seven years – the nymph Calypso detains Odysseus on the island of Ogygia. There is a third island to which the phrase 'all islands resemble one another' could refer. In Homer's poem, Odysseus returns home to Ithaca and is, at first, unable to recognize the place or be recognized by his loved ones.

In all probability, Brodsky, summing up his own life in the city of Leningrad, had Vasilevsky Island in mind. Even in his very early poems, this symbolized a place to return to at the end of one's days. As early as 1961, in 'July Intermezzo' ('You will return home. So what . . .'), he wrote, 'How nice it is there is nobody to blame, / nobody in this world has any obligations to you, / how nice it is nobody is obliged to love you / till death do you part' (I: 87).[9] This presages Odysseus' letter to Telemachus.

The Trojan War in Brodsky's poetry is not just the Second World War[10] or simply 'an ironic code for the "war with the state machine"'.[11] It can be seen also as the Civil War which, beginning in 1917, continued, in various forms, throughout all the years of the Soviet regime and, as an ideological struggle, continues to this day. For Brodsky, the war ended with exile. That cessation of hostilities forced him to concentrate on existential questions: 'When, in the face of violence, extermination and terror, primitive fear makes its appearance, the other, secret fear, the fear of existence itself, evaporates'.[12]

Brodsky's 'A New Life' (1988) has a direct bearing on the problem of existence and the ending of the war and needs to be viewed in the context of both 'Odysseus to Telemachus' and the mythical subtext: 'Imagine the war is over, that peace reigns [. . .] There where the horizon lies the sail is his judge. / The eye prefers the remnant of a piece of soap to a rag or foam. / And if anybody asks, 'Who are you?' answer, 'Who am I?' / 'I am Nobody'. As once Odysseus replied to Polyphemes' (III: 167, 168–9).

The lines 'It must have been the Greeks: / only the Greeks could have forsaken / so many corpses abroad' are remarkable not only because Greeks is clearly a euphemism for Russians – that has been noted by everybody who has written about this poem. Greeks outside Greece was a theme Brodsky was musing upon as early as 1966 in 'A Halt in the Desert'.[13] There he talks frankly about Greek culture as the foundation of Russian culture and about the responsibilities its upholders must shoulder: 'There are so few Greeks now in Leningrad, / and, in general, outside of Greece there are few. / At least too few to preserve the buildings of the faith. / And to have faith in what we build, / nobody demands that of them. / It is one thing, / probably, to christen a nation / but to carry a cross that is something else altogether. / They had just one obligation. / They have failed to fulfil it. / The unploughed fields have grown wild' (II: 12).

The lexical congruence of the phrases *vne Gretsii* [outside Greece] and *vne doma* [abroad] indicates a direct link between the two texts; in 'A Halt in the Desert' Brodsky is an observer who does not identify himself with the Greeks; however, in 'Odysseus to Telemachus' he becomes a participant because he himself is now 'abroad'. The poem about the Greek church ends with a meditation on a loss of spiritual orientation, a loss of place in time, in history, culture, ethics: 'At night I look through my window / and think, where have we got to?' (II: 13).

Bearing in mind the significant number of interpretations, which go beyond Homer's poem and self-reference, we will direct our attention to the intertextual links of the poem. Until now, as far as I know, only V. Kulle has ventured into this territory. Comparing 'Odysseus to Telemachus' with 'A Letter', a poem by Umberto Saba[14] which Brodsky translated from the Italian, Kulle directs our attention to how Brodsky inserts a reference to Telemachus in his translation:[15] 'If the text of this Mediterranean daydream, / tapped out on a typewriter, / will give [you] pleasure, be so kind / as to put it in the blue notebook / I left behind at my departure / where there are verses / about Telemachus. Soon, I venture, / we will meet again. The war is over. And you, / you forget, that I too survived' (III: 314).

The word 'survived' is particularly significant here. Its semantics link Brodsky's text with the substratum of the texts of Mandelshtam[16] and Akhmatova. Brodsky sketches a situation contrasting with that which concludes Mandelshtam's 'Out of the bottle the stream of golden honey poured so slowly . . .': 'Golden fleece, but where are you, golden fleece? / The whole journey the sea's weighty waves thundered, / And leaving his ship, its canvas worn out on the seas, / Odysseus returned, filled with time and space'.[17] Odysseus' return, in the ancient mytho-symbolic sense, corresponded to 'a return from the dead', to 'resurrection', 'a conquest of death'. The golden fleece of Odysseus here takes on the meaning of a triumph over death, over the inert, uncreative, primordial forces at the heart of the material world. The acquired time and space is 'sad and stony' Taurida ennobled through work with honey, wine, garden and flower beds.[18] Brodsky's Odysseus does not return, time is lost, space is not to be conquered, our hero finds not Taurida but 'some filthy island'.

However, whilst incapable of mastering space and time, the golden fleece of Mandelshtam's poem, Brodsky's Odysseus does affirm with his very first words his possession: 'My Telemachus'.

The triple repetition of this construction, is not so much an invocation as the casting of a spell of affirmation. It is a question of grammar: the placing of a possessive pronoun in front of a proper noun is not a typical Russian form of address, it is a clear expression of possession.

In the poem 'The Golden Honey Flowing...' there is a direct question, 'Do you remember in the Greek house, the wife dear to all? – / Not Helen, the other – how long she spent embroidering?' To that question Brodsky replies, 'I don't'.[19] 'Odysseus to Telemachus' also has close ties with another poem of Mandelshtam's, 'The Day Stood at Five Heads...', from the Voronezh cycle (1935), though Mandelshtam neither mentions nor alludes in any way to the figure of Odysseus.[20] In another text of Mandelshtam's, 'This Blue Isle was Famed for its Potters', they are linked with the figure of Odysseus:[21] 'This was, and was sung and turned blue / long before Odysseus, / before food and drink were called "mine" and "my"' (I: 252).

The images of 'pine-needle meat' in Mandelshtam and of 'watery meat' in Brodsky are linked with problems of perception, with loss of sensitivity and, therefore, with staging posts in the cessation of existence. The poet under armed escort is losing his sight, Odysseus his hearing. The verb *zastit* normally means to impede vision, thus it follows that the image of fading hearing in Brodsky's poem is a product of failing sight.[22] Deciphering the image of 'pine-needle meat' in Mandelshtam's poem, it is possible to suggest that it is not simply prompted by a view of pine woods but is derived from the phrases 'sharp glance', 'penetrating look', 'keen eye', etc. Another phrase linked with 'pine-needle meat' is *dikoe miaso* [proud flesh] – an unhealthy growth on a wound which hinders its healing. It is a term that was known to Mandelshtam and it is twice metamorphosed in 'The Fourth Prose' (in relation to the linguistic metaphor *dikoe* as *lishnee* – superfluous): 'Things have gone so far that I only value the wild flesh around the wound in the word trade, only the insane excrescence' (III: 171). When comparing the two images of 'pine-needle' and 'watery meat' it seems of most significance that whilst Mandelshtam depicts a bodily change – the eye is metamorphosed,[23] Brodsky's 'watery meat' is not a bodily growth but is external to its subject.

The sharpening of sensitivity is, in both poets, a result of organic tension so extreme as to be painful, indeed such as to prevent the organ's proper functioning. Mandelshtam's metaphor begets not only the line 'and watery meat obstructed the hearing', but also the preceding 'the eye soiled by the horizon, weeps'. In the latter metaphor, three poetic sources, at the very least, can be traced. It is, to a large extent, anticipated by Mandelshtam's discourse on the powers of sight in his 'Journey to Armenia'. This contains images of the sea, stretching out, extreme tension, dust motes, tears, the horizon.

The horizon defined in the dictionary as an imaginary line, in Brodsky assumes an acutely sensed materiality, becomes an object which is painful unto the limits of physical endurance: 'Everything has its limit: / the horizon for [the eye's] pupil, for despair – memory' (II: 330); 'In my flight of the fateful line, / I crossed another – the horizon, / whose blade, Mary, is sharper than a knife's' (II: 338). The horizon in 'Odysseus to Telemachus' appears in a diminished form,[24] and Brodsky interprets it as a graphic sign: 'Just like Theseus from the minotaur's lair / emerging into the air, carrying out its hide, / I see not the horizon, but a minus sign / on spent life. This cutting edge is sharper than his sword / and the better part has been shorn off by it [. . .] One wants to weep. But there is nothing to weep for' (II: 293).

In Brodsky the horizon is always found in association with the weeping motif. The link between these concepts, tropes and motifs, Greeks, victory/defeat, the boy and tears as well as Mandelshtam's 'pine-needle meat' and poetry in general is distinctly to be seen in 'Post aetatem nostram' (1970): 'The losing Greek / counts his drachmas; the victor orders / an egg hard-boiled with a pinch of salt / [. . .] The Greek opens a terrifying black eye, / and the fly buzzing with horror, wings away / [. . .] Poetry, obviously, consists in / the absence of distinct boundaries. / An incredibly blue horizon. The rustling of the breakers. / [. . .] The tramp-Greek calls the boy to him [. . .] / turning he sees the sea / [. . .] Unlike animals man / can leave behind him / what he loves (only in order to distinguish himself from animals!) / But, like a dog's saliva he bestows the tribute to his animal nature in the form of a tear / [. . .] and there rose to meet him / a crest of pines where the horizon should have been' (II: 245–54).

Brodsky continues his discourse on the eye in a much later text, 'Report to the Symposium' (1989), which grows into a summing-up of Mandelshtam's 'Armenian Lessons' and of his own imagery. What soils the eye is generalized into a concept of inimical surroundings which sharpen the sensitivity of the perception of that organ's autonomy, overcoming the body's mortality: 'Eyesight is an adaptive device of / the organism in an inimical environment. Even when you / have wholly adapted yourself to it that environment remains absolutely inimical. / The enmity of the environment grows / commensurate with your habituation to it; / and sight grows sharper' (III: 182). On the other hand, loss of hearing in Brodsky's poetry is related to Mandelshtam's 'Sleep Was Senior to Hearing'.

In Brodsky's text, as well as the 'watery meat' and the eye soiled by the horizon, there is the metaphor of stretched-out space. 'As if Poseidon had, while we were there / wasting time, stretched out space', is also related to Mandelshtam's 'I, shrinking, was proud of space because it sprouted on yeast' (I: 214).[25] Mandelshtam's metaphor of growing space (in a construction in which space is the grammatically active element – the subject of the action) depicts a marvel of which the man involved in it can be proud, even if he is forced to shrink. In Brodsky, space itself does not grow, it is stretched out by Poseidon and there is no reason for the victim to be proud of the fact. What for Mandelshtam is marvel is, for Brodsky, merely violence.

The verb *rastianut'* [to stretch] is used not of space but of time. However, it is characteristic that the meaning of a linguistically dead metaphor, 'to stretch time', is defined using verbs normally applied to the parameters of space – (*udlinit'*, *prodlit'*) to lengthen, draw out the time for the accomplishment, transpiration or application of something. In Odysseus' wanderings, time too is stretched out. In Brodsky, the characteristics of time are ascribed to space (as language dictates) and time is described as something they wasted. Brodsky, preserving the usual sense of the expression *teriat' vremia* [to idle, to busy oneself with trivialities] (comparable with Mandelshtam's words 'a whole five days' in his poem about the journey into exile) but applying it to a victory in war, incorporates an existential meaning: loss of time as loss of life (for many physical death, for Odysseus loss of time – time subtracted from the sum of his lifetime). Thus, the metaphorical meaning of a stock phrase assumes in Brodsky a metaphysical sense.[26]

Brodsky's 'watery meat' is an image which is, of course, linked with the potential extension of the meaning of the word 'meat', i.e. its being applied to any flesh. But, additionally, because in Russian the word is applied not just to flesh but food as well, watery meat indicates a certain thickening of the element into some jelly-fish-like medium, one which provokes feelings of nausea.[27] And, actually, following that noun and adjective come the repulsive images of 'some sort of filthy island [. . .] the snorting of swine'. Odysseus' feelings as depicted by Brodsky can, indeed, be summed up in the word nauseous. A similar sense of inedibility – of the impossibility of assimilating reality – is present in the Mandelshtam text: besides the image of the eye as meat (see my remarks above on the cannibal motif) there is time as a damp swelling dough, a direct indication that reality is a fairy-tale that sticks like a lump in the throat: 'Crusty Russian fairy-tale, wooden spoon, halloo!' In Mandelshtam, consciousness is presented as a marginal condition divided between sleep and hearing. In Brodsky's poem, 'and your brain / is already confused, trying to count the waves' is the completely logical outcome of a situation in which 'watery meat obstructs the hearing'.

In Brodsky's poetics water and waves are forms of time[28] and the counting of waves is the equivalent of an idiosyncratic Odyssean calendar. There is another metaphor which is important here: 'And if we are indeed partly synonymous with water, which is fully synonymous with time . . .' (W: 124). In which case 'and the watery meat obstructs the hearing' is related to the titles of Mandelshtam's book *The Noise of Time*, and of Akhmatova's *Flight of Time* (cf. Бег времени and «волны набегают» – 'the waves dash'). One must bear in mind that water = time is a revival of the archetypal metaphor 'the flow of time' as well as of the literary (Derzhavin) metaphor 'the river of time'. The likening of water and time to man is affirmed on numerous occasions in Brodsky's work, and the comparison of waves with the convolutions of the human brain can be found in, for example, 'Kellomäki' (1982):[29] 'Tiny, flat waves of the sea beginning with "B", / strongly reminiscent from afar of the thoughts of oneself, / rolled like convolutions / onto the desert shore / and froze into wrinkles' (III: 59). The metaphor 'watery meat' is decoded and developed by Brodsky in the 'Fourth (Winter) Eclogue' (1980): 'Time is the meat of a dumb universe' (III: 14).[30] In the same text there is an explication of how consciousness goes awry in its counting of time: 'In winter in fact Tuesday is the same as Saturday. It's easy to confuse days' (III: 15). In his counting of waves Odysseus/Brodsky can be seen as echoing Mandelshtam's: 'The wave wavefully, wilfully dashes breaking wave's backbone' (I: 220).[31] In that case the action of time upon man, as well as the process and effect of self-knowledge as a result of which the brain goes awry, is related to the Mandelshtam backbone breaking metaphor.[32]

Waves in Brodsky's poetry are metamorphosed not just as segments of time, as cerebral convolutions and wrinkles ('All those years the river flowed by / like wrinkles in quest of an old man (III: 224), but also as rhyming lines in poetry: 'I was born and grew up in the Baltic marshes beside / grey zincous waves for ever dashing in twos – / and hence, all the rhymes . . .' (II: 403). The noise of the sea is the very 'sound of time', and speech itself: 'Throwing the vocabulary to the shore (I: 374); 'The sea, Madam, is someone's speech [. . .] I drank and I was filled with speech . . . [. . .] Remember me at the sight of waves! [. . .] what rhyming pairs gave us we return to her in the form of days' (I: 369); '. . . I have already lived in Holland somewhat longer / than the local waves that roll on afar / leaving no address. Like these verses' (III: 225). The general linguistic basis for the comparison of waves and rhymes is the use of the term *volny* [waves] in its acoustical sense (and the corresponding graphical representation), the transferral of the image of the wave – both watery and acoustical – into the emotional sphere:[33] *volnovat'sia* is a verb which can be applied to a choppy sea and to an agitated person, and there is also the expression *nastroit'sia na odnu volnu*, to be in tune with someone's emotions, be on the same wavelength. Of course the phonetics of *reka* and *rech'* [river and speech] are traditional bases for tropes in poetry.

There is an obviously constant and growing tension in the first part of the poem (at the Ulyssean myth level), and that tension is released in the second part. That growing tension and its subsequent release are connected with the process of forgetting. The poem's first stanza ends with the words 'I don't remember'. In the second stanza Odysseus' psychological portrait has changed: he remembers. In the first part there are five enjambments where the words take on a double edge. These syntactical hesitations make the reader sensible of meanings opposed to those eventually realized: 'The Trojan war (goes on, continues) / is over . . . so many corpses (there were many on both sides) / only the Greeks . . . / and, nevertheless the way leading home / [the way did eventually lead home] turned out to be too long . . . while we there / [a) we are now there, b) were fighting] were losing time . . . and your brain / [recalls] is already confused, trying to count the waves'.

The semantic dislocations are accompanied by dislocations of grammar. Thus, up to the enjambment Trojan War is the subject, after the enjambment it is the object. The phrase 'so many corpses' up to the enjambment is in the nominative case forming a nominative proposition; after the enjambment it is in the accusative and the phrase is transformed into the grammatical object. The phrase 'leading home' up to the enjambment is, in an actual parsing of the sentence, rheme, after the enjambment it becomes the theme, the emphasis being transferred from the 'leading' to 'too long'; the syntactical relation of the particle remains dual: does the road nevertheless lead home or is the road, nevertheless, too long? The word 'there' changes its spatial significance, 'in that place', to the temporal, 'at that time', 'then' remaining strongly accented at the enjambment, thanks to its semantic indeterminacy the pronominal adverb takes upon itself the function of a particle. The phrase 'there / we were wasting time' in the temporal sense becomes in Brodsky iconically figurative: in the pronominal adverb 'there' the meaning of space is widened, thus narrowing the meaning of the time which they 'wasted'. All of the enjambments have a figurative function. The irregularities in the syntactical structure and in the lexical significance are analogous to the movement of waves. The syntagma 'and the brain is already confused' sums up that succession of enjambments: its rhythmical break-up iconically models the brain's confusion.

The poem 'Odysseus to Telemachus' is the second epistle carried through stretched out space, subjected to the new ordeal of the contrary forces of time and violence, to be received within the dimension of poetry. In 1993, that is roughly twenty years after 'Odysseus to Telemachus', Brodsky wrote the poem 'Ithaca':

Воротиться сюда через двадцать лет,
отыскать в песке босиком свой след.
И поднимет барбос лай на весь причал
не признаться, что рад, а что одичал.

Хочешь, скинь с себя пропотевший хлам;
но прислуга мертва опознать твой шрам.
А одну, что тебя, говорят, ждала,
не найти нигде, ибо всем дала.

Твой пацан подрос; он и сам матрос,

и глядит на тебя, точно ты – отброс.
И язык, на котором везде орут,
разбирать, похоже, напрасный труд.

То ли остров не тот, то ли впрямь, залив
синевой зрачок, стал твой глаз брезглив;
от куска земли горизонт волна
не забудет, видать, набегая на.

(III: 232)

To return here after twenty years, / to seek in the sand your
own barefoot trace. / And the mongrel dog's barks fill the whole
wharf / not to show his gladness but because he's gone wild. /
/ If you want to, you can throw off those sweat-soaked rags; /
but the servant is dead who would recognize your scar. / And
the one, they say, who waited for you, / is nowhere to be found
for she gave herself to all. / / Your boy has grown tall: he himself is a sailor, / and he looks at you as if you were scum. /
And the language they all shout in making / it out seems to be
a vain labour. / / Whether it's not that island or it is indeed,
inundating / a dark-blue pupil, your eye becomes fastidious: /
from a patch of earth the horizon waves / will not forget, evidently, dashing on.

The parallels between that text and 'Odysseus to Telemachus' are
quite obvious, for example the line 'Your boy has grown tall: he
himself is a sailor' corresponds to 'Grow tall, my Telemachus,
grow';[34] the words 'Whether it's not that island' echo 'All islands
resemble one another'. In both texts eye, horizon, waves appear.
But the two poems are written in different languages: that *mladenets*
(infant) is replaced by *patsan* [lad] marks this stylistic opposition.
There is a significant change from metaphors of overcharged sight
to the careless, negligent desemanticized *vidat'* [evidently]. And
the object being meditated upon in Ithaca is 'language' itself.

   The thought expressed in the words 'and the language they
all shout in / making it out seems to be a vain labour' is iconically reproduced in the syntactic anomalies which begin with the
line 'and the mongrel dog's barks fill the whole wharf / not to
show his gladness but because he's gone wild'. In the text the
question is raised but not answered – whose language is it that

has changed? The homeland's or that of the one who has returned? Note that the text contains no proper names, the word *odnu* [the one] losing its meaning of uniqueness and taking on a demonstrative function and, at the same time, acting as an indefinite pronoun. There is, here, a possible echoing of Mandelshtam's line 'Not Helen, another one – how long has she been embroidering?' The word *barbos* [mongrel dog] orthographically transformed from a proper to a common noun becomes a sign of alienation. The verb *odichal* [became wild] is so positioned as to make one wonder to whom it is applied – to dog or wanderer? In the final stanza the words become involved in an absolute tangle which not only mirrors in form and content the returning wanderer's frame of mind but also reflects the attempts of the author to master a new language and whose brain, in the process, 'becomes confused'. In that last stanza the word *zaliv* [a bay] is grammatically and semantically ambiguous; up until the enjambment it is a noun and, after, it becomes a gerund (a part of the common phrase *zalit' glaza* [to get drunk]. With some effort it may be possible to make some, hypothetical, sense out of the confused fragments: 'the wave dashing toward the horizon from the fragment of earth will not forget that island'. However, it could mean quite the opposite 'the wave dashing into the fragment of earth will not forget the horizon'. This attempt to unravel the linguistic riddle which was, no doubt, deliberately posed by Brodsky, forces one to concentrate one's efforts on the verb 'will not forget' which becomes the antithesis of the leitmotif 'I don't know' of 'Odysseus to Telemachus'. The poem ends with a postposition of the English type which reveals what so tormented Brodsky – his loss of 'a part of speech' – for the whole of Brodsky's opus is an affirmation that language is the final refuge and salvation of the poet.

The testing ground for such a construction was the use, on many occasions, of a preposition in the enjambment position by both Tsvetaeva and Brodsky himself. The elliptical and euphemistic origins of the construction which transforms a preposition into a postposition give the widest possible scope for changing the position of any word. For this reason the construction *nabegat' na* could be continued with the words horizon, earth, eye, me, life, etc. It is, possibly indicative of what 'Ithaca' is about, the taboo recollection of happy moments in life. At the same time the incompleteness of the phrases models the destructive action of water/time. The influence of these destructive forces overcomes the last bulwark of existence – language – whose ruins can be seen in the poem's final stanza. In the linguistic confusion the mind of the poem's character, of the author and, consequently, of the reader, is so disorientated that even the name of the island *Itaka* ('Ithaca' which is the title of the poem) can be taken to be a product of the Russian officialese *itak* [therefore] a word used to open the final paragraph in reports, speeches, articles, etc. That would be an absurd assertion were it not for the lexical matching with the lines from 'Letter in a Bottle':

Итак, возвращая язык и взгляд
к барашкам на семьдесят строк назад [. . .]
поскольку я не вернусь домой:
куда укажешь ты, вектор мой?

(I: 366)

Therefore, returning tongue and glance / to the white-caps of seventy lines ago / [. . .] in so far as I will not be going home: / in what direction will you point, vector mine?

Brodsky's poem itself comes to resemble an expanding crystal. That is evident not only in its autobiographical aspect when the author, countering his own arguments, translates his existential reflections into their intonational and stylistic antipodes but also, from V. Kulle's observation that Brodsky has carried on from where Saba left off and that his work has, in its turn, been continued by Tomas Venclova.

Notes

1. See Joseph Brodsky's interview with John Glad, 'Nastignut' utrachennoe vremia', in *Vremia i my* (Moscow, New York, 1990) p. 285.
2. The metre of 'Letter in a Bottle' is a very similar to that of Kipling's famous ballad 'Oh, East is East. West is West, and Never the Twain Shall Meet', in E. Polonskoi's Russian translation: Kipling, *Izbrannoe* (Leningrad, 1980) p. 460. This translation was very popular with Brodsky, his friends and that generation of young writers in the Soviet Union. Incidentally there is a short poem of Kipling's, written in the same metre, which is very relevant to the Homeric theme

in Brodsky's poetry and to this article. It begins 'When 'Omer smote 'is bloomin' lyre . . .' (ibid., p. 424).

3. A. Kalomirov, 'Iosif Brodskii. Mesto', *Poetika Brodskogo. Sbornikstatei*, ed. L. Loseff (Tenafly, NJ: Hermitage, 1986) p. 223.

4. For the differences between Brodsky's and Ovid's interpretations of the Odysseus theme see K. Ichin, 'Brodskii i Ovidii', *Novoe literaturnoe obozrenie*, no. 19 (1996) pp. 230–1.

5. In the 'perestroika' years, when Brodsky's work began to appear in print in the USSR, this was the poem that particularly angered Soviet critics, who termed Odysseus' forgetfulness hypocrisy and mockery, typical of 'returning prodigals', see P. Gorelov's 'Mne nechego skazat' . . .', *Komsomol'skaia pravda*, 10 March 1988. Evidently, that was how the poem was first interpreted in Russia.

6. Kees Verheul, 'Iosif Brodsky's "Aeneas and Dido"', *Russian Literature Triquarterly*, no. 6 (Spring, 1973) part II, pp. 499–500.

7. Mikhail Kreps, *O poezii Iosifa Brodskogo* (Ann Arbor, 1984).

8. I. V. Shtal', *Odisseia – geroicheskaia poema stranstvii* (Moscow, 1978).

9. See Brodsky's 'You are no longer here, and there will be no more, / it's time I too was on the road away from these parts. / There's no forgetting. Nor anguish, nor pain. / You are no longer here. And thanks to God' ('Strel'ninskaia elegiia', 1960, I: 46) and also 'and death comes far from the one's native land. And thanks to God' ('In memory of E. A. Baratynsky', 1960, I: 60).

10. The post-war motif runs throughout Brodsky's early poetry, for example 'Book' (1960), 'March is coming . . .' (1961), 'Three chapters' (1961): 'The wars are over. The generation is growing' (I: 36); 'Meanwhile wearily the streets roar / with the sound of my semi-military century (I: 60); 'in my noisy Baltic homeland / in the midst of a lean semi-spring / walking shoes beat a tattoo / on a semi-war staircase' (I: 51). See also A. N. Vorob'eva, 'Poetika vremeni i prostranstva v poezii Brodskogo', in *Vozvrashchennye imena russkoi literatury. Aspekty poetiki, estetiki, filosofii. Mezhvuzovskii sbornik nauchnykh trudov*, ed. V. I. Nemtseva (Samara, 1994) p. 187.

11. Kreps, *O poezii Iosifa Brodskogo*, p. 155.

12. N. Mandelshtam, *Vospominaniia* (Moscow, 1989) p. 79.

13. In Brodsky 'so many corpses' hints broadly at a certain nation, 'The age has been, in the end, / not bad. Possibly there is a surplus of corpses' ('Fin de Siecle', II: 193).

14. Brodsky cites Saba as one of those who had a decisive influence on his life. See his 'How to Read a Book', in *On Grief and Reason* (New York, 1995) p. 102.

15. Viktor Kulle, '. . . Tam, gde oni konchili, ty nachinaesh', in *Bog sokhraniaet vse*, ed. V. Kulle (Moscow, 1992) p. 6.

16. Odysseus is one of the central figures of Mandelshtam's writing and this fact is, of course, a vital one for Brodsky. The names of Odysseus and Mandelshtam are linked anecdotally in the context of a telephone conversation with Enukidse (see S. Lipkin's 'Ugl', pylaiushchii ognem', in *Osip Mandel'shtam i ego vremia* (Moscow, 1995) p. 303) and as cultural memory in Galich's 'Return to Ithaca' (1969) dedicated to Mandelshtam:

'They are bringing Odysseus in a cattle wagon', Galich, *Vozvrashchenie. Stikhi, pesni, vospominaniia* (Leningrad, 1995) pp. 69–71.

17. Osip Mandelshtam, *Sochineniia v dvukh tomakh* (Moscow, 1990) p. 116. All further references are to this edition.

18. See Faryno's 'Zolotistogo meda struia . . .' in *Text and Context. Essays to Honour Nils Ake Nilsson*, ed. Peter Jensen (Stockholm, 1987) p. 118.

19. It is possible that Brodsky was here thinking of Mandelshtam's 'I have forgotten the word I meant to say . . .'. For the semiotic significance of forgetting in the context of this poem, see Faryno's 'Ia pomniu (chudnoe mgnoven'e . . .) . . .' and 'Ia (slovo . . .) pozabyl . . .', *Wiener Slawistischer Almanach*, Band 16 (Wien, 1985) p. 35.

20. O. Mandelshtam, *Sochineniai v dvukh tomakh* (Moscow 1990) pp. 214–15. One's attention is drawn to this poem because one is struck by the similarity of the two strange metaphors: 'watery meat' in Brodsky and 'pine-needle meat' in Mandelshtam.

21. There is also this line 'and the vessel's algid power / sundered into sea and eye'.

22. In 'The Journey to Armenia' Mandelshtam defines 'the eye as the organ possessing an acoustic' (*Sochineniia v dvukh tomakh*, vol. II, p. 120).

23. Cf. also 'What if Ariosto and Tasso whose monsters with azure brains and scales of moist eyes fascinate us' (I: 196).

24. For Brodsky's growing shortsightedness, see V. Polukhina's 'Poeticheskii avtoportret Brodskogo', *Zvezda*, no. 5–6 (1992) pp. 187–90.

25. In other poems by Mandelshtam space is compressed, 'And you, the chimes of the Kremlin's clock, you are the very tongue of space, pressed to a single point' (I: 212).

26. Recall that 'I Like Ulysses' also deals with loss but not of time but in time (himself? opportunities?) and the language is rather more bookish in tone, 'how much I will lose / in time' (I: 152).

27. See Brodsky's 'The New Jules Verne': 'A captain differs from the Admiralty / in his solitary thoughts about his self, his repugnance for blue / [. . .] When I strain my eyes / I make out some arches and vaults. / There's a powerful ringing in my ears. I will try to investigate the digestive system / it's the only road to freedom. Yours faithfully Jacques. / Picture to yourself an evening, candles. On every side – octopuses [. . .] Octopus (shorten it to Osia)' (II: 387–91). This is comparable with 'watery meat' equating as it does water, time and man, bearing in mind that, in Russian, octopus is *Os'minog* and *Osia* is short for Joseph.

28. 'I always adhered to the idea that God is time, or at least that His spirit is. [. . .] if the Spirit of God moved upon the face of the water, the water was bound to reflect it', *Watermark* (London: Hamish Hamilton, 1992) p. 42. The shortest and most direct formulation in Brodsky's poetry is 'Time is a wave' (I: 365). See also Polukhina, 'Landshaft Iiricheskoi lichnosti v poezii Brodskogo', in *Literary Tradition and Practice in Russian Culture*, eds V. Polukhina, J. Andrew and R. Reid (Amsterdam: Rodopi, 1993) pp. 227–45.

29. The figurative system of the poem 'Kellomak' dedicated to M.B. is

also connected with the Mandelshtam poem 'The day stood at five heads . . .': 'In a small town one usually eats / the same as the rest. And to distinguish oneself / from them was possible only by copying from a rouble note / the Kremlin spire, which tapers to a star / or by seeing your things everywhere' (III: 60).

30. Is it only coincidence that in Russian the third person singular of the verb 'to be' is a homonym of the infinitive of the verb 'to eat'?

31. Cf. Brodsky's 'Thus the tongue comforts the singer, / excelling nature herself, / changing its endings without end / according to case, number, gender, / God knows for whose pleasure, / looking into the waters with the eyes of a swimmer (II: 22).

32. For the semantics of water and wave in Brodsky and how they relate to the classical tradition see also K. Ichin, 'Brodskii i Ovidii', pp. 232–3.

33. An erotic image connected with waves (Or – dancing waves reflecting, as if in a dull / mirror what was going on beneath the blanket', II: 390] has no direct relation to the poem we are analysing here, but it is an extremely pertinent image in relation to the theme of poetry.

34. Recall the lines '. . . twenty years from now my offspring / unable to bask in the glory of my laurels / has to earn himself a living . . .' (II: 50); in comparing the various Brodsky texts which return time and again to the same image, we may begin to perceive a very personal 'stylistic wave'.

3

'On the Death of Zhukov'*

Na Smert' Zhukova

MIKHAIL YU. LOTMAN

Вижу колонны замерших внуков,
гроб на лафете, лошади круп.
Ветер сюда не доносит мне звуков
русских военных плачущих труб.
Вижу в регалии убранный труп:
В смерть уезжает пламенный Жуков.

Воин, пред коим многие пали
стены, хоть меч был вражьих тупей,
блеском маневра о Ганнибале
напоминавший средь волжских степей.
Кончивший дни свои глухо, в опале,
как Велизарий или Помпей.

Сколько он пролил крови солдатской
в землю чужую! Что ж, горевал?
Вспомнил ли их, умирающий в штатской
белой кровати? Полный провал.
Что он ответит, встретившись в адской
области с ними? «Я воевал».

К правому делу Жуков десницы
больше уже не приложит в бою.
Спи! У истории русской страницы
хватит для тех, кто в пехотном строю
смело входили в чужие столицы,
но возвращались в страхе в свою.

* Translated from the Russian by Chris Jones.

44

Маршал! поглотит алчная Лета   ' U I U ' U I ' U U I ' U
эти слова и твои прахоря.   ' U I U ' I U U ' I U U '
Все же прими их – жалкая лепта   ' U I U ' U I ' U U I ' U
родину спасшему, вслух говоря.   ' U U I ' U U I ' I U U '
Бей, барабан, и, военная флейта,   ' I U U ' I U U ' U U I ' U
громко свисти на манер снегиря.   ' U I U ' I U U ' I U U '[1]

(II: 34)

*   *   *

'On the Death of Zhukov'

I see columns of stock-still grandsons / the coffin on a gun-carriage, the backside of a horse. / The wind here does not carry the sounds to me / of plangent Russian military horns. / I see, in its regalia decked, the corpse: / To death journeys firey Zhukov. / /

Warrior before whom fell many / walls, though his sword was blunter than his foes' / with a brilliant manoeuvre, of Hannibal / reminiscent, mid the Volga steppes. / His final days, solitary, in disgrace / like Belisarius or Pompey. / /

How much he spilt of soldier's blood / in foreign lands! Did he grieve? / Did he remember them as he lay dying in his civilian / white bed? A complete blank. / What does he answer meeting with them in hell's / domain? 'I was waging war'. / /

In a just cause Zhukov's right hand / no more exerts itself in the fray / Sleep! In Russian history a page / suffices for those who in military formation, / marched boldly into foreign capitals / but returned in fear to their own. / /

Marshal! Avid Lethe will swallow / these words and your dust. / Nevertheless take them and a pitiful *lepta* / for one who saved the home country – say it out loud. / Beat, drum, and, military flute, / trill shrilly in the bullfinch manner!

*   *   *

'*On the death of . . .*' poems occupy a special and very important place in Brodsky's legacy. Of course, first of all, in keeping with tradition, they are about the deaths of poets. (Of particular interest in this respect is the poem, 'On the Centenary of Anna Akhmatova', which whilst, formally, celebrating that anniversary is, in content, one of Brodsky's poems 'on the death of . . .'). However, that is not the whole story. Brodsky wrote poems on the deaths of friends, relatives and lovers. Some are named, some given initials, some not designated in any way. Thus, the poem 'In Memory of N. N.' begins with the words 'I have forgotten you', whilst 'On the Death of a Friend' begins 'For you whose name's better omitted'.[2] One even gets the impression that Brodsky is more interested in death itself than in the person who has died. Such poems as '*Bobo's Funeral*', '*The Autumn Cry of the Hawk*' illustrate this trait and '*Fly*' and '*Butterfly*' are of particular interest. The insignificance – as it were – of the dead serves to underscore the significance of death itself. In his analysis of Tsvetaeva's poem 'Novogodnee' [New Years' Greetings] Brodsky feels the need to rationalize this approach:

> Every 'on the death of' poem, as a rule, serves not only as a means for an author to express his sentiments occasioned by a loss but also as a pretext for more or less general speculations on the phenomenon of death *per se*. In mourning his loss (be it the beloved, a national hero, a close friend, or a guiding light), an author by the same token frequently mourns – directly, obliquely, often unwittingly – himself, for the tragic timbre is always autobiographical. In other words, any 'on the death of' poem contains an element of self-portrait. [. . .] It may be that the only shortcoming of these wholly natural and otherwise respectable sentiments is that we learn more about the author and his attitude towards his own possible demise than about what actually happened to the other person. On the other hand, a poem is not a news report, and often a poem's tragic music alone informs us of what is happening more precisely than a detailed description can. Nevertheless, it is difficult, sometimes simply awkward, to combat the feeling that the writer is situated in regard to his subject as a spectator is to the stage, and that his own reaction (tears, not applause) is of greater consequence to him than the horror of what is taking place; that at best he simply occupies a seat in the front row of the orchestra. (*LTO*: 195–6)[3]

Though the tone of this would suggest that Brodsky is not intending us to apply this reasoning to himself, the poem under examination begins by fixing the relative positions of the narrational subject and the object of his discourse. The subject, in the light of the above extract, gives every appearance of being a spectator – the poem begins with a demonstrative 'Вижу...' [I see...] which is anaphorically repeated in the fourth line.[4] The text, at least its beginning, is constructed on the same principles as a news report: I am giving you a direct account of what I can see. However, this particular spectator is certainly not 'at the scene' nor, even, in the front row of the orchestra: the distance separating him from the action he is observing may be defined in terms of the difference between the faculties of seeing and hearing. The textual 'I' is near enough to see everything in detail but too far away to hear anything; on the one hand there is the 'I see' and, on the other, 'the wind here does not carry the sounds to me'. Thus the 'I' is a mere spectator (in the etymological sense of that word) – a witness. Here, this distancing of subject and object has nothing to do with the subject's being seated in the front row of the theatre's orchestra or, even, in the gallery, but has everything to do with the moving away of the object.

What is more, the character of the depiction leads one to suppose that this witness is not to be found in the general throng of onlookers, nor on the same level but, in some way above it (for example, looking out of a window or from a balcony, to use Brodsky's own figurative terms). Knowing the place and the manner of Zhukov's funeral it may be, though only as an intellectual exercise, possible to try and answer the question – where is the poem's subject physically positioned? But one has now to remember that in 1974, when Zhukov died, when this poem was published, unlike his lyrical *alter ego* Brodsky was not only unable to hear the sound of Zhukov's funeral but unable to witness it at all.[5] One can thus, really, only speak of the mental presence of the lyrical subject and one has to reject identifying the latter with the poet himself.

'On the Death of Zhukov' differs both stylistically and thematically from the general run of 'on the death of' poems. It concerns a man who was not at all close to Brodsky (either biographically, socially, psychologically or emotionally); is about someone who was, in every respect, distant. That distance (one feels the need to use the Lomonosov term *dalekovatost'* here) and –

more widely – incompatibility in general, becomes one of the motifs of the text.

The absent presence of the author is not the only incongruity in this particular text. It is marked throughout by lack of proportion and clumsiness, firstly in style and syntax and last, though not least, though the personalities involved are grander than those usually met with in Brodsky's poetry, there is one who is never named but whose absent presence plays an extremely important role in the text's semantic structure. The missing name is that of Suvorov.

From the very first words of the poem the reader is, as it were, posed a riddle. And, while in the course of the text's unfolding this riddle seems to remain unresolved, the poem's final word, 'the bullfinch', contains, if not a direct answer, at the very least a decisive hint. The poem's metre, used by Brodsky here for the first and last time, is one seldom encountered in the general metric repertory of Russian poetry and holds for the knowledgeable reader an unambiguous association with a specific poem – Derzhavin's 'Bullfinch', an ode (and that was the poem's genre according to the author himself, any formal indications to the contrary) on the occasion of Suvorov's death.[6] Here is the text of that poem:

Снигирь

Что ты заводишь песню военну	′U ׀U ′U ׀ ′U ׀U ′U
Флейте подобно, милый снигирь?	′U ׀U ′U ׀ ′U ׀U ′
С кем мы пойдем войной на Гиену?	′ ׀U U ′ ׀U ′ ׀U U ′U
Кто теперь вождь наш? Кто богатырь?	′U U ׀ ′U ׀ ′ ׀U U ′
Сильный где храбрый, быстрый Суворов?	′ U U ׀ ′ U ׀ ′ U ׀U ′U
Северны громы в гробе лежат.	′ U U ׀ ′ U ׀ ′ U ׀U
Кто перед ратью будет, пылая,	′ ׀U U ′ ׀U ′ ׀U ′U
Ездить на кляче, есть сухари;	′ U׀U ′U ׀ ′ ׀ ′U U ′
В стуже и в зное мечь закаляя,	′ U׀U ′U ׀ ′ ׀ ′U U ′U
Спать на соломе, бдеть до зари;	′ ׀U U ′U ׀ ′ ׀ ′U U ′
Тысячи воинств, стен и затворов,	′ U U ׀ ′U ׀ ′ ׀U U ′U
С горстью Россиян все побеждать?	′ U׀U ′U ׀ ′ ׀ ′U U ′
Быть везде первым, в мужестве строгом,	′ ׀U U ′ ׀U ′ ׀U U ׀ ′U
Шутками зависть, злобу штыком,	′ U U ׀ ′U ׀ ′ ׀U ′U ′
Рок низлагать молитвой и Богом,	′ ׀U U ′ ׀U ′ ׀U ′U ′U

Скиптры давая, зваться рабом,
Доблестей быв страдалец единых,
Жить для царя, себя изнурять?

Нет теперь мужа в свете столь славна:
Полно петь песню военну снигирь!
Бранна музыка днесь не забавна,
Слышен отвсюду томный вой лир;
Львинова сердца, крыльев орлинных,
Нет уже с нами! – что воевать?

'Bullfinch'

Why do you start to sing a martial song / like a flute, sweet bullfinch? / With whom will we go through war to Gehenna? / Who is our leader now? Who our hero? / Where is strong valiant swift Suvorov? / Our Northern thunder in his coffin lies. / /

Who will advance, blazing, at the head of our host / astride his nag munching rusks; / his sword in the hard frost and the intense heat tempering / sleeping on straw, vigilant till dawn / thousands of warriors, fortress walls and gates / with a handful of Russians conquer all? / /

First in every place in manhood stern, / envy with jests, malice with bayonet, / Fate laying low with prayer and God, / sceptres bestowing, calling himself a slave, / of his own virtues being the martyr, / to live for the Tsar and wear oneself out? //

There is now no man so famed on earth / / Enough of your war song bullfinch! / Martial music does not amuse today / audible on all sides is the lyre's languid wail: / He of the lion heart, of the eagle's wings / Is no longer with us! – How will we wage war? / /

The metrical basis of 'Bullfinch' is a caesua-ed four-foot dactyl with truncation before the caesura (D4tc1): _UU_UI_UU_(U) or D2$_f$ + D2$_{f/m}$. Nineteen of the poem's lines follow that scheme whilst four further lines contain a slight modification to it with a displaced caeusura: _UU_IU_UU_(U) (i.e. $D2_m$ + Am2); one line is a 'pure' D4; however, the caesura follows the fifth syllable causing it to seem to be $D2_f$ + AM2. Brodsky, in comparison with Derzhavin, simplifies the metrical structure, reducing the variants to two, which are, however, distributed in more equal proportions: 17 of the 30 lines are D4c1 and 13 are D4. Their distribution within the stanzas, however, is uneven: in stanzas I and II there are two lines that are D4, in stanza III just one, while in the IVth and Vth there are four. Thus, from the metrical point of view the poem is divided into two parts: stanzas I, II, III and stanzas IV and V.

The rhythmical structure of Brodsky's poem differs in principle from Derzhavin's. In the latter there are no omissions of expected stress, though there are supplementary stresses, most of these being concentrated in the first inter-ictic interval of the opening line of a stanza ('kto *teper'* vozhd' nash', 'kto *pered* rat'iu', 'byt' *vezde* pervym', 'net *teper'* muzha polno *pet'* pesniu', 'tomnyi *voi* lir', 'net *uzhe* s nami'). Brodsky, on the other hand, avoids supplementary stresses and omits stress where one expects to find it (mainly, in keeping with the Russian tradition in dactylic verse, on the first, but once on the third, i.e. the first post-caesuran ictus) The 'heavy' disharmonious rhythm of Derzhavin is 'lightened' in an essential way by Brodsky.

The characteristic differences can also be seen in the distribution of word intervals in the poem:

	Masc.	Fem.	Dactylic
Brodsky	17.6%	57.7%	24.7%
Derzhavin	27.8%	58.3%	13.9%

Whilst the index of feminine intervals is the same in both, in Derzhavin the number of masculine endings is decidedly greater than the dactylic. In Brodsky's poem the contrary is true. Derzhavin constructs his text on the contrast between masculine and feminine intervals whilst, with one exception, he uses dactyls only in the first few words of a line. Moreover, in the first and, in particular, in the fourth stanza, there is a decided predominance of feminine intervals (compare the first couplet which consists of them entirely), whilst in stanzas II and III they are equally balanced with masculine intervals. The preponderance of dactylic intervals has a function analogous to that of omitted stress – a lightening of the verse.

It should be noted that Brodsky who, in general, displays an exceptional sensitivity to poetic structure (which does not, however, prevent him in his essays from committing errors in the nomenclature of metric forms) shows particular attention to the breaks in the poem, the caesura and the intervals generally. Thus, again in the Tsvetaeva essay we read: 'In the final analysis every writer strives for the very same thing: to regain or hold back time past or current. Towards this end the poet has at his disposal caesura, unaccented feet, dactylic endings . . .' (*LTO*: 180).

For us it is unimportant just how universally an avowed principle is applied, there is no need whatsoever to doubt Brodsky's practical poetic ability. Time is also one of the central characters of this poem though, as with Suvorov, it is not named outright.

In comparison with 'Bullfinch' the stanzaic construction of 'On the Death of Zhukov' is simplified in one significant respect. The whole of Derzhavin's poem has a unifying chain rhyming scheme: AbAbCd EfEfCd GhGhId JkJkId. The sextains are paired together by the rhymes of the concluding couplets, whilst each sextain ends with the same rhyme. (Note that at that time, called by M. L. Gasparov the 'first period of crisis in Russian rhyme', *lezhat / pobezhdat' / iznuriat' / voevat'* were fully canonic rhymes.) Brodsky keeps the sextains but, from the point of view of rhyme, makes them self-enclosed and, what is more, the rhyme scheme for the first sextain (AbAbbA) differs somewhat from what follows (AbAbAbAb). The difference in length of the poem means that because of the five-stanza construction there is a purely mechanical isolation of the third, middle, stanza. The special position of stanza III manifests itself at the level of sound, through both its vowel and its consonant orchestration. From the point of view of stressed vowels the basic 'subject' of the poem is the opposition between the compact vowels (A, O and E) and the diffuse vowels (I and U); in particular the opposition of A (the most compact of sounds) and U. Most revealing, in that sense, is the distribution of stressed vowels in the rhymes. In the first stanza all the rhymes are stressed on U; in the second stanza A and E alternate; in the third all are stressed on A; in the fourth I and U alternate while, in the fifth, it is again the turn of A and E. Though compact vowels predominate over diffuse in all the stanzas, the absolute peak of compactness occurs in the third stanza where the ratio of compact to diffuse vowels is 7 to 1, whereas in the first stanza that ratio is just 1.4 to 1, in the second 6.3 to 1, in the fourth a mere 1.1 to 1 and in the fifth 5 to 1. If it were not for the third stanza we would see a regular alternation of 'non-compact' and 'compact' stanzas throughout the poem. From the psycho-physiological point of view diffuseness and compactness are very important parameters in Russian vocalism. According to K. F. Taranovsky they evoke very well-defined synaesthetic reactions; diffuseness is associated with instability and incompleteness, whilst compactness, on the contrary, evokes feelings of stability and completeness.[7] If now, with that in mind, we turn to the semantics of the poems, then we must note that Brodsky goes directly counter to this sound symbolism. The third stanza, the compositional centre of the poem and, moreover, the most 'stable' phonically, is, from the semantic point of view, the most unbalanced, in it the phrase 'polnyi proval' [a complete blank] assumes an ironic shade which mirrors the reader's feelings at that point in the poem. That feeling is supported (it would really be more correct to say prompted) by the syntax; the third is the only stanza to contain three enjambments and interrogative constructions (all three of them). If in the other stanzas there are two or three sentences, in the third there are six.

As far as any orchestration of consonants is concerned, we only have to turn our attention to one parameter, the number of consonants. (As B. O. Unbegaun noted, in syllabatonic poetry, while there is a predetermined number of vowels in a line, the poet is free in his choice of the number of consonants.) The third stanza is where, leaving to one side any other dissonance, the most consonants are to be found, if on average there are 15.1 consonants to a line (in the fifth stanza 13.5) in the third there are 16.7.[8]

From the point of view of grammatical construction, of most interest in the distribution of tenses. The first stanza is restricted to the present tense, the second to the past. Beginning with the third stanza, the temporal unity is disrupted. In lines 1 to 4 the past tense of the preceding stanza continues, but in the fifth and sixth lines there is an abrupt change to the future tense. The fourth stanza is a mirror image of the third, the fifth starts with the future and ends with the present.

Tense as a grammatical category is usually closely linked with the temporal semantics of the text – the more so in Brodsky's case given his acute sensitiveness towards Chronos. We have already noted the 'journalistic' beginning of the poem and its concomitant difficulty for the interpreter. The report is imagined.[9] It seems pertinent to ask what its function is. Obviously, it is not a matter of trying to impart a greater air of verisimilitude to the writing. It seems to have some other function here. A report is usually about something or someone important (or of great interest – a sports report for instance) and the author uses this to attune his reader to the grand, triumphant key of his ode. That same end is also served by the chosen metre, unambiguously associated as it is with Derzhavin's well-known ode.[10] In the second stanza, which is in the past tense, we are given with the help of comparative constructions a specimen of the so called 'pluperfect' tense or, in other words, of history. Two matters are of particular interest at this point: firstly, history itself is not (yet) mentioned and, secondly, there is no mention here of the person who immediately springs to mind as being a suitable comparison. 'A brilliant manoeuvre reminiscent of Hannibal...' is a reference to Hannibal's most famous manœuvre, his crossing of the Alps. Zhukov did not cross the Alps but they were crossed by that Russian general for whom, from his earliest years, Hannibal was the very epitome of the art of war – Suvorov. (As a matter of fact, the very first intimations of the 'Derzhavin' rhythm of the poem evoke immediate associations with Suvorov.) The beginning of the third stanza continues the narration in the past tense, but there are changes of modality and intonation: there is a move from narration to the use of the rhetorical devices of interrogation and exclamation. This stanza deals with something essentially antithetical to history – the ephemeral nature of the soldiers' life and the ephemeral feelings they evoke (they are shorn not just of individuality but even of independent existence, they do not exist, not just in the singular but also in the plural: soldiers' blood is not really the blood of soldiers but some independent inanimate substance).

Finally, in the fourth stanza, the image of History itself appears, but in a paradoxical fashion; it is not the past but the future which is being dealt with here. (Note that 'boldly marched into foreign capitals / but returned in fear to their own' is again, firstly, about Suvorov). In the fifth stanza the image 'avid Lethe' evokes fresh associations of Derzhavin – this time of his deathbed ode 'On Mortality', better known by its opening line 'The River of Time').

The temporal structure of the text is constructed in such a way that the alternation of past–future–past–future at its centre is framed by the present of both its beginning and its end. Thus, the composition of the poem is rondo-like but there is a remarkable thematic contrast: the demonstrative 'visuality' of the beginning is counterpoised by the just as demonstrative 'acousticality' of its conclusion. There is yet another circular motion to be noted; Brodsky ends where Derzhavin begins. One of the poem's fundamental themes is the linearity of time (Brodsky's favourite theme in fact) but the structure of the poem itself is a logical realization of the directly opposing principle – circularity.

Now a few remarks on style. 'Bullfinch', as is usual with Derzhavin, is constructed on antithetical principles ('sceptres bestowing, calling himself a slave . . . to live for the Tsar and wear oneself out', etc.) verging at times on oxymoron (for just one example, 'Our Northern thunder in his coffin lies' – where the antithesis is additionally underscored by a pseudo-etymological figure – agnominatio. Antithesis also permeates the text's stylistic structure; the lofty odic style is constantly being brought into conflict with low style: on the one hand, not *polkovodets* [commander] but *vozhd'* and *bogatyr'* (grand archaism),[11] not *armiia* [army], not even *voisko* but *rat'* (a grand archaism again), not the realistic *shpaga* [sword] but the poetic *mech'*, etc., and on the other hand, *kliacha* [nag[, *sukhari* [rusks], *soloma* [straw] . . . none of them neutral but deliberately low in style. A particularly powerful effect, however, is produced by this clashing of styles: 'Who will advance, blazing, at the head of our host / astride his nag munching rusks'.[12] The same conflict of styles is to be found in Brodsky's poem where archaisms (not just lexical but grammatical) mix with officialese and colloquialisms. However, unlike Derzhavin's changes of register, there does not appear to be any system to it; one would say that Brodsky wrote down the first word that came into his head, without a care about stylistic regis-ter. But that is certainly not the case. Firstly, for Brodsky, it is the breadth of stylistic register which is important; secondly, stylistic disorder itself, just like the disorder of life (compare *Pomnish' svalku veshchei* . . .) the disorder of the 'scrap heap', is worthy of remembrance – unlike all the great deeds and words which will be swallowed up by avid Lethe.

As for the strictly semantic structure of the text we must distinguish two levels: the *propositional* level (the level of assertion) made up of words combined in sentences, and the *sememic* level, the level of semantic units composed of the smallest units of meaning, of parts of words.[13] The two levels are very closely linked. In fact, words making up assertions are, in their turn, combinations of semes. Nevertheless, that link is by no means automatic and, in poetry, those structures are quite often in conflict one with the other.

What is so interesting in Brodsky is that, contrary to our usual notions of poetry in general and of lyric poetry in particular, he is a poet – if one can put in this way – of heightened propositionality. It is not the suggestivity of his imagery but the chain of his rhetorically developed and logically strengthened assertions which, at first glance, form the semantic fundament of his poetry. It is, therefore, all the more instructive to examine the creative forces at work at his 'sublexic' level.

The poem is, to use Brodsky's own words, devoted to the death of a 'national hero'; that Zhukov can also be categorized as one of the 'masters of thought' is questionable. According to the rules of the genre which are followed, in part, also by Derzhavin, this type of poem should deal with greatness and death. Those two themes may be accompanied by thoughts on the art of poetry, a meditation on language and death. An examination of the way in which the rules are followed in our selected poem is instructive.

Death usually (and in the European tradition especially) involves thinking about its antithesis, life. The two contraries 'living/not living' are closely correlated with two others 'static/dynamic'. The very first substantive of the poem we are examining, 'columns', yields a wide spectrum of interesting motifs. The first and basic meaning has architectural connotations and, considering the context of Brodsky's work as a whole, one can venture the assertion that it has reference to a specific imperial architecture. The reader acquainted with Soviet ceremonial practice will visualize the Hall of Columns. Here, however, because that does not seem to fit, one is forced to think along the following lines: column also refers to a particular military formation, introduced to Russia by Rumiantsev (thus the eighteenth-century motif makes its appearance). And, finally, columns in the widest sense has come to mean any significant gathering of people. Though, obviously, that last meaning is precisely what we have been looking for, the first two cannot be dismissed out of hand: they introduce the themes of monumentality, of stasis and of military science which loom so large in the text. 'Stock-still grandsons' carries those themes forward. One needs to direct one's attention to the recurrent incongruity that the living are described as immobile and cold but the dead Zhukov (he isn't borne away he moves) as active zealous and fiery. What is more, etymologically, yes and purely phonically, the word *zamershie* [stock-still or frozen] is linked with death. Thus, starting with the very first images of the poem there is an apparent incongruity, almost a contradiction, between the propositional and the sememic structure. If, from the point of view of the first, the dead body of Zhukov is led past crowds of people formed into columns, from the point of view of the second, the relation between the living and dead is significantly more complex – the living are encoded into terms normally reserved for the dead and vice versa. In this context one needs to examine the very strange image of the funeral: the body of Zhukov 'departs into death'. An analogous absurdity appears in the final stanza where *Lethe* is connected and rhymed with *lepta* but it is not the dying man who hands the coin to the ferryman Charon, the latter receives his payment from the author himself.

Of all Brodsky's poems on death this one is different because it is devoted to a general, to a man for whom, therefore, death and blood-letting are, in a manner of speaking, his basic vocation. And it is precisely there that 'On the Death of Zhukov' confounds our expectations: it deals exclusively with the deaths of *his own* soldiers, which contrast in the extreme with that of the man who led them to the slaughter, who dies in some quiet corner with his boots off. Thus, in the system of oppositions which form the semantic co-ordinates of the text, there is yet another, *one's own/foreign*, which is also realized in a completely untraditional way. The usual correlation *reliable/dangerous* is destroyed: one's own is more dangerous than that of the foreigner. Though the soldier's blood is spilt on foreign soil, it is not spilt by the enemy (the foreigner) but by their own leader for whom, in his turn, the entry into the foreign capital is less dangerous than the return to his own. Brodsky's semantic chaos is not lack of structure, the contradictions to be found in his poem are more straightforward than those in the antithetical Derzhavin's. Brodsky's chaos does not precede order but is the result of the former being developed to the maximum and that, quite naturally, produces ruins (look at the theme of ruins in his poetry).

Beyond the typically Brodskian cold-blooded logic in the

unfolding of his narrative, we get a clear view of that same chaos, the abyss, which also horrified and inspired Pascal, Kierkegaard, Dostoevsky, Nietzsche, Camus. . . . All of which leads us into Brodsky's own particular brand of 'imperial discourse' and, further, into the very imperial Brodskian imagery where everything is absurd, where there is a promiscuous intermingling of all styles and epochs (see 'Post aetatem nostram' or 'Plato elaborated', for instance). Imperial life is the life of the absurd where ruins prop up new constructions and where the fundamental law is the law of abrasion. A ruined totality engenders a ruined discourse, a melting pot of themes, quotations, languages and styles held together by elementary particles, hints, allusions. . . . And that discourse is realised most naturally of all in the 'On the death of' poems.

Notes

1. Symbols indicate: _ – strong position (ictus), ∪ – weak position, ´ – stressed ictus, | – word boundary.
2. The subject of this particular poem not only did not die at the time but has outlived the author of his verse obituary: the urge to write poetry about death was so great that any unconfirmed news of the death of an acquaintance was welcomed by Brodsky, almost as if he were prepared for it in advance.
3. Joseph Brodsky, *Less than One: Selected Essays* (London: Penguin, 1987). Hereafter referred to as *LTO*.
4. The Russian present tense can have as many as three different meanings: (a) the actual present, the moment of writing and speaking; (b) the continuous present and (c) the gnomic present indicating that something is 'always' true. In this last function the present approximates to the infinitive (*Iiubish katat'sia – Iiubi i sanochki vozit'*). Obviously 'I see' belongs here in (a).
5. One could, in theory, conjecture that he is watching the funeral on television or at the movie theatre; some of the descriptions could be seen as camera-eye views of the scene (for example, the backside of a horse could be a close-up). However, the next phrase 'The wind here does not carry the sounds to me' makes that supposition impossible – he could not be that far from the screen.
6. See, for example, Petr Vail's penetrating 'Snegir' na pokhoronakh Zhukova', in *Panorama*, no. 294 (1986) pp. 20–2.
7. See, for example K. F. Taranovsky, 'Zvukovaia faktura stikha i ee vospriiatie', in *Proceedings of the 6th International Congress of Phoneticians* (Prague, 1970) pp. 883–4.
8. It is remarkable that the index of consonants in Brodsky's poem is

no lower than in that of Derzhavin's: a poet noted for his deliberate dissonance. In 'Bullfinch' there are, on average, 15 consonants to a line. Because, especially for Brodsky, the visual parameters are of particular importance here – the more consonants the longer the line – the letters and not the actual sounds have been counted; this has no practical bearing on the results.

9. We should also note that by beginning the poem with an account of the sounds to be heard, Brodsky is engaging in a polemical interchange with Derzhavin – Brodsky's lyric hero is too far away to hear, he can only see.

10. It is curious to note that if Derzhavin's text significantly departs (in a purely technical way) from the odic traditions of the eighteenth century Brodsky's poem is specifically orientated towards that century in general and its odic tradition in particular.

11. Of course, all of Derzhavin's readers knew that the real Suvorov was of diminutive stature.

12. This clash of styles reflects for Derzhavin Suvorov's own unconformity, his scorn for the latest 'stylistics' of society.

13. A closer differentiation has been proposed by I. I. Revzin, who distinguishes periphrastic from categorical meaning: the former differs from the latter in that it cannot be phrased differently (or translated) (I. I. Revzin, *Sovremennaia strukturnaia lingvistika* (Moscow, 1977) pp. 37–8). None the less, we cannot use Revzin's terminology here because, for us, the hierarchic relationships between the different aspects of sense are equally important.

4

'1867'*

ROMAN TIMENCHIK

В ночном саду под гроздью зреющего манго
   Максимильян танцует то, что станет танго.
Тень воз-вращается подобьем бумеранга,
   температура, как под мышкой, тридцать шесть.
Мелькает белая жилетная подкладка.
   Мулатка тает от любви, как шоколадка,
в мужском объятии посапывая сладко.
   Где надо – гладко, гле надо – шерсть.

В ночной тиши под сенью девственного леса
   Хуарец, действуя как двигатель прогресса,
забывшим начисто, как выглядят два песо,
   пеонам новые винтовки выдает.

Затворы клацают; в расчерченной на клетки
   Хуарец ведомости делает отметки.
И попугай весьма тропической расцветки
   сидит на ветке и так поет:

"Презренье к ближнему у нюхающих розы
   пускай не лучше, но честней гражданской позы.
И то и зто порождает кровь и слезы.
   Тем паче в тропиках у нас, где смерть, увы

распространяется, как мухами – зараза,
   иль как в кафе удачно брошенная фраза,
и где у черепа в кустах всегда три глаза,
   и в каждом – пышный пучок травы."

(II: 368)

*   *   *

* Translated from the Russian by Lev Loseff and Barry Scherr.

'1867'

At night in the garden under a bunch of ripening mango / Maximilian dances that which will become the tango. / His shadow keeps co-ming back like a boomerang, / the temperature, like an armpit's, is thirty six [F96.8]. / / The vest's white lining gleams. / A mulatto girl is melting from love like a chocolate bar, / sweetly and heavily breathing in a male embrace. / She is smooth where she is supposed to be smooth and woolly where she is supposed to be woolly. / / In the stillness of night, under the canopy of virginal forest, / Juarez, acting like an engine of progress, / distributes new rifles among peons / who have no memory whatsoever of how two pesos would look together. / / The rifle bolts a-clanging, Juarez marks / boxes on the square-ruled form. / And a parrot of quite tropical colouring / Sits on a tree branch and sings: / / Among rose-smellers, contempt for fellow humans / is, perhaps, not better but more honest than striking a civic pose. / Both generate blood and tears. / Especially here, in the tropics, where death, alas, / / is being spread, like infection by flies, / or like a well-turned phrase in a cafe, / and where skulls in the bushes always have three eyes, / with a rank tuft of grass in each.

*   *   *

This is a dance in verse, inspired by memories of the author's trip to Mexico in 1975, a round-dance of multi-national Muses: Mexican History, French Painting (Edouard Manet, 'The Execution of Emperor Maximilian'), Austrian Lyrical Poetry (the Emperor of the poem was also a poet, Franz Grilparzer's correspondent, and, incidentally, in his poetry one finds the following line: 'Hispan'sche Nacht ist Melodie'[1]), Argentinian Music ('El Choclo', op. Angel Villoldo, 1905; the title translates as 'sweet corn' but its phonetical echo in the sixth line of Brodsky's poem is a chocolate bar; in the English-speaking world this tango used to be known as 'The Kiss of Fire'), Russian Urban Folklore, American Hollywood Film, as well as the Muse of Wanderlust and, perhaps, some other Camenae.

The musical motif 'gleams' rhythmically through the verse as the white silk lining of the vest worn by the tangoing Emperor in the poem gleams through the darkness of the tropical night. The implied music causes words to display a double semiotic allegiance: they help form the verse structure and also belong to the melodic structure. Each word is not just said but played out in a kind of verbal auto-reflexion, e.g. the word рас-про-стра-ня-ет-ся [is-be-ing-spread] *is* spread or stretched on the rhythmic frame, or the word воз-вращается [comes back] *does* come back as in a tango step, because the hyphen also functions here as a syncope. Words become signs of themselves just as in some art forms objects become signs of themselves.

'Film is the most important art form for us' (Lenin), or 'We all came out of the movie theater's darkness' (Brodsky). The movie in question was made in Hollywood: *Juarez* (1939; dir. Wiliam Dieterle, based on the drama, *Juarez and Maximilian* by Franz Werfel, 1924). It was made on the eve of the Second World War and has as its main theme the superiority of the democratic form of government: the Austrian Archduke, who was alien to the Mexican people, is sacrificed on the altar of democracy. Benito Juarez, on the other hand, is an instrument of historical justice (cf. in Brodsky's poem: Хуарец, действуя как двигатель прогресса . . .). Some lines of the poem correspond directly to scenes from the film, e.g. в расчерченной на клетки Хуарец ведомости делает отметки. However, on the whole, Brodsky quotes from his cinematic source structurally, substituting his own material for the film's. In the film Maximilian and Carlotta listen to the local song, 'La Paloma', and Carlotta translates its sweet lyrics from Spanish; later, before his execution, Maximilian requests this song. In the poem, the hero, who is the author's *alter ego* (a European in America) projected on to the past, dances the tango, which will be born only fifteen years later but which is the author's favourite. In his memoir, *The Spoils of War*, Brodsky wrote:

> Or else it could be 'La Comparsita' – the greatest musical work of this century, as far as I am concerned. After this tango, no triumph is meaningful, either your nation's or your own. I've never learned to dance, being both self-conscious and truly awkward, but I could listen to these twangs for hours and, when there was no one around, move in time to them.[2]

Incidentally, it seems that despite a popular dictum, 'It takes two to tango', but like the famous solo tango of Ostap Bender in the *Golden Calf*, the Maximilian of the poem also dances with an imaginary partner: the mulatto girl is but a personification of erotically charged guitar twangs. Historically, the chronological inversion and distortion of the Hollywood prototype are justi-fied, for in real life the melody of 'La Paloma' was used for an anti-Maximilian song of the 'Europeans, go home!' kind.

In composing Russian verses for American music, Brodsky was following an old tradition, which originated, it seems, with Innokenty Annensky, who, in the fall of 1904, while sitting on the terrace of a Yalta restaurant and listening to a Romanian cymbalist playing over and over a new-fangled Afro-American tune called 'cake-walk,' composed his 'Cake-Walk for Cymbals'. It is a poem about life's transience and at the same time about life as a palimpsest: Palestrina lurks in the Romanian interpreta-tion of Afro-American music, as does Palestine (Jerusalem), and all set against the background of a fish restaurant menu. Simi-larly, Brodsky's quotational palimpsest compacts the three stages in the cultural history of the tango: its cultivation, its profana-tion, and its retro-cult.

The first encounter between Russian poetry and the tango took place in 1913, the year Paris went tangomaniac ('*Cependant, la vague de trop langoureux Tangos envahit l'Europe, et ces musiques trompeuses bercent ceux qui seront tués dans la grande guerre qui éclate en 1914*'[3]), and at first, as it happens, they did not recognize each other.

Akhmatova recalled a St Petersburg party with Konstantin Balmont:

> Balmont was the reigning monarch. To us all this was completely unnecessary. [. . .] We went into the next room, someone sat down at the piano, and a couple started dancing. Then little red-haired Balmont suddenly appeared in the doorway, leant his head against the jamb, put his feet in this position [at this point she folded her hands crosswise] and said 'Why am I, such a sensitive person, obliged to see all this?'[4]

What makes this episode delightful, in a historico-cultural way, would not be clear unless one knew *what* the young couple were dancing. They were dancing the tango. The episode took place in November 1913, when tangomania had reached Petersburg:[5] everybody was learning how to dance the tango, which was the subject of tempestuous ethical discussions. It had an aura of subversive sexuality: cf. the following account of a Muscovite, who in 1913 was six years old:

[N]ot far from us was the 'Aquarium', a variety theatre. My parents went there and when my father began telling his friends that they saw 'the real Argentinian tango', mother took me out of the room: the tango was considered so indecent that it could not be mentioned in the presence of children.[6]

Even Balmont, a mexicophile and bard of sexual emancipation, who wrote about his desire to be 'daring and bold and to rip the clothes off' his female partner, could not find a soulmate in the tango, with its 'greedily posessive and obediently submissive rhythm',[7] its 'sinful artificial music' full of 'southern ardour and passion and, at times, of northern languor and suffering'.[8]

Talk of the tango's indecency accurately reflected the dance's stylistic history: originally tango lyrics dealt with the suburban bordellos of Buenos-Aires and Montevideo, glorified in transparently obscene metaphors.[9] The memory of this genre informs the salacious line 8 of '1867'. Popular Odessa songs with the 'El Choclo' motif – 'Believe me, it is not necessary to be in Argentina' and 'They opened a new beer hall in Deribasovskaya street' – were obliged to contain a minimum of one obscene passage.[10]

In 1913 this new barbarism, the 'tango,' with its languid nasal phonetics, or, to use a line from another Brodsky poem, 'nasopharynxal celebration', gave rise to world-wide associations and boundless exoticism. Here is a characteristic ditty of the period:

ТАНГО
(забавная песенка)

Марго быстрей, чем Конго,
Марго опасней Ганга,
Когда под звуки гонга
Танцует танец танго![11]

Tango
(a funny song)

Margo is faster than the Congo, / Margo is more dangerous
than the Ganges, / When to the sounds of a gong / She dances
the tango dance.

Igor Severianin displayed the same kind of boundless exoticism
when he made the boomerang a part of Mexican daily life[12] and
thus invoked a reprimand from Valery Briusov.[13] We see that
even in this sense the spirit of 1913 lives in the deliberately
confused *couleur locale* of Brodsky's 'Mexican' poem. Remember
that for Brodsky 1913 was the period of 'art's better days,' when
'one felt like singing: bobbaobby'.[14]

In Russian poetry 'El Choclo' was inaugurated in 1916, when
Vladimir Mayakovsky inserted a line of music from it into his
long poem 'War and Peace' (Figure 1).

FIGURE 1

In January of 1918 Aleksandr Blok heard a poem, inspired, it
seems, by the same 'El Choclo'. Blok himself already had experience in grafting, unwittingly as it were, a Latino-American melody
on Russian iambic verse, when he quoted the *habanera* from
'Carmen' ('О да, любовь вольна, как птица . . .' [Oh, yes, love is
free like a bird . . .']): Georges Bizet had borrowed this melody
from an Afro-Cuban song, which is believed to be one of the
immediate antecedents of the tango.[15] Having heard a poem about
the tango, in his diary Blok commented on the subject as an apoca-
lyptic sign of expanding decadence: '[D]ecadent poem (rhymes,
assonances, alliterations, tango)'.[16] The poem was read by Valentin
Stenich, whom Blok nicknamed 'the Russian dandy':

Tango macabre

Сияя сумеречным серебром Коро,
Слезящийся туман на слизистой скале пал.
Платаны сочными сонетами корон
Свилися над провалами слепого склепа.

О, близко с липко-льстивой лживостью скользя,
Продли, сомнамбула, соблазны сна, продли же!
Тебе с пути змеистого сползти нельзя,
И пес кладбищенский застылый мозг подлижет.

Со свистом голосит извилистый фальцет,
El queso tango радостные трупы воют,
Схватились за руки в стремительном кольце,
Задравши саван над бесстыжей головою.
Скользи, сомнамбула, с луною на лице!..
О, плечи пахнут глиной гробовою.¹⁷

Shining with the twilight silver of Corot, / The teary mist fell
on slimy rock. / Planetrees entertwined sleepy sonnets of their
crowns / Over the crevices of a blind crypt. . . . Oh, closely slith-
ering with sticky-unctuous mendacity / Extend, somnambulist,
temptations of dream, do extend them! / You cannot creep off
your reptilian way / And a cemetery hound will lick the
congealed brain off. . . . The sinuous falsetto wails whistling, /
Joyous corpses howl *el queso tango*, / They clutch each other's
hands in a swiftly moving ring, / Pulling their shrouds over
shameless heads. / Slither, somnambulist, with the moon on
your face!.. / Oh, shoulders reek of the grave's clay.

This sonnet by Stenich confirms that already by the middle of
the 1910s every tango became a 'tango of death'¹⁸ (as in 'The
Man from the Pink Cafe' by Jorge Luis Borges).

Death 'spreads' over the final part of Brodsky's verse tango,
indicating that this Mexican improvization with its semi-ribald
'lining' is not just a joke. The seriousness of this seemingly almost
parodic piece is determined by the fact that it is concerned with
a problem which has always been deathly important for Russian
poetry. This is a poem about a poet who let himself be seduced
by power, i.e. who was, so to speak, 'kissed by fire'. In other

words, it is a poem about the incompatibility of 'smelling the roses' with 'civic poses', although that was exactly what Gumilev, whose death perfectly 'rhymes' with that of Franz-Maximilian, dreamt about.[19] And this was the proposition rejected by Khlebnikov before he died:

Мне гораздо приятнее
Смотреть на звезды,
Чем подписывать
Смертный приговор. [. . .]
Вот почему я никогда,
Нет, никогда, не буду Правителем![20]

To look at the stars / Pleases me much more, / Than signing / A death sentence.[. . .] / That's why I never, / No, never, will be a Ruler!

Notes

1. Euphemia von Ferro, '*Erzherzog Ferdinand Maximilian von Osterreich Kaiser von Mexico als Dichter und Schriftsteller*', Inaugural-Dissertation zur Erlangung der Doktorwurde vorgelegt der philosophischen Fakultat der Universitat Lausanne, Lausanne, 1910.
2. Joseph Brodsky, *On Grief and Reason: Essays* (New York: Farrar, Straus & Giroux, 1995) p. 18.
3. Valentin Parnac, *Histoire de la Danse* (Paris, 1932) p. 69.
4. Anatoly Nayman, *Remembering Anna Akhmatova*, trans. Wendy Rosslyn (New York: Henry Holt, 1991) p. 86.
5. See 'Vse tantsuiut tango', *Argus*, vol. 12 (1913) pp. 112–13; Yuri Tsivian, 'Russia, 1913: Cinema in the Cultural Landscape', *Griffithiana*, vol. 50 (May 1994) pp. 135–9.
6. V. Morkovin, 'Memoirs', *Russian Literature*, vol. 1 (1993) p. 193.
7. V. Gorskii, *Tango, Poezy* (Moscow, 1914) p. 2.
8. Vl. Krymov, *Khorosho zhili v Peterburge!* (Berlin, 1933) p. 190. This is a reprint from V. P. Krymov's own magazine, *Stolitsa i usad'ba*. See S. Frederick Starr, *Red and Hot: The Fate of Jazz in the Soviet Union* (New York, 1985) pp. 29–30.
9. Deborah L. Jakubs, 'From Bawdyhouse to Cabaret: The Evolution of the Tango as an Expression of Argentine Popular Culture,' *Journal of Popular Culture*, vol. 18 (1984) no. 1, p. 136; Peter Manuel, *Popular Music of the Non-Western World: An Introductory Survey* (Oxford University Press, 1988) p. 60.
10. The most recent publication of 'They opened a new beer hall in Deribasovskaya street' has its obscene passage edited «Но нет,

Арончик был натурой очень пылкой / Ударил Розочку по кумполу бутылкой, / Официанту засадили *вилкой в бок* – [должно быть: в ж . . . вилкой] / На этом кончилось поломное танго» [But no! Aronchik was of explosive temper and he struck Rosa with bottle over her noggin, somebody stuck a fork in the waiter's *side* [originally: ass], and this was the end of the disastrous tango']. In *V nashu gavan'zakhodili korabli* (Moscow, 1995).

11. A. Belenson, *Zabavnye Stikhi* (St Petersburg], 1914) p. 43.
12. In his poem, 'M-me Sans-Gene.'(Это было в тропической Мексике . . .'): Краснокожий метал бумеранг' [A lady-traveller's story ('It was in tropical Mexico'): A redskin threw his boomerang . . .]. Cf. in 'After a Journey, or Homage to Vertebrae': 'One morning I walk out of the hotel and see Aleksander Vertinsky's couplet sailing into the harbor: "When we see the tall Brasilian cruiser, sailors'll tell us tales about a geyser"' (*On Grief and Reason*, p. 63); these lyrics are also by Severianin.
13. V. Briusov, *Sredi stikhov* (Moscow, 1990) p. 504.
14. From the poem 'Classical Ballet is a Castle of Beauty . . .' (1976): 'Бобэоби' ['bobbaobby'] is an onomatopaeic neologism from Velemir Khlebnikov's 'Lips' Song Was Bobbaobby . . .') (1908–9); this borrowing from Khlebnikov is not preserved in the English translation by Alan Myers (Joseph Brodsky, *A Part of Speech* (New York: Farrar, Straus & Giroux, 1980) p. 77).
15. Nicholas Slonimsky, *Perfect Pitch: A Life Story* (Oxford University Press, 1989) p. 223.
16. A. Blok, *Sobranie sochi nenii*, vol. 7 (Moscow, Leningrad: Khudozhestvennaia literatura, 1963) p. 324.
17. L. F. Katsis, 'V. Stenich: Poetry of a "Russian Dandy"', *Literaturnoe obozrenie*, vol. 5–6 (1996) p. 72. We can add that Aleksandr Vvedensky's 'Argentinian Tango' could be among young poets' manuscripts handed to Blok in January of 1921; its contemporary publishers could not help mentioning Brodsky's '1867' in their commentary (A. A. Kobrinskii, M. B. Meilakh, 'Vvedenskii i Blok: Materialy K poeticheskoi predistorii Oberiu' in *Blokovskii sbornik*, vol. x (Tartu, 1990) pp. 77–80).
18. See Yu. Tsivian, 'The Tango', *Experiment/Эксперимент: A Journal of Russian Culture*, vol. 2 (1996) pp. 307–35.
19. See N. Gumilev, *Pis'ma o russkoi poezii* (Moscow: Sovremennik, 1990) pp. 358–62.
20. V. Khlebnikov, *Tvoreniia* (Moscow: Sovetskii pisatel, 1986), p. 173.

5

'I, Instead of a Wild Beast, Entered the Cage'*

Ia vkhodil vmesto dikogo zveria v kletku

VALENTINA POLUKHINA

> Кто прожил жизнь, однако же не став
> ни жертвой, ни участником забав.[1]
> JOSEPH BRODSKY, 1961

Я входил вместо дикого зверя в клетку,
выжигал свой срок и кликуху гвоздем в бараке,
жил у моря, играл в рулетку,
обедал черт знает с кем во фраке.
С высоты ледника я озирал полмира,
трижды тонул, дважды бывал распорот.
Бросил страну, что меня вскормила.
Из забывших меня можно составить город.
Я слонялся в степях, помнящих вопли гунна,
надевал на себя что сызнова входит в моду,
сеял рожь, покрывал черной толью гумна
и не пил только сухую воду.
Я впустил в свои сны вороненый зрачок конвоя,
жрал хлеб изгнанья, не оставляя корок.
Позволял своим связкам все звуки, помимо воя;
перешел на шепот. Теперь мне сорок.
Что сказать о жизни? Что оказалась длинной.
Только с горем я чувствую солидарность.

---

* Translated from the Russian by Chris Jones with the author.

Но пока мне рот не забили глиной,
из него раздаваться будет лишь благодарность.

                    24 мая 1980 г.

                              (III: 7)

            *   *   *

'I, Instead of a Wild Beast, Entered the Cage'

I, instead of a wild beast, entered the cage, / burnt my own
sentence's length and moniker with a nail in the barrack, / lived
by the sea, played roulette, / dined with the devil knows who
in a tail-coat. / From the heights of a glacier I surveyed half
the globe, / thrice drowned, twice was ripped apart. / Abandoned the country that had nurtured me. / Those who've forgotten me could make up a city. / I mooched around the steppes
which remembered the howls of the Hun, / wore what's again
in fashion, / sowed rye, black-felted the barn, / and the only
thing I didn't drink was dry water. / I let into my dreams the
burnished steel pupil of my guard, / gobbled down the bread
of exile, not leaving a crumb. / Permitted my vocal chords all
sounds save wailing; / changed to a whisper. Now I'm forty. /
What's there to say about life? That it turned out to be long. /
Only with grief do I feel solidarity. / But whilst my mouth is
not yet packed with clay, / It'll only resound with gratitude.

            *   *   *

This, one of the poet's own favourite poems – he would read it
at festivals and poetry readings more often than any – can be
regarded as an epitome of Brodsky's creative work. It opens the
third English collection *To Urania* as well as the third volume of
his *Collected Works*. It is to be found in anthologies and in numerous
articles, interviews and reminiscences. His own translation of it
was subjected to harsh, and not always competent, criticism by
certain English poets.[2]
    The poem is written in a free dolnik which changes to accentual

verse whilst retaining a constant ending and a regular feminine rhyme scheme (ABAB), and its poetics are, at first glance, in many ways untypical of Brodsky's output during the seventies and eighties. Firstly, there is no enjambment. At that time, as in most of his preceding poetry, his enjambments were always both very unexpected and extremely daring. Brodsky also veers from the usual vector of his poetics in the syntactic sphere. His syntax here is not overfraught, there is no inversion and he does not go counter to the rhythm of the poem.[3] Every line is either a complete semantic unit or its end coincides with the end of a sentence. Nevertheless, despite the absence of obvious signs of the ailing syntax to be found in other poems written at this time, one cannot call the syntax healthy. Its simplicity is the simplicity of an official communiqué. Its minced phrases sound very like someone answering questions at a police interrogation. This kind of style allows unfavourable details to be omitted, along with any admissions of weakness, cowardice, fear or reproach. On the other hand, it is this same syntax that accounts for the poem's aphoristic quality.[4] Its stylistic double is to be found in the poem 'The Thames at Chelsea' (1974):

> Эти слова мне диктовала не
> любовь и не Муза, но потерявший скорость
> звука пытливый, бесцветный голос;
> я отвечал, лежа лицом к стене.
> "Как ты жил в эти годы?" – "Как" буква "г" в "ого".
> "Опиши свои чувства". – "Смущался дороговизне".
> "Что ты любишь на свете сильней всего?"
> "Реки и улицы – длинные вещи жизн".
> "Вспоминаешь о прошлом?" – "Помню, была зима.
> Я катался на санках, меня продуло".
> "Ты боишься смерти?" – "Нет, это та же тьма;
> но, привыкнув к ней, не различишь в ней стула".

(II: 351)

These words were dictated to me not / by love or the Muses, but the slackening speed / of a plaintive colourless voice; / I answered, lying face to the wall. / 'How did you live in those years?' / 'Like the letter "h" in "oh"' / 'Describe your feelings'. 'I was embarrassed by the high cost of living'. / 'What do you

love on earth with most passion?' / 'The rivers and the streets
– the long things in life'. / 'Do you remember about the past?'
'I remember it was winter. / I was sledging and caught cold'. /
'Are you afraid of death?' 'No, it is the same old dark; / only,
once accustomed to it, you can't make out the shape of a chair'.

At first glance, 'I, instead of . . .' is not a very original beginning: the first person pronoun is to be found at the beginning of
about thirty other poems by Brodsky. It also gives the impression of being a text in which, despite the considerable number
of tropes, the rhetoric has been deliberately damped down. Its
unembroidered simplicity of style is alien to Brodsky, though he
was in the habit of saying that that was precisely what he was
striving for.[5] It would seem that in this poem he was making
some effort to neutralize his tropes. Thus, the metaphor of substitution ('I, instead of a wild beast entered the cage') is weakened both by the presence of the personal pronoun and by the
use of the adverb *vmesto* ([instead of] which makes it virtually a
description of an actual situation. The grammatical structure of
the metaphors of personification ('. . . in the steppes which
remember the howls of the Hun'; 'Let into my dreams the burnished
steel pupil of my guard') ensures that they are just as restrained.[6]
Even the oxymoron 'and the only thing I didn't drink was dry
water' is such a master-stroke that it does not give the impression of being the author's own original trope; the phrase seems
so proverbial.[7] The poet's favourite metonyms – 'pupil', 'vocal
chords', 'mouth', because of their frequent use in other poems,
are toned down by that accrued range of just perceptible meanings.

What makes this poem original? This essay will attempt to show
that its virtuosity lies in the choice of lexicon, in Brodsky's inherent
tendency to bring together both high and low styles, in its strangely
moving blend of humility and pride, irony and grief. Organically of a piece with the rest of his work, this poem follows in
the footsteps of Horace, Derzhavin and Pushkin as a poem-
monumentum. It expresses, in a very aphoristic form, the life credo
of the poet, its style being dictated by the fact that it is, in many
aspects, a summing-up. A summing-up, above all, in biographical terms: everything recounted in the poem is factual, there is
nothing invented here, nothing 'romantic'. It paints a portrait
both of Brodsky the man and Brodsky the poet: in his case, fate
and character were as one. Writing on his fortieth birthday, the

Joseph Brodsky

poet attempts to clarify, as it were, his relationship with his own destiny, recalling all the main events of his life: arrest, prison, exile in the North ('a cage', 'in the barrack'), work on a collective farm in Norenskaia ('sowed rye', 'black-felted the barn').

It refers to the period between 1963 and 1965 when he was already the author of a handful of universally praised poems, and to an even earlier period, that of his poetic apprenticeship when, between 1959 and 1962, he participated in geological expeditions and tourist excursions, travelling all over a large part of one sixth of the globe: from the Baltic marshes to the Siberian taiga, from northern Yakutia to the mountains of Tian-Shan, where he did 'drown',[8] travelling on foot across the tundra and 'mooched around the steppes which remembered the howls of the Hun'. His enforced exile in 1972 is depicted as a voluntary act ('Abandoned the country that had nurtured me') and his life in the free world as an ordeal ('gobbled down the bread of exile, not leaving a crumb'), whilst there is a persistent memory of the unfree world he once inhabited ('Let into my dreams the burnished steel pupil of my guard'). Totalling up the 'unavoidable percentage of misfortune' (I: 90) that fell to his lot the poet does not complain ('Permitted my vocal chords all sounds save wailing'). He accuses no one in particular, apart from himself ('Abandoned the country which had nurtured me').[9] He does not rue the past, does not idealize it, but gives thanks. To whom? To fate? To the Almighty? To life itself? To all of them? He had something to thank them for in that jubilee year. At the end of 1978 he had undergone open heart surgery for the first time ('ripped apart'). He spent the whole of 1979 making a slow recovery: there are no poems at all dating from that year. In 1980 his third collection of poems in English was published to very flattering reviews. That same year, he was first nominated for the Nobel laureate, news of the possibility of his receiving the prize reaching him a few weeks before his fortieth birthday.

The poem is also a summing-up at the thematic and linguistic level. All of his fundamental motifs are present, sometimes in variant form: lack of freedom, homeland, exile, life, ill-health, death, time, poetic gifts, man and society, God and man. Also present is one of the major themes of his poetry – grief.[10] That theme which declared itself at a very early stage in his career, in the poem 'Pilgrims' (1958), is one which sounds insistently throughout his work, e.g. 'Song, no matter how resonant, is less distinct than a cry of grief' (I: 311); 'When there are so many things behind us, in particular grief' (II: 160, see also, I: 313, II: 129). The line 'Only with grief do I feel solidarity' could be taken as the key to the poem if we had not already heard, in a poem written in exile, his prayer that he might be released from the overwhelming burden of his grief:

Боже, услышь мольбу: дай мне взлететь над горем
выше моей любви, выше стенаний, крика   (I: 310).

God, hear my prayer: let me soar above grief / higher than my love, higher than lament or keening.

It is precisely that desire not to be weighed down by the 'burden [. . .] of grief' (II: 361), not to consider oneself the victim of any misfortune, that supplies the link between the theme of grief and the theme of courage and stoicism which was, with time, to supersede it.[11] The theme of, to use Tillich's words, 'the courage to be', is one which is fundamental to the poem under analysis. Brodsky early came to the conclusion that in the twentieth century neither despair nor pain nor grief 'was an infringement of the rules' (II: 210) but the norm. And in this poem the desire 'to understand the essence of one's fate' (I: 79) transforms the lyrical 'I' into an observer who comments from the sidelines on his own life and tries thus to make some evaluation of what is going on. And there is a certain ambivalence in that evaluation. On the one hand the urge to avoid a tendency to self-dramatization forces the poet to renounce his preferred stance of denigrating his own actions ('I [. . .] was ripped apart', 'mooched about the steppes', 'gobbled down the bread of exile'). Everywhere there is a deliberate emphasis upon his own ordinariness, even insignificance: 'And of the worthless children of the world / perhaps he is the most worthless of them all', as Pushkin put it in 'A Poet' (II: 110). On the other hand, one feels the stirring of some wilfulness: I will tell you what happened to me but none of it is very important, the essence of life does not consist in this, it lies in your attitude to what happens – in stoicism and humility. The tone of the poem bears no trace of either judgement or melodrama but, the critically inclined reader cannot help but notice an element of pride: the poet not only accepts everything but even accepts what others have burdened him with. This gesture of a proud soul is to be glimpsed in the very first line, 'I, instead of a wild beast, entered the cage', not they put me in the cage because, like a wild beast, I was dangerous. From the very first line of the poem fate is seen as just. The desire not to consider himself a victim forces Brodsky to reject the traditional metaphor of the poet as a bird, and a bird in a cage as a sign of his lack of freedom. A similar psychological complexity lies hidden in the phrase, 'Abandoned the country that had nurtured me' when, in actual fact, it was the country that drove him into exile. Behind that simple grammatical strategy of translating a passive voice into an active one is concealed much strength of will, product of an ethic of self-constraint and humility. It is worth noting that all three denials are, semantically, assertions: 'and the only thing I *didn't drink* was dry water', i.e. I drank everything; 'gobbled down the bread of exile, *not leaving* a crumb', i.e. I eat everything; 'But whilst my mouth is *not yet packed* with clay', i.e. for as long as I live. The line 'Those who've forgotten me could make up a city' is not unambivalent: with the stress on the word 'city' he underlines his belief that he knew thousands of people whilst, with the stress on 'of those who have forgotten me', the emphasis lies on the tragedy of forgetting and the abdication of human love. It was evidently not pride which allowed Brodsky to rise above his grief but a titanic reworking of himself and of his talents. 'In essence a writer's life may be thought of as the product of his work: his work begins to define the nature of his life. What someone praises, rejects or ignores has to do with his work not with what precedes it.'[12] The independence of his personality and the non-conformity of his poetic style made Brodsky, in the conditions which then prevailed, an outsider and dangerous.

Brodsky always remained 'one of the freest men' in the most unfree of countries.[13] And it was when he was seized and incarcerated, like a wild beast in a cage, that the real process of his stepping outside himself began. 'In those days it was what we called *self-defence*. When they grabbed you, led you to your cell and so on, you would turn yourself off. And that stepping out of yourself is a very dangerous thing because it very quickly turns into an instinctive state, with one eye you're looking at your own life, at your own experience and you give a chirp. . . .'[14] The more society tied him to the role of dissident poet or prophet 'whose opinion must be bowed down to' the stronger the tendency to step outside himself, to denigrate himself, grew. It is precisely this psychological gesture of self-estrangement that defines the intonation of this poem.

Being a summing-up, the poem contains not just the fundamental themes but also the basic tenets of his poetics. Moreover, the poet emphasizes them precisely because he temporarily renounces their most evident traits – the enjambments, the mosaic rhymes, the topsy-turvy syntax. In this poem he puts into practice what he theorized about in prose: ' . . . in a poem, you should try to reduce the number of adjectives to a minimum. So if somebody covered your poem with a magic cloth that removes adjectives, the page would still be black enough because of nouns, adverbs and verbs. When that cloth is little, your best friends are nouns. Also, never rhyme the same parts of speech. Nouns you can, verbs you should not, and rhyming adjectives is taboo' (L: 314–15). And, really, in the whole fabric of this poem there are only four adjectives to be found ('wild', 'black', 'dry', 'long') and two participles ('forgotten' and 'remembered'). Its basic vocabulary is made up of nouns (39%), verbs – almost a third (28%), pronouns (15%): this is excluding *kem* [with whom] and *vse* [all], which are directly related to the first person singular; *ia* [I] appears five times, *svoi* [mine] three times, *menia* [me] twice, *mne* [me] twice, *na sebia* [on me]. There are only two adverbs (*syznova* – again; *teper'* – now) and three numerals.

The craftsmanship of the poem is already perceptible in that distribution of the parts of speech. Substantives dominate in the rhymes – 98%. There is just one adjective in the rhyme position and that is rhymed with a noun (*dlinnoi/glinoi*) and one verb, also rhymed with a noun (*polmira/vskormila*). 'Three things about rhyme. First of all, the aspiration of a poet is to make his utterance stick. Rhyme is, apart from everything else, a terrific mnemonic device, it imparts an air of inevitability to your utterance. The most interesting thing is that the rhyme simply uncovers the dependencies within the language. It brings together those things heretofore unconnected.'[15] And in this poem the rhymes, as so often with Brodsky, enrich one another's meaning with their semantic congruities and incongruities. They set up, one with the other, complex echoes of both sound and sense. In the cage or under armed guard we are all liable to wail.[16] In the latter case the choice of the preposition *pomimo* rather than *krome* means that as well as wailing there were other sounds.[17] In the cold boundless steppes a hun doesn't just shout he also wails. Only a man who has entered a cage instead of a wild beast, who has lived in prison and barracks, allows the burnished steel pupil of his guard into his dreams and then, subsequently, sees himself in a position to secure a Nobel prize (how else are we to interpret 'dine with the devil knows who in a tail-coat'?) is capable of rhyming in the 'barrack' with in a 'tail-coat'.[18] It as if, like the style of dress, the poet's fate has altered: however, like water, it does not change its essence.

Hidden meanings are hinted at by the way in which the sounds of the rhymes are orchestrated. The rhyme *voia/konvoia* is surrounded by three other stressed 'o's giving an echo effect, whilst the stressed 'u' of *gunna/gumna* responds to the unstressed 'u' of the rhymes *modu/vodu*. His use of the short particle *rasporot* [ripped apart] in the rhyme position is also extremely interesting. Only what has been sewn together can be ripped apart: a sack, clothing, a thing, not a man. This expression is also used in fairy-tales of animals, e.g. of the wolf's belly in 'Litte Red Riding Hood'. Hinting at his two major operations, Brodsky chooses a particularly self-deprecating trope completely lacking in pathos, not just in order to avoid melodrama but in order to remind both himself and his readers (once more) of the general vector of man's fate, of what time does to us, transforming our body into a thing and ourselves into a part of speech, a number, a sign in general.[19] And with that 'thought about death – frequent, aching, palpable' (III: 165) Brodsky lived all his life. As Olga Sedakova has pointed out, 'this early and extremely powerful intimacy with, mortality, death, temporality [. . .] frees one from petty demands, insults and ties'.[20] The rhyme *rasporot/gorod* [was ripped apart/a city] combines a physical pain with an emotional one;[21] *rasporot* is related phonetically to *raspiat* [crucified] and morphologically to *vyporot* [flogged]. The pain is held at bay by grammatical means: by using a non-normative link verb *byval* [used to be] in *byval rasporot* [used to be ripped apart] instead of the normative *byl rasporot* [was ripped apart], he conveys the sense of something repeated many times, just as the verbs *khazhival* [used to walk], *nashival* [used to wear], indicate habitual actions, which used to happen and will happen again.[22] The rhyme *korok/sorok* [crumbs/forty] is coloured with the rich Biblical semantics of the number forty. Brodsky makes the rhyme *glinoi/dlinnoi* [clay/long] into a metaphor: clay, the basis of life, (the Creator's material) is presented here as the final substance of death. Thus in the wake of

their phonal links come the semantic bonds between the rhymes
which lay claim to the prismaticism of metaphor and fill the whole
right hand margin of the poetic fabric.

The right-hand margin, heavy with the semantic weight of its
nouns, is balanced in turn by the left-hand margin's own semantic
weight. If nouns dominate in the rhyme position, it is verbs that
cluster at the beginnings of lines and phrases: 'I entered, burned,
lived, dined, drowned, abandoned, mooched, wore, sowed, drank,
let, gobbled, allowed, changed, to say, resound'. It is verbs that
provide the narrative, the canvas backing of the poetic fabric,
portraying the various important acts in the life of the poet. The
distribution of the actions on the left hand and the nouns on the
right does not mean that the left-hand side is less important than
the right. Grammar often enters into the semantics of this left
side to provide additional weight. In the long array of verbs
beginning twelve of the poem's twenty lines, there is to be seen
a curious alternation of perfective and imperfective aspects.
Following the first five imperfective verbs telling of the poet's
many vicissitudes, 'entered, burned, lived, dined, drowned', there
appears a verb in the perfective aspect, the sole verb redolent of
an irrevocable act, 'I abandoned the country'.[23] It is interesting
that that sentence should begin and end with a perfective verb,
as if to draw our attention to the quality and equilibrium of their
semantic weight at the beginning and end of all the sentences to
come, 'Abandoned the *country* that had nurtured me'. At the centre
of that sentence is a possibly no less interesting inversion: the
country nurtured me and I abandoned the *country*. Such a
semantically and grammatically balanced phrase sums up the first
third of the poem. There follows a whole set of imperfectives:
'mooched, sowed, black-felted, drank', interrupted by a perfective: 'Let into my dreams the burnished steel pupil of my guard'.
Like the two previous perfectives 'abandoned' and 'nurtured' the
verb *vpustil* [let into] signals something final and irreversible from
which there is no escape, even in sleep – as if to confirm Pascal's
words: 'Nothing of what has been, ceases to exist'.[24] In the last
part of the poem the succession of verbal aspects is repeated but
the rhythm differs; there are three imperfectives (gobbled, leaving, permitted), three perfectives (changed, to say, turned out).
Another imperfective (I feel) is followed by a perfective (packed)
and the poem ends with an imperfective (resound). Ordering the
hierarchy of his actions the poet makes extensive use of the internal

bonds of the language itself, sometimes testing them to the limit,
e.g. semantization of the copula 'to be' leads to a contradiction
between the passive form of *rasporot* [ripped apart] and the active
byval [used to be]. There is a piling up of verbs at the left-hand
margin of the poem but these also penetrate the centre and even
the rhyme position, showing that they stand by their rights even
though Brodsky strives to make the noun the central grammatical category of his poetry. 'And that is natural', remarks Sedakova
in an article on Brodsky, 'the semantics of the verb connecting
the utterance with the person, time and character of the action,
bespeak a consciousness with an ability to co-ordinate itself well
in reality.'[25] The verbs, like the rhymes, have their phonetic focus;
the left part of the poem is permeated with sibilants and hush-
ing sounds: *vyzhigal, zhil, trizhdy, Iz zabyvshikh, rozh, zhral, pereshel,
na shepot, Chto skazat' o zhizni*. The repetition of '*sh*' in '*pereshel
na shepot* (changed to a whisper) is especially significant since it
is oxymoronic: a poet, deprived of a voice, speaks.

Douglas Dunn has made a curious suggestion as to the criteria
to be used in evaluating the aesthetic quality of a poem. If a poet
only burdens a poem semantically at the right-hand margin, he
is a good poet. And if the left margin of a poem also has semantic
weight he is a very talented poet. But if the centre sags under
the semantic burden, he is a genius.[26] Let us examine what lies at
the centre of our poem. At first glance the verbs are of a less
dramatic semantic hue than these to the left: 'played, know, surveyed, happen to be, and make up'. We have already spoken of
the function of the verbs 'used to be' and 'knows'. One's attention
is drawn to the bookish verb *oziral* [surveyed]. There is only one
other use of the verb in Brodsky's poetry and that is in a poem
also dating from 1980, 'Who is to know? Perhaps that is how /
God surveyed His own work on the eighth day and after' (III:
14). A somewhat blasphemous parallel is only possible in the context
of the poet's own verse: 'It seems to me that / my Last Judgement, the judgement of my heart is in the balance' (I: 135).[27] Bearing
in mind that 'glacier' is an archetypal metaphor of eternity,[28] the
line 'From the heights of a glacier I surveyed half the globe' refers
to metaphysical rather than physical heights, although, by the time
of his fortieth birthday, Brodsky had literally looked around half
the globe, including the heights of Tian-Shan glacier. Now he is
examining his own life and passing judgement, above all else, on
himself, not the world, remembering literally his own youthful

decision to 'create yourself and your life create / with all the strength of your unhappiness' (I: 127). The world gains the poet's forgiveness; his final two verbs, 'packed' and 'will resound', bear witness to that:

> Но пока мне рот не **забили** глиной,
> из него **раздаваться будет** лишь благодарность.

> But whilst my mouth is not yet packed with clay, / It'll only resound with gratitude.

These two verbs at the centre of their respective lines contain almost the whole fundamental seme of the poem, for in them one can read the ethical credo that guided Brodsky in life: acceptance of all of life's trials with gratitude. That the concluding line is indeed Brodsky's own credo is evident once one has examined the fate of the word 'gratitude' and the other words related to it by root throughout his work. It is to found at the opening of the poem 'Procession': Пора давно за все благодарить, / за все, что невозможно подарить' [It has long been time to give thanks for everything, / for everything that is impossible of bestowal (I: 95)] as well as in many other poems: 'with all my heart I give thanks to you / one saved by you' (I: 351); 'can you hear, every line / gives thanks to you for the fact that you did not perish (I: 353). Gratitude becomes an invocation: 'Let it [poetic song] ring out and in the hour of death / as gratitude of mouth and eye / to Him who forced us, at times, to look into the far-off distance' (I: 414). With the years the feeling of gratitude became part and parcel of the poet's stoic ethic: 'There, up above, / you listen, one thing: I thank you because / you took everything that I, in my time, / possessed [. . .]. / I thank you / or rather the last fragment of my mind / thanks you for not fixing me / to those of the tabernacle, to that framework and lexicon' (II: 212); 'A throat . . . um . . . gives thanks to fate' (II: 388).[29] The line 'whilst my mouth is not yet packed with clay', i.e. while I still have breath in me, refers us to several poets: to Mandelshtam's 'Да я лежу в земле, губами шевеля, / И то, что я скажу, заучит каждый школьник' [Yes, I lie in the ground, but my lips are moving, / and what I am about to say every schoolboy will memorize], the concluding line of which, 'Покуда на земле последний жив невольник' ['whilst the last slave yet lives on this Earth'][30] in turn recalls Pushkin's: 'И славен буду я, доколь в подлунном мире / Жив будет хоть один пиит' [I will be famed as long as in this sublunar world at least one poet remains alive] ('Exegi Monumentum', II: 385). It also reminds us of Heine's 'Zum Lazarus' with its motif of death – a mouth filled with soil symbolizing the loss of speech:

Так мы спрашиваем жадно
Целый век, пока безмолвно
Не забьют нам р от землею . . .
Да ответ ли это полно?[31]

But in Brodsky's poem what we hear most clearly is an echo of Akhmatova's 'Poem without a Hero':

И со мною моя "Седьмая"
Полумертвая и немая,
Рот ее сведен и открыт,
Словно рот трагической маски,
Но он черной **замазан** краской
И **сухою землею набит**.

And with me is my 'Seventh', / Mute, half-dead, a / Puckered grimace its mouth, / That could be the mouth of a tragic / Mask, but for the black daub, / The stuffed-in dry earth.[32]

Bearing in mind that Brodsky said, on more than one occasion, that it was Anna Akhmatova who showed him the path of truth, that he learned from her the humility and ability to forgive both individuals and the state,[33] it is impossible to overestimate the importance of that reference.[34] It is perfectly feasible to suppose that it is simply for the sake of those last two lines that the whole poem was written, 'in order to meditate on one's fate' (I: 123) and once again give 'thanks to Fate with Cyrillic letters' (II: 422). Brodsky always refused to separate ethics from aesthetics. For him, a poet is a part of the language (a voice of the language) just as talent (gift – *dar*) is part of *blagodarnost'* [gratitude], i.e. a man giving thanks.

   Also at the centre of the text lies one of its two participles, *pomniaschikh* [which remembered] which forms an antonym to *zabyvshikh* [who've forgotten]. What people easily forget the steppes and Nature in general remember: 'wood and meadow all recall. Everything around will recall' (I: 413). This antithesis of forgetting and remembering is sustained by the contrast of sleep and waking (Let into my dreams . . .') and also by the all-embracing opposition of life and death (drowned, ripped apart, whilst my mouth is not yet packed with clay). To the existential antinomies correspond spatial polarities: the cage and half the globe, the height of the glacier and the flat lands of the steppes, the shut-off-from-the-world land of his birth and the wide-open place of his exile beyond its bounds. These polarities shape the multi-spaciality of the poem (closed/open, up/down, north/south, inside/outside). The spaces which the lyrical 'I' occupies are placed at the text's centre ten times out of thirteen. The number of references to an quotations from Classics and his own works hint at the dimensions of the pretextual space. Almost all the words in the poem bring with them the semantics and metaphors of other Brodsky poems.

Thus, profound light is thrown upon the words to be found at the text's centre by examining their lexic forerunners. 'Wild beast' has its equivalent in 'herded beast' (II: 8), in 'of a wild beast' (II: 230) and 'stinking beast' (II: 48) as well as the straightforward 'beast' (II: 290) and 'beasts' (II: 383).[35] The unpretentious epithets 'black' and 'dry' also acquire additional semantic weight given the context of their metaphorical use in other poems. Black is one of the poet's favourite epithets and retains all the attributes of its traditional symbolism as well as being singled out by the frequency with which it is used. Black can, in Brodsky's poetry, be used of water (I: 26), glass (I: 80), boughs (I: 93), the horse of the Apocalypse (I: 192–3, 347). There are also 'huge, black damp, Leningrad' (II: 175), 'black cities' (I: 241), 'black wound' (I: 400), 'marriage in black' (II: 82), 'the black bars of prison' (II: 304), 'black nowhere' (II: 321). Finally, of poetry itself, there is a 'deposit / of black on the page' (II: 458). In the context 'black-felted barn' takes on a sinister shade, given the neighbouring metaphor of the burnished steel pupil of my guard', which can be interpreted as a metaphor for the guard's weapon (the barrel of his gun) rather than for the black all-seeing eye of the guard, a sort of devil in uniform. The oxymoron 'dry water', a synonym for something which does not exist in nature, joins a long line of epithets and predicates from earlier poems 'the fountain [. . .] is dry' (II: 149), 'reason is dry' (II: 252), 'dry foam' (II: 439), 'dry abundance' (III: 9), 'a dry clotted form of light. – / snow' (III: 13).[36]

'Life', as one of the most common and all embracing of concepts, is subject to a variety of tropic transformations in Brodsky's poetry.

It can be personified: 'How strange to find on the clock's face / all one's life with unclasped hands' (I: 110), and reified: 'Life is a form of time' (II: 361). Those two extreme transformations of life can be combined, 'Life which, / as with things given, you don't look into the mouth of, / bares its teeth at every encounter' (II: 415); or reduced to speech, 'Life is only conversation in the face / of silence (II: 127); 'all life is like a shaky honest phrase' (II: 324). Life absorbs classical allusions: 'In the dark wood of middle / life – of a winter's night, repeating the steps of Dante' (I: 309); and the modern semantics: 'Life is a take-away: / torso, penis, forehead. / And a dash of geography / to time is fate' (II: 457). The motif of life dragging itself out (III: 13, 15) is varied in 'What is there to say about life? That it turned out to be long'.[37] Life in Brodsky is often viewed from a religious or philosophical point of view: 'Tell me, soul, how does life look?' (I: 39); 'and my life will move forever beyond the parentheses of the eyelids, its eyebrows / forever raised' (I: 355). Being such a central concept the word life is to be found at the centre of the poem under discussion.

The three metonyms, 'vocal chords', 'sounds', 'mouth' are frequently encountered in Brodsky's poetry as metonyms for song (I: 303, 307, 325), poetry and speech in general: 'dictated by the mouth' (II: 330). That is why 'mouth', 'that wound of Thomas' (II: 325) is frequently accompanied by a verb 'to open' (I: 131, I: 401, II: 270), or a participle 'gaping mouth' (I: 34). The word *sviazki* [vocal chords] – 'That develops the vocal chords' (II: 364) – is a metonym for the voice and throat: 'The throat sings of ageing' (II: 290) and also a synonym for sound. Sound itself can be interpreted in this poem, as in others written in 1980, to mean intonation, melody, even poetic genre: 'And of urban elegies the new sound' (I: 109); 'No, the Muse wouldn't mind, / if from her adorned lyre / a commonplace motif would suddenly burst, / a sound, indifferent to taste' (I: 253). Sound is, sometimes, the only link the poet has to life: 'Here buried alive / I wander through the stubble in the twilight [. . .] without memory, with the same one, monotonous sound' (I: 386). Sound is animated and conceptualized: 'the love felt by sound / for sense' (II: 329); 'the orphan / of sound, Tomas, is speech' (II: 330); 'Striving upward, / sound throws out its ballast' (II: 451). The poet completely identifies himself with sound in a 1978 poem: 'I was, more truly, a sound' (II: 450). It is interesting that the line 'Permitted my vocal chords all sounds' is the most well organized in terms of sound orchestration: 'Pozvolial svoim sviazkam vse zvuki'. Other alliterations are less noticeable: *kletku; klikukhu; brosil stranu, chto menia vskormila: voronenyi zrachok; pereshel na shepot.* The placing of the tropes of substitution for both poet and poetry at the centre of the text together with the personal pronouns *ia, menia, mne* gives the centre of the text the same semantic resilience and multiplicity of meaning as the left- and right-hand margins. The metonyms 'mouth' and 'pupil' figure in a poem of 1964, 'To the Northern Land', written shortly after his arrival in exile at Norenskaia in Russia's North: 'Northern land, give me shelter [. . .] / And leave just the pupil [. . .] / Harness me up and close my mouth' (I: 327). *Zrachok* [pupil] rhymes with *volchok* [judas in the door of a prison cell], in another poem from 1964 (I: 336) and has the same semantics as in the metaphor 'the burnished steel pupil of the guard'. Pupil, like mouth, is part of Brodsky's basic poetic vocabulary, 'and blinding my pupil in the Fontanka, / I split myself into a hundred' (II: 257).

A variant of the metaphor 'bread of exile'[38] is also to be found in a poem of 1964, written on March 25th of that year in the Archangel transit prison camp, 'compressing the ration of exile' (I: 319). Both versions assimilate the idiom '*gorek khleb izgna'ia*' (the bitter bread of exile) and can be read as 'I ate bitter things in prison, deportation and exile'. The repetition of the exile motif passes through several stages from the prophetic, 'I will drink the cup of exile' (I: 152), through the experiential, 'Truly, each one who in exile longs for home' (I: 331), the detached, 'through war or the exile of the singer / demonstrating the authenticity of the age' (I: 372) to the universal, 'allude indistinctly, centuries later, to / the reasons for exile' (II: 383). The last quotation comes from a poem of 1976, with allusions to Dante, called 'December in Florence'. Less direct allusions to Dante appear in the poem we are examining, such as the metaphor 'the bread of exile' and 'I abandoned the country that had nurtured me':

Ты **бросишь все**, к чему твои желанья
Стремились нежно; эту язву нам
Всего быстрей наносит **лук изгнанья**.

Ты будешь знать, как горестен устам
Чужой ломоть, как трудно на чужбине
Сходить и восходить по ступеням.[39]

Thou shalt leave everything loved most dearly, and this is the
shaft which the bow of exile shoots first. Thou shalt prove how
salt is the taste of another man's bread and how hard is the
way up and down another man's stairs.[40]

Thus, the loading to the extreme of every part and of every
formal structure, correlating and binding them together is, without doubt, what makes this poem such a master-work. The poem
is a summing-up from yet another point of view: all of its basic
vocabulary consists of words to be found in other poems written
before 1980.[41] Apart from the verbs, all of which are part of the
poet's active vocabulary, also of great interest are the nouns. Many
of them are not only found with great regularity in the poetry
written prior to 1980 but form part of Brodsky's basic armoury
of conceptual metaphors. The sea is conceptualized with almost
the same intensity as are life and sound: 'and the sea is getting
more and more wrinkled and the faces' (II: 264), 'The sea, Madam,
is someone's speech (I: 369). Brodsky really did live by the sea,
both in the North, 'in a damp city that freezes by the sea' (III:
17), and in the South, in the Crimea with the Tomashevskys:
'I'm writing from the sea' (I: 420; see also II: 285), but he did not
domesticate the sea and, instead, developed it as a concept, placed
it, as he did water in general, alongside the main themes of his
poetry: space and time. If the city, be it Leningrad, London, Venice
or Rome is the leading character in many of his poems, the
metonym of country stands usually for Russia: from the prophetic
words of an early poem, 'In every suburb of that country, / on
every stoop, by every wall, / late or soon, dark or fair / will appear
my spirit, in two persons one' (I: 190) to the sarcastic 'country,
epoch – spit on them and tread it in' (II: 43). After his exile from
Russia it is accompanied by the epithets 'big' or 'large': 'Just the
thought of oneself and a big country throws one into the night
from wall to wall' (II: 364); 'I was born in a big country' (II: 447).
   One of the most important characteristics of Brodsky's poetry
is its lexic daring, which manifests itself in its non-discriminating
vocabulary. In Gordin's words, 'he united a great many dispar-
ate elements. Once again in Russian culture, in the Russian
language a poet has brought a whole lot together. He simply
implemented that same principle, employed by Pushkin and
Pasternak, introducing a new poetic substratum at a new level.'[42]
In his poems distant registers of the language are brought into

close proximity: from the camps (barrack, guard); from prison slang (moniker); from the language of the emotions (gratitude, solidarity); from the language of the common people (*sloniatsia* – mooched, *syznova* – again, *zhral* – gobble) and from the grand style (survey, nurture). Brodsky carried on his great work – adopting and making his own another 'language', smelting down and removing the dross from Sovspeak. Refusing to be dependent on history or to consider himself in debt to society, yet 'using the language of that society, working in its language, the poet, especially when he makes a good job it, takes, as it were, a step toward society'.[43] That poet to whom, indeed, fell the lot of carrying on the task of Pushkin, of opening the door of poetry to all aspects of the living Russian language, including foul language, prison slang, the whole of Sovspeak, that poet was exiled from the living language, a separation which often drove him to distraction and made him subject to despair deeper than any 'longing for home' as imagined by those who have never left their country. But beyond the borders of his own language and of Russian culture Brodsky continued to serve 'his native tongue and letters' (II: 292), to respect the democracy of language.

In conclusion, it must be noted that this poem is not the only poem composed by Brodsky on his birthday. The first such poem, 'Robin Redbreast', is dated 24 March 1964, at which time Brodsky had already been sentenced and sent into exile in the North. Comparing himself with the small song-bird, Brodsky employs the traditional poetic lexicon, stating the fact of his lost liberty in a manner which is both unaffected and unforced. The second such poem, dated 24 March 1965 (I: 423), written in remand prison, marks an important milestone in his life – his quarter century. Like the poem on his fortieth birthday, it takes in a wide lexical compass: the vocabulary of prison life (cell, judas, duty-officer, barbed wire, guard), alternates with slang (filth, i.e. policeman), foul language (fuck) and mythological figures (Phoebus, Apollo). It is, in that sense, a foretaste of the pattern that was to emerge in the 1980s. The same denigrating self-portraiture: 'and even to myself I seemed like a waste bin / where Fate shovels its rubbish, / where all the filth direct their spittle'; 'The barbed wire lyre' is followed by a very lofty conclusion, in much the same way as 'I, instead of . . .', 'And a guard on a heavenly backdrop / is Phoebus' very self. / Where hast thou strayed Apollo!'.

It is remarkable that in all of these three poems written on his birthday Brodsky abandons the classical tradition in which it is usual to refer to the place and date of that event and to mention your name. One needs only to recall the tenth elegy of Ovid's *Tristia*, the first autobiographical poem.[44] In Brodsky's case life begins with his arrest and imprisonment: *srok* [sentence] is what time turns to in prison, and instead of his name he gives us his prison nickname or moniker (*klikukha*). There is also something even more vital which links Brodsky with Ovid – a belief in his gifts, in the power of his poetic spell:

Слушай, дружина, враги и братие!
Все, что творил я, творил не ради я
славы в эпоху кино и радио,
но ради речи родной, словесности.
За каковое раченье-жречество
(сказано ж доктору: сам пусть лечится)
чаши лишившись в пиру Отечества,
нынче стою в незнакомой местности.   (II: 292)

Listen, liege men, brethren and foes! / Everything I've done, I've done not for fame in the age of movies and radio, / but for my native tongue, for literature. / For this kind of sacrificial zeal / (it is said, physician, heal thyself), / deprived of a cup at the feast of my Fatherland, / I now stand in an unknown locality.

We read much the same thing in Ovid: 'ingenio tamen ipse meo comitorque fruorque: / Caesar in hoc potuit iuris habere nihil' (Tr. III vii. 47–8).[45] That is why, in Brodsky's view, 'exile does not impair the quality of the writing'.[46]

The fates and works of Ovid, Dante, Pushkin, Mandelstam, Tsvetaeva and Akhmatova form the cultural backdrop to this poem. But it is Brodsky's fate more than the immense cultural riches of the poem which makes of it a worthy successor in genre to *Exegi monumentum*. These two aspects, moreover, are closely intertwined. Thus, 'sowed rye, black-felted the barn' for all its biographical reference takes the poem beyond the purely biographical level, its very mundaneness making of it a universal experience. 'Sowed rye, black-felted the barn', these are strange details to be noted by a poet, but do recall Akhmatova's lines 'I was with my people there where my people, unhappily, were' (I: 361). In such cases the ever present personal pronoun 'I' transcends itself by means of an incredible spiritual leap and the whole poem becomes the biography of a generation. However, unlike other poems of that genre, in it Brodsky does not catalogue his great deeds; quite the reverse, he emphasizes the ways in which he shared the fate of millions of Soviet people. He is grateful to fate for the authenticity of that life, even with its prison sentence and nickname. All the state's attempts to violate his fate (arrest, prison, exile) have ended in failure. In the two-thousands-year-old opposition between poet and emperor (in the Soviet version, poet and tyrant), it is the poet who triumphs as the voice of the language. In other words, the real victor is the 'empire' of language. Whether it was his wish to avoid melodrama or whether it was a result of the struggle to curb his pride, his new-found humility and Christian capacity for forgiveness ensured the ethical restraint of the poem. This restraint went on developing to become a stylistic trait of the whole of Brodsky's poetry. The last poet of the grand style writes his own kind of poem-memorial on his birthday. Thanks to the concurrence of both biographical and poetic planes, Brodsky conceptualizes his life, constructing his own legend. That legend continues to grow in persuasiveness.[47]

Notes

1. 'Who lived out his life, neither participating / in their games nor falling victim to them', in *Sochineniia Iosifa Brodskogo*, vol. I (St Petersburg: Pushkinskii fond, 1992) p. 96.
2. See Christopher Reid's review of Brodsky's third English collection, *To Urania*, 'Great American Disaster', *London Review of Books*, vol. 10 (8 December 1988) no. 22, pp. 17–18. And also, Craig Raine, 'A Reputation Subject to Inflation', *The Financial Times Weekend* (16 and 17 November 1996) p. xix.
3. See the chapter 'Poeziya kak sistema konfliktov', in E. Etkind, *Materiia Stikha* (Paris: Institut d'Etudes Slaves, 1978) pp. 84–184.
4. According to the Voronezh poet, Elena Fanailova, for someone of her generation (the provincial intelligentsia now in their thirties and forties) 'every fourth line of that poem has been quoted, has become proverbial: "dined with the devil knows who in a tail-coat", "wore what's again in fashion", "the only thing I didn't drink was dry water"'. From a letter to the author of this article, 8 April 1997.
5. During a telephone conversation in the late seventies I asked him whether it was true that he was cleansing his poetry of all metaphor; Brodsky's answer was: 'Not only of metaphor but of all tropes in general.'

6. For the interactions between grammar and semantics in tropes see V. Polukhina and Ü. Pärli, *Slovar' tropov Brodskogo* (Tartu, 1995).
7. In the opinion of Professor L. Zubova, the linguistic paradox *sukhaia voda* [dry water] is linked with the polysemic nature of the word 'dry' as well as with the contrast between 'living and dead' water in folklore. It can also be linked with 'dry spirit' and 'dry wine'.
8. Brodsky's friend, Georgii Ginzburg-Voskov, dedicatee of the 1961 poem 'V pis'me na iug' [In a letter to the South] (I: 84–5) and his hiking companion on the trip through the Tian-Shan mountains told me that Brodsky did indeed nearly drown twice in the course of one summer. He was with him on both occasions. From a telephone conversation, March 1997.
9. The intonation which dominates this poem contrasts with the tone of poems written by two of Brodsky's great poetic forebears, Ovid and Pushkin, who served him as archetypes of exile. See Ovid, *Tristia*, III, xiii, 'A Birthday at Tomis': *'dure, quid ad miseros veniebas exulis annos?'* ['Cruel one why hast thou come to increase the wretched years of exile'] (London: Loeb Classical Library, 1958) pp. 150–1, trans. A. L. Wheeler. Pushkin, like Ovid, bewailed his fate. The poem 'Dar naprasnyi, dar sluchainyi' ['Fruitless Gift, Chance Gift'] was written on 26 May 1828 – his birthday. See A. S. Pushkin, *Sobranie sochinenii v desiati tomakh*, vol. II (Moscow, 1974) p. 139. Also see stanza XLIV of the sixth canto of *Eugene Onegin*.
10. In Fazil Iskander's opinion, 'grief was the chief theme of his poetry'. See Vecher pamiati I. Brodskogo, *Mansarda*, no. 1 (1996) p. 70.
11. As the title of his last collection of essays *On Grief and Reason* (New York: Farrar, Straus & Giroux, 1995) suggests, the archetypical personification of grief gradually became a symbol of time itself.
12. Iosif Brodskii, 'Ia prinadlezhu russkoi kul'ture', an interview with Dushan Velichkovich in *Sobesednik*, no. 4 (October 1989) p. 12.
13. Vladimir Ufliand said of this, ' . . . he was one of the freest men I know [. . .] at the time when freedom was a very rare thing indeed, when there was practically no-one around who managed to preserve their intrinsic freedom, he did', in V. Polukhina, *Brodsky through the Eyes of his Contemporaries* (Basingstoke: Macmillan Press; New York: St Martin's Press, 1992) p. 148.
14. From a conversation between Amanda Aizpuriete and Brodsky, published in *Rodnik*, no. 3 (1990) p. 73.
15. From the transcript of a debate between Brodsky, Seamus Heaney, Derek Walcott and Les Murray, 'Poet's Round Table: A Common Language', *PNReview*, vol. 15 (1988) no. 4, p. 43.
16. Cf. Akhmatova's *Requiem*: 'Budu ia, kak streletskie zhenki, / Pod kremlevskimi bashniami **vyt'** [Like the wives of the Streltsy, / I'll wail under the Kremlin towers'], *Sochineniia*, vol. I (Munich: Inter-Language Literary Associates, 1967) p. 363.
17. The ambiguity of the word *pomimo* might be interpreted, in this context, as an absolute prohibition of crying as unmasculine behaviour. Polysemy betrays what Brodsky does not even wish to allow himself to think.

18. Professor Loseff has suggested that Brodsky might have remembered a song about a bandit who *'nosit fraki, zhivet v barake i liubit draki, kogda serdit'* ['wear a tail-coat, lives in a barrack and loves a fight when he is angry']. There could be one more biographical fact reflected in this line: Véronique Schiltz told Loseff that during the 1970s Brodsky was invited to a film festival and had to wear a tail-coat. The syntactical ambiguity of the phrase 'dined with the devil knows who in a tail-coat' leaves it open to interpretation as to whether both the lyrical subject and his companion are wearing tail-coats. There is another ambiguity in the expression 'the devil knows who'. It cannot be excluded that we are here dealing with the motif of the double so characteristic of Brodsky's poetics. See my article 'Metamorfozy "ia" v poezii postmodernizma: dvoiniki v poeticheskom mire Brodskogo', *Modernizm i postmodernizm v russkoi literature i kul'ture*, vol. 16 (Helsinki: Slavica Helsingiensa, 1996) pp. 391–407.

19. For the conceptual function of reification in Brodsky's poetry, see the work of the present author, in particular *Joseph Brodsky: A Poet for Our Time* (Cambridge University Press, 1989); 'Similarity in Disparity' in *Brodsky's Poetics and Aesthetics*, ed L. Loseff and V. Polukhina ((Basingstoke: Macmillan Press, 1990) and *Dictionary of Brodsky's Tropes* (see n. 5).

20. Olga Sedakova, 'A Rare Independence', in *Brodsky through the Eyes of his Contemporaries*, p. 245.

21. This rhyme refers us to Khlebnikov's little poem *'Moskva kolymaga'*, see his *Tvoreniia* (Moscow: Sov. pisatel', 1986) p. 122.

22. And indeed, it did happen again: in December 1985 Brodsky underwent a second open-heart operation.

23. It was Professor Gerald Smith who first examined the function of verbal aspect in this poem, in his lecture 'Brodsky as Self-Translator: the Fortieth Birthday Poem' in either 1987 or 1988. I would like to take this opportunity to thank Professor Smith for sending me his lecture notes.

24. Blaise Pascal, *Pensées*, II (Bibliotheque de Clunes, 1948) p. 825.

25. Olga Sedakova, 'Pobeg v pustyniu', *Tat'ianin Den'*, *Pravoslavnaia Gazeta*, Moscow State University (January 1997) p. 20.

26. Douglas Dunn during his poetry reading at Keele University, 28 February 1997.

27. When asked by a journalist to which faith he belonged, Brodsky answered that he 'might well call himself a Calvinist. In the sense that you are your own judge and jury and you judge yourself more severely than the Almighty. You show no mercy to yourself, you forgive nothing. You yourself are the last and often rather dreadful court of judgment'. From an interview with Brodsky conducted by Yuri Radyshevskii, published in *Moskovskie Novosti*, no. 50 (23–30 July 1995) p. 21.

28. Correlating 'a glacier' with 'burnt' we obtain the primordial antithesis of ice and fire as a sort of parallel to the poet's cool, detached position allied to a passionate temperament.

29. Gratitude is also a main motif of his 'Roman Elegies' (III: 48) and

'On the Centenary of Anna Akhmatova' (II: 178).

30. Osip Mandelshtam, *Sochineniia v dvukh tomakh*, vol. I (Moscow: Khudozhestvennaia literatura, 1990) pp. 308–9.

31. Also fragen wir beständig, / Bis man uns mit einer Handvoll / Erde endlich stopft die Mäuler / Aber ist das eine Antwort?' Heinrich Heine, *Poems* (Oxford: Blackwell, 1961) pp. 100–1. Russian translation by M. Mikhailov, see Genrikh Geine, *Stikhotvoreniia. Poemy. Proza* (Moscow, 1971) pp. 329–30.

32. Translated by D. M. Thomas, in Anna Akhmatova, *Selected Poems* (London: Penguin, 1985) p. 123.

33. In Helsinki, in the autumn of 1995, answering questions from the audience, Brodsky said 'The chief lesson I, both as a poet and as a man, gleaned from my acquaintance with Akhmatova was restraint; restraint in relation to everything that may happen to you in life – the pleasant as well as the unpleasant. It is a lesson I think, that I learnt for keeps. In that sense I really am her disciple. As for the rest, I wouldn't go so far but, as far as the aspect goes, and it is a decisive one, I am her fully worthy disciple.' *Sobesednik*, 8 September 1995, p. 12. See also Volkov's interview with Brodsky, 'Vspominia Annu Akhmatovu', *Kontinent* (1987) no. 53, pp. 337–82 and D. M. Thomas's interview with the poet in *Quarto*, December 1981, pp. 9–11.

34. It is very easy to underestimate. Craig Raine, for one, has done so. He has either misread or, worse, failed to understand these two lines at all: 'It is no use pointing out that burial after death seldom involves the undertaker in the task of cramming clay (of whatever complexion) down the throat of the deceased. The melodrama is entirely of Brodsky's making.' Craig Raine, 'A Reputation Subject to Inflation'.

35. The image of a wild beast occurs fairly frequently in Ovid's *Tristia*; see V. vii, 6.

36. Compare with Mandelshtam's 'Poiu, kogda gortan' *syra*, dusha – *sukha*' [I sing when my throat is wet and my soul is dry] I: 239.

37. Replacement of an adjective of time, *dolgoi* [long] with an adjective of space, *dlinnoi* [long] is in accordance with Brodsky's interpretation of these two philosophical categories.

38. This metaphor can also be seen as a tribute to Stephen Spender, who wrote one of the very first, and very positive, reviews of Brodsky's first collection of poems in English, *Selected Poems* (London: Penguin, 1973). The review entitled 'Bread of Affliction' appeared in the *New Statesman* of the 14 December of that year (pp. 915–16). Brodsky could not possibly have forgotten what he wrote, 'Brodsky is someone who has tasted extremely bitter bread and his poetry has the air of being ground out between his teeth. He sees things from a point of view which is ultimately that of Christians who have devoured bread and gall as the sacraments of the Mass. . . .'

39. Dante's *Divine Comedy* in M. Lozinsky's translation, *Paradise*, canto 17, ll. 55–60, p. 448 (Moscow, 1967). Also of significance from Dante's great poem, not from the *Paradise* but from the *Inferno*, are '*dikii les*' (I: 5) – a wild wood; 'Pri vide *zveria*' (I: 43) – at the sight of the

beast; 'Smotri, kak etot *zver'* menya stesnil' (I: 88) – See how that beast hampers me; 'I ty uslyshish *vopli* isstupleni'a' (I: 115) – thou shalt hear cries of frenzy; 'kak *zver'*, kogda mereshchitsia emy' (II: 48) – as a beast shies at an imagined thing; 'Nikto pospeshnei ne bezhal ot *goria'* (109) – no-one fled so swiftly from grief; 'Ot *zveria* spas tebia' (II: 119) – From the beast I saved thee; 'A te pod livnem *voiut*, slovno suki' (VI: 19) – they howl in the rain like curs; 'Tak rukhnul *zver'* (VII: 15) – thus the beast tumbled down; 's *voplem* vechnym' (VII: 27) – with their eternal yelling; 'Chto ia podnes' blagadariu Tvortsa' (VIII: 60) – for that I render thanks unto my Creator; 'Skvoz' chernyi vozdukh' (IX: 6) – through the black air; 'I *zver'* i pastyr' ot nego bezhit' (IX: 72) – and beast and herdsmen fled, etc. The words most frequently repeated are: *zver'* – beast; *volp'* – cry; *voi* – yell; *gorod* – city; *son* – sleep, dream; *chernyi* – black; *zhizn'* – life; *zhil* – lived; *oziral* – surveyed; *izgnan* – driven out, exiled. So dense a cluster of lexic reference to Dante gives the theme of the poet's exile a universal character.

40. *The Divine Comedy* of Dante Alighieri, III, *Paradiso*, trans. John D. Sinclair (London: Bodley Head, 1946) p. 245.

41. I would like to take this opportunity to express my gratitude to Tatiana Patera whose *Concordance of Brodsky's Poetry* (in preparation) has helped to confirm my own observations as to the frequency with which certain words of his poem are repeated throughout Brodsky's work as a whole. Her *Concordance* shows that only ten words of this poem are unique to it: *vyzhigal* [burnt], *klikukha* [moniker], *ruletka* [roulette], *obedal* [dined], *polmira* [half the globe], *rasporot* [ripped apart], *slonialsia* [mooched], *gunna* [hun], *solidarnost'* [solidarity], and *zabili* [packed] – less than 10% of its lexicon.

42. Ia. Gordin, 'A Tragic Perception of the World', in Polukhina, *Brodsky through the Eyes of His Contemporaries*, p. 45.

43. For Brodsky's own views on this see his interview with the editor of the journal *Amerika*, no. 426 (1992) pp. 35–6.

44. See Ovid, *Tristia. Ex Ponto* (London: Loeb Classical Library, 1953) pp. 197–207. For more on the theme of exile in the work of the two poets see K. Ichin, 'Brodskii i Ovidii', *Novoe literaturnoe obozrenie*, no. 19 (1996), pp. 227–49.

45. 'My mind is nevertheless my comrade and my joy; over this Caesar could have no right', Ovid, *Tristia. Ex Ponto*, p. 131.

46. 'Dante left Florence and because of that we have the *Divine Comedy*. Ovid wrote *Tristia. Ex Ponto*, and completed 'Fasti' in Sarmatia – far from Rome, but they work better than anything they were writing in Rome at the time. And the best Russian poet of this century (in my opinion), Marina Tsvetaeva, wrote her finest poems while living for almost twenty years outside Russia . . .', Joseph Brodsky, 'To be continued', *PENewsletter*, no. 43 (May 1980) p. 10.

47. I would like to thank Elena Fanailova for her valuable comments made via E-mail, while I was working on the analysis of this poem. My special thanks to Olga Sedakova, Professor Liudmila Zubova and Tatiana Patera for their critical readings of the first version of this article.

6

'To Urania'

K Uranii

BARRY P. SCHERR

1 У всего есть предел: в том числе, у печали.
2 Взгляд застревает в окне, точно лист – в ограде.
3 Можно налить воды. Позвенеть ключами.
4 Одиночество есть человек в квадрате.
5 Так дромадер нюхает, морщась, рельсы.
6 Пустота раздвигается, как портьера.
7 Да и что вообще есть пространство, если
8 не отсутствие в каждой точке тела?
9 Оттого–то Урания старше Клио.
10 Днем, и при свете слепых коптилок,
11 видишь: она ничего не скрыла
12 и, глядя на глобус, глядишь в затылок.
13 Вон они, те леса, где полно черники,
14 реки, где ловят рукой белугу,
15 либо – город, в чьей телефонной книге
16 ты уже не числишься. Дальше, к югу,
17 то есть, к юго–востоку, коричневеют горы,
18 бродят в осоке лошади–пржевали;
19 лица желтеют. А дальше – плывут линкоры,
20 и простор голубеет, как белье с кружевами.

(III: 64)

* * *

'To Urania'

To I. K.

1 There is a limit to everything, including sorrow.
2 A glance is caught in a window, like a leaf in a fence.
3 One can pour out some water, rattle some keys.
4 Loneliness is a person squared.
5 Thus a dromedary, wrinkling its nostrils, sniffs at a rail.
6 The emptiness is drawn apart, like a curtain.
7 And besides, what is space if
8 not the body's absence at every point?
9 That's why Urania is older than Clio!
10 In daytime, or by the light of blackened oil-lamps,
11 You see that she hides nothing
12 and, in looking at a globe, you're looking at a pate.
13 There they are, the forests filled with blueberries,
14 the rivers where sturgeon are caught with bare hands,
15 or the town in whose phone book
16 you are no longer listed. Further to the south
17 that is, to the south east, rise brown mountains,
18 and Przewalsky horses roam amidst the sedge grass;
19 the faces grow yellower. And still further, battleships steam
20 and the expanse turns blue, like lace underwear.[1]

*   *   *

Not the least of the questions that arises upon first reading Brodsky's 'To Urania' is how he gets from the sorrow of l. 1 to the lace underwear with which he concludes the poem. The issue is not trivial, for to elucidate the relationship between the beginning and the end of the poem, and in many cases the connections between one line and the next, requires more than a little effort. After the powerful first line comes a set of images relating to the cause of the sorrow: the loneliness (and presumed sense of loss) that is mentioned literally in l. 4. But why then the dromedary in l. 5? What motivates the introduction of Urania, and why is she older than Clio? For that matter, is this poem even about the Muse of astronomy? How do the last eight lines of the

94 Joseph Brodsky

poem, which appear to involve a whirlwind tour over some part of the globe, relate to the more abstract earlier sections?

Like most of Brodsky's poetry, 'To Urania' contains elements that resist ready interpretation or that a first reading will often fail to see entirely. A full appreciation of any poem by him requires a careful consideration of structural elements that point to the manner in which the ideas are presented and emphasized, an awareness of possible sources for the use of certain key words or images, and finally a willingness to join Brodsky in 'poetic thinking', which he is careful to distinguish from 'ordinary literary scholarship'. The poet operates through 'intuitive synthesis,' a process which comments on the real world but involves not so much analysis as inspiration and abstract thinking.[2]

At first glance the structure of 'To Urania' seems to offer little that is of special interest. Brodsky often creates unusual stanzas with unique or nearly unique rhyme schemes,[3] but here the poem's twenty lines are not broken down into stanzas at all and the rhyming does not appear to be out of the ordinary: the rhymes are consistently feminine (i.e. stretch over the last two syllables of the line) and alternating (ABAB). While it is more common for poets to alternate masculine and feminine rhyme, Brodsky shows a certain predilection for feminine rhyme and for creating poems entirely with those endings, as he does here.[4] Most of the rhymes are approximate rather than exact, but the differences often involve closely related consonants (e.g. the first rhyme pair, *pechali/kliuchami*, where the *l* and the *m* are both sonorants);[5] such rhymes are hardly rare or experimental by the standards of modern Russian poetry.[6] This kind of approximate rhyming in feminine rhymes is typical of Brodsky, as is the use of nouns for the great majority of his rhyme words.[7] Thanks in no small part to the approximate rhyming, Brodsky generally manages to avoid 'easy' grammatical rhymes; again, the first rhyme pair (the genitive singular of one noun with the instrumental plural of another) is indicative, as are the cases when a noun is used to rhyme with another part of speech (*rel'sy/esli*; *Klio/skryla*).[8] In short, the rhymes are hardly dull, and yet there seems to be little to draw more than passing attention.

Still, a search for the central ideas in a poem often begins with Brodsky's rhymes.[9] For that matter, as Natal'ia Galatskaia has shown in her analysis of 'Nochnoi polet', the rhymes provide one of the structural cornerstones in many of Brodsky's poems.[10]

Not only do many of the semantic features of the poem become emphasized through the rhyme words, but the ordering of lines by rhyme may create natural thematic groupings, while the sound correspondences of the rhymes may echo back further into the line and play an important role in creating the sound harmony for the poem as a whole. Such in fact turns out to be the case for 'To Urania'.[11] From the very start the rhyme scheme helps delineate the poem's chief structural elements: an eight-line opening section, which can be further broken down into two groups of four, with the first dealing more with loneliness and the second with notions of space; a central four-line cluster, where Urania is mentioned directly for the only time in the poem; and then a final eight-line section, with a break in the middle (instead of at the end) of l. 16, where the theme shifts from the nearby landscape to more distant lands.

These major groupings are emphasized not only by the rhymes but also by enjambment (or by the lack of it). Brodsky employs enjambment quite frequently – for instance, it appears in about a third of the lines of the cycle *Chast' rechi*. And often the device is used in a striking manner: to link stanzas or sections of a poem, or to divide a preposition at the end of a line from the rest of the phrase on the next line.[12] Here, atypically, Brodsky begins with six consecutive sentences that end with periods, lending something of a staccato effect to the opening section – all the more so since each line is self-contained in terms of the particular point it makes. Line 4, for instance, does not necessarily flow from l. 3, nor does 5 lead directly into 6. Only ll. 7 and 8 are tied together by the strongest instance of enjambment in the entire poem, and they are used to summarize the theme of the opening section as well as to provide a sense of closure for that portion. The middle section contains a period after its introductory (ninth) line, but the next three lines form a single unit, creating a somewhat different flow from that over the first part of the poem. Then, over the final eight-line section, only the twentieth and last line ends with a period. Here, more characteristically for Brodsky, the rhymes are particularly important for marking line endings, since the syntax generally does not create strong breaks between lines. More importantly, the sharp differences between the syntactic structures of each section help contrast the first and third parts of the poem, and also single out ll. 9–12 as forming a bridge between them.

A closer look at the rhymes themselves shows that they too bring out contrasts among the three sections. The first quatrains are each distinguished by the use of so-called 'shadow rhyme', a consequence of twentieth-century approximate rhyming.[13] Take ll. 1–4, where Brodsky uses the same rhyme vowel in both rhyme pairs. Given his rhyming technique, it is clear that he intends to rhyme ll. 1 with 3 and 2 with 4, yet, for instance, the words at the end of ll. 3 and 4, *kliuchami* and *kvadraty*, are sufficiently similar that they could well be rhymed in another context. In ll. 5–8 Brodsky again uses the same rhyme vowel in each of the four concluding words, and, similarly, it would be possible for a modern poet to rhyme *tela* with *esli* or *rel'sy* as well as with *port'era*. By using shadow rhyme in each of the four-line groupings, Brodsky makes each of the quatrains more self-contained, thereby high-lighting the shift in focus from one to the next. At the same time the rhymes, by implying connections among the lines that comprise each four-line unit, compensate for the periods that conclude ll. 1–6 and which would otherwise tend to isolate each of the lines. In this regard too the first eight lines of the poem again contrast with the last eight, where virtually any hint of shadow rhyme is absent. The middle quatrain, ll. 9–12, not only contains shadow rhyme but is further distinguished by the most salient echoes among the four rhyme words. *Klio* rhymes with *skryla*, but its four sounds (with the single substitution of hard 'l' for soft) reappear as the final four letters in each rhyme word of the other set: *koptilok* and *zatylok*. And *skryla* itself shares the four phonemes that conclude the other two rhyme words in the set. Note too the manner in which the rhyme words contain thematic as well as phonetic echoes. The device is used frequently in Brodsky[14] and appears elsewhere in the poem, as in the massiveness implied by the rhyme pair *gory* and *linkory* toward the end of the poem. A crucial theme in these middle four lines is the tendency of Clio to mask things (a point brought out more directly in Brodsky's own translation of the poem) as opposed to Urania's openness. Hence, Clio rhymes with the verb to hide, and between them are the 'cloudy lanterns' that could make visibility problematic. Conversely, Urania is connected less with the rhyme words than with the sharp alliteration of the fourth line in the quatrain, where the cluster of words deals with sight and openness. The powerful set of connections permeating these lines helps draw attention to these middle lines, which in some ways are the most difficult to interpret.

TABLE 1

Lines 1–4	Lines 5–8	Lines 9–12	Lines 13–16	Lines 17–20
2-2-2-2-1	-2-0-2-1-1	2-2-2-1-1	2-2-2-1-1	2-2-4-1-1
-2-2-2-1-1	2-2-4-1	-2-2-1-1	-2-2-1-1	-2-1-3-1
-2-1-2-1-1	2-2-2-1-1	-2-2-1-1	2-1-2-1-1	-2-2-2-1-1
2-2-2-1-1	2-2-1-1-1	1-2-2-1-1	2-1-2-1-1	2-2-3-2-1

The poem is written in the 'loose dolnik' that Brodsky developed over the years.

Unlike the so-called classical metres, such as iambic or anapaestic verse, where there is a fixed number of metrically weak syllables between the ictuses (the positions in the line that potentially carry stress in accordance with the metre) the dolnik allows for either one- or two-syllable intervals between stresses. As in iambic or trochaic poetry, poems in dolniki may omit stress on an ictus, thereby creating intervals of as many as four or five syllables between stresses. Perhaps the best analysis of Brodsky's looser type of dolnik remains G. S. Smith's article on the long poem 'Kellomäki'.[15] The lines there do not exhibit a fixed number of strong syllables (or ictuses) but instead vary, although the majority of the lines have four or five stresses. Since the number of stresses is not fixed, it is difficult to say whether Brodsky is omitting stress on a particular line or whether he is simply using longer than usual intervals of unstressed syllables. In the poem analysed by Smith, intervals between stressed syllables range from zero syllables (an atypical feature for the usual dolnik line) up to six, though most are in fact one or two.

'To Urania' is similar in that the poem appears to be written in dolniki, but the number of stresses per line may vary, and some of the intervals between stresses fall outside the usual one- or two-syllable norm (Table 1). Most lines contain four or five metrical stresses, though hypermetrical stressing (stressing that is not predicted by the metre) does occur, especially in the fourth of the five rhyme units. Twelve consecutive lines (7–18) have precisely four metrical stresses, and except for the last two of these lines, all the unstressed intervals contain either one or two syllables: in other words, for a significant portion this poem adheres to the norms of the conventional four-stress dolnik. Several features are typical of the modern dolnik: the two-syllable intervals between stresses outnumber those with one syllable, one-syllable intervals

TABLE 2

	1	2	3	4	5	6	7	8	9	10	11	12	13	14
1			×	\		×	\		×			×		
2	×		×			×	\			×		×		
3	×		×		×				×		×			
4		×			×				×		×			
5	×		×	×				×		×				
6		×			×				°			×		
7		×			×	\			×		×			
8		×			×			×		×				
9		×			×				×		×			
10	×		×			×			×					
11	×		×			×			×					
12		×		×				×		×				
13	\		×	\		×	\		×		×			
14	×		\	×				×		×				
15	\		×	×				×		×				
16	\		×	×				×		×				
17	\		×			×					×		×	
18	×		×		×					×				
19	×		×			×				×		×		
20			×			×		°		×			×	

occur most often toward the end of the line, and instances of what might appear to be omitted stresses tend to occur toward the end of the line rather than the beginning.[16]

However, in order to appreciate the rhythmic qualities of the poem it is best to view each line graphically (see Table 2).

In Table 2, an '×' is used to indicate a metrical stress, a backwards slash (\) for a hypermetrical stress, and ° for a possible weak stress. A solid line delineates quatrains. Here it is evident that the lines vary in length from 10 to 14 syllables, with most having 11 or 12. The first and last four line-groupings contain the most syllables (totals of 50 and 52); the middle four the fewest (43). The first line of the poem is a regular anapaestic tetrameter, but none of the other lines adheres fully to one of the so-called classical metres. The anacrusis, the part of the line that occurs before the first metrical stress, contains either zero or two syllables in all but l. 12. When there is both a two-syllable anacrusis and a two-syllable interval after the first metrical stress (so that the first two metrical stresses fall on syllables 3 and 6, as in ll. 1, 4, 6–9, etc.) the lines assumes a kind of anapaestic rhythm at the start.

If, on the other hand, a metrical stress falls on the first syllable and on the fourth (e.g., ll. 2–3, 10–11, etc.) the rhythm at the beginning of the line is dactylic. These two basic lines types account for all but four of the poem's lines: ll. 15–16, which are rhythmically identical, begin more like trochees (and therefore the weak stress on the first syllable of each line is difficult to analyse: it might be possible to see each of these lines as containing five metrical stresses rather than four). Line 12 is amphibrachic at the start, while in l. 5 the zero interval between the second and third stresses provides a sharp interruption to the rhythm that begins over the first four syllables.

How do the metre and rhythm affect the poem's structure? As with the line lengths, there are certain parallels between the first and fifth quatrains, as well as the second and fourth. Note, for instance, that in ll. 1–4 and 17–20 the middle two lines of the rhyme cluster are similar rhythmically, as are the first and last. Thus, while the first and third as well as second and fourth lines in each quatrain are joined by rhyme, these rhythmic parallels pair-off the lines in another way and help suggest a strong set of interwoven linkages within each of the quatrains. The second and fourth quatrains, ll. 5–8 and 13–16, offer the fewest parallels. The fifth line is simply unique; while the internal lines of the quatrain, ll. 6–7, are again similar, l. 8 resembles them more than it does the first line of the quatrain – which is perhaps fitting, since l. 8 represents a continuation of the idea in l. 7. Lines 15–16, also tied together by enjambment, are identical rhythmically and different from all other lines in the poem. Lines 13 and 14 have structures that are similar to other lines in the poem, but not to each other or to the other lines in the unit. In contrast, the tightest parallels occur within the middle quatrain, ll. 9–12. As with the first two quatrains, the middle two lines have more of a dactylic beginning while the first line in the quatrain begins with an anapaestic rhythm. Here the middle two lines are in fact identical in terms of stress placement, while ll. 9 and 12 both maintain strong ternary rhythms until the interval preceding the final ictus. The conciseness of these lines as well as the strong sense of order again helps highlight the importance of this middle section.

Brodsky uses the rhythms of individual lines in still other ways. Note, for instance, that he tends to begin each four-line unit with a strongly marked line, be it the regular anapaests of l. 1, the consecutive strong stresses on syllables four and five of l. 5, or the hypermetrical stressing of l. 13. The syntax, either by itself or in conjunction with the rhythm, also plays a role in this regard: the self-contained, general statements in ll. 1, 5 and 9 all serve to introduce what immediately follows.

In short, rhyme, enjambment, syntax and rhythm all help create a structure in which each of the quatrains takes on a degree of independence. For the poem as a whole, the movement from quatrain to quatrain involves both elaboration and contrast. On the one hand, there is a straight-line development, with the poem going from the more abstract to the more concrete and also from a tighter order to a freer form, as evidenced by the more chaotic rhythm toward the end: cf. the large amount of hypermetrical stressing in l. 13, the different form of ll. 15–16, and then the long intervals of unstressed syllables between ictuses in ll. 17, 18 and 20, creating a somewhat 'looser' dolnik toward the end of the poem. On the other hand, the parallels suggest more of a circular structure, with the middle four lines singled out as distinct from the rest.

The structural elements lay out the paths along which the imagery and the import of the poem follow. Take ll. 1–4, where the opening two lines set the manner for much of what is to follow. Brodsky begins with a statement – that everything, including sorrow, has a limit – which he will then elaborate throughout the entire poem. From here he can go in many different directions, and the poem with its second line already takes on a quality of unpredictability. Lev Loseff caught this feature of Brodsky's poetry precisely when he compared him to the English metaphysical poets, noting that 'the metaphysician seeks only the initiatory metaphor, expands it and then the metaphor leads him to results which in all probability stun the poet himself'.[17] And the second line is indeed surprising: a person's gaze gets caught in a window, like a leaf in a fence – a wonderfully concrete comparison that concisely expresses a feeling of profound sorrow.[18] Yevgeny Rein has pointed to Brodsky's 'prosaic kind of talent'; to his sight which can take in 'whole continents' but also objects as ordinary as 'a fleeing cat' – or a leaf stuck in a fence.[19] This talent appears as well in l. 3, with its ordinary actions that are likely to be undertaken by one coping with grief. In the fourth line Brodsky rounds off the theme of sorrow by returning to a more complex image; loneliness is a person 'squared', an unbearable expansion of feeling that becomes larger than the vessel containing it.

The second quatrain contains a shift of scene. The image of a dromedary sniffing at rails is both concrete and abstract at the same time, for its relation to the preceding and following lines is problematic.[20] The rails recall the inanimate and similarly metallic keys and fence in preceding lines. A more general linkage looks back to loneliness and forward to emptiness. In his poem 'Lullaby of Cape Cod' ('Kolybel'naia Treskovogo Mysa') he says that 'Loneliness teaches the essence of things, for their essence is also / loneliness'.[21] The figure of a single dromedary suggests both the loneliness of l. 4 and the desert, or the abstract emptiness, in l. 6, which is further combined with the concrete image of a curtain opening: here to reveal Brodsky's definition of space, 'prostranstvo'. As Era Korobova has pointed out, Brodsky refers to space frequently, but within the context of any given poem it can take on different and sometimes contradictory meanings.[22] In 'Nature morte' Brodsky remarks that a thing is the space outside of which the thing does not exist.[23] He seems to be saying something similar here: empty space is the absence of a body at each of its points. This complex set of images, taken within the context of Brodsky's other poetry, points to the central concern of these opening eight lines: 'Smert' – eto tozhe ekvivalent pustoty, prostranstva, iz kotorogo ushli, i imenno ona – smyslovoi tsentr vsego tsikla' [Death is also the equivalent of emptiness, of a space which people have left, and death itself is the semantic centre of the entire cycle].[24] Significantly, while not referring directly to 'To Urania' at this point in their article, the Lotmans use the two key words of the second quatrain, *pustota* and *prostranstvo*, emptiness and space. David Bethea has pointed out that Brodsky's poetry deals frequently with the death not just of poets and friends, but also of acquaintances and even animals and insects.[25] The first large section of this poem quite possibly offers a meditation on death, or possibly on parting or absence – in any case, on what it means to be alone once the vastness of space has been emptied of another being.

The crucial distinction between Urania and Clio appears in l. 9. Clio is traditionally the Muse of history, a definition that does not appear to be totally out of context here, but it is harder to know what to make of the reference to Urania. In the Classical period, she was regarded as the Muse of astronomy. However, in much later times the figure later became identified as the Muse of Christian poetry, an interpretation that influenced Spenser and Milton, among others.[26] Urania is also a name for Aphrodite, and the term uranian has been used synonymously with homosexual. By extension from astronomy, Urania has been interpreted as referring to science in general. Baratynskii, one of Brodsky's most beloved poets, refers to Urania in his well-known poem, 'Poslednii poet' ('The Last Poet'): 'Poklonnikam Uranii kholodnoi / Poet, uvy! on blagodat' strastei' [To the followers of cold Urania / He sings, alas, of the passions' grace]. 'He' is the poet, while Urania in this case is clearly meant to refer not so much to astronomy as to science in general, which is opposed to poetry.[27] The conflict is presented in darker terms than those used by most other contemporary commentators,[28] and thus the attitude toward Urania would appear to be quite hostile.

However, Urania seems much more positive in Brodsky's verses than in Baratynskii's, and none of the traditional accounts given above can account for the image of her in this poem. It is helpful to turn to Brodsky's, 'Profile of Clio', a lecture that he gave a decade after writing 'To Urania'. In a passing reference he again notes that Clio is younger than Urania, 'who, being the Muse of Geography, curbs many of history's notions significantly'.[29] Exactly how Brodsky arrives at the notion of Urania as representing geography is not clear. However, earlier in the same paragraph he mentions the various manners in which Clio is depicted. He does not say anything about Urania in this regard, but she is often seen holding a globe and sometimes scientific instruments such as a compass. Brodsky could well have had in mind a statue or a painting that shows her in this manner, especially given the reference to a globe in l. 12, and he might have viewed these accoutrements as representing the tools of a geographer rather than those of an astronomer.

Here, Brodsky's English version provides a valuable hint by expanding the contrast between the two muses: 'she [Urania] hides nothing, unlike the latter [Clio]'. In his essay, Brodsky quotes (but does not name) the Auden poem, 'Homage to Clio', which became the title for an entire collection of Auden's verse.[30] If Urania is the Muse of geography, then Clio, according to Auden/Brodsky, is the Muse of time, not just history. Brodsky calls himself Clio's admirer, but he claims that historians (and, in a different way, theologians) have tried to 'domesticate' her by trying to discover various laws and principles. To Brodsky, the essence of Clio is her unpredictability; the 'only law of history . . . is chance'.[31]

The poem, then, is not just a meditation on sorrow, on a sense of loss, but a discourse on history and geography, time and space. A crucial shift is signalled at the end of the central quatrain, in l. 12, with its striking alliteration and unique rhythm for this poem. Brodsky uses geographical realia with striking frequency in his poetry,[32] and here, even without naming specific places, he appears to be writing from a particular perspective, most likely his own. In the lines following the twelfth he describes both what he knows intimately (cf. the reference to a head, presumably the poet's own, in l. 12) and the vast earth (the globe of that same line). The blueberry-filled forests could well be those around Brodsky's Leningrad, while the rivers in which sturgeon can be caught by hand are those of European Russia. The scene then shifts to the south-east (perhaps toward the Pamir mountains?) and toward the horses of the eastern plains; Mongol faces replace those of Slavs. And finally the verses look out toward the Pacific and the great expanse of the sky, taking on a vast perspective from above, again not atypically for Brodsky,[33] before it rushes back to earth and the mundane object, the lace underwear, that anchors the poem once again in the world of people and intimacy.

But why this concern with concrete places? How do they relate to the sorrow and sense of loss at the beginning of the poem? The key lies in Brodsky's view of history and time, which, as indicated above, he sees as both unknowable in its behaviour and as indifferent to people; the main trait of both the past and the future is our absence from them, as he notes more than once.[34] History, though, is only perceived by the living; preceding history, and thus older than it, is space, or geography. To the extent that the individual is linked with things, with places, the person retains a tie to the world, to the berries in one's local forest as well as to distant mountains and seas, that can overcome or at least place a limit on sorrow. Urania, or space, is thus both superior to Clio (time) and kinder to humans. Note how the inorganic, 'cold' objects of the poem's opening lines (the window, a fence, keys, rails, etc.) are replaced over the last section by references to life and vitality: the berries in the forests, the rivers teeming with fish, the people in a town, the horses and people in the east. And with the emphasis on life comes a burst of colour as well, not just the verbs referring to brown, yellow and blue, but also nouns such as *chernika* and *bel'e*, formed from roots of colour words. Hence, the structure of the poem focuses on the centre, where the contrast between an open and life-affirming Urania and an indifferent if not untrustworthy Clio is brought out, at the same time that the poem as a whole presents a progression – from the absence and lifelessness caused by the workings of time, to a sense of vitality and of belonging to one's home and to the earth; from the formal orderliness of an elegy, to the more chaotic yet exuberant homage to geography, with which it concludes.[35]

Notes

1. For Joseph Brodsky's own translation of this poem, see *To Urania: Selected Poems 1965–1985* (New York: Farrar, Straus & Giroux, 1988) p. 70.
2. Joseph Brodsky, Preface to *Modern Russian Poets on Poetry*, ed. C. R. Proffer (Ann Arbor: Ardis, 1976) pp. 7–8.
3. Barry Scherr, 'Strofika Brodskogo', in *Poetika Brodskogo: Sbornik statei*, ed. L. Loseff (Tenafly, NJ: Hermitage, 1986) pp. 97–120.
4. Scherr, 'Beginning at the End: Rhyme and Enjambement in Brodsky's Poetry', in *Brodsky's Poetics and Aesthetics*, eds L. Loseff and V. Polukhina (Basingstoke: Macmillan Press, 1990) pp. 180, 184.
5. M. L. Gasparov, 'Rifma Brodskogo', *Russian Literature*, vol. XXXVII (1995) pp. 195–6.
6. Scherr, *Russian Poetry: Meter, Rhythm, and Rhyme* (Berkeley: University of California Press, 1986) pp. 215–18.
7. Scherr, 'Beginning at the End', pp. 180–82; on the latter point see also Kari Egerton, 'Grammatical Contrast in the Rhyme of Joseph Brodsky', *Essays in Poetics*, vol. 19 (1994) no. 1, pp. 7–24.
8. As Egerton has noted, from his early poems through *Uraniia* Brodsky sharply reduced the frequency of instances when he would rhyme nouns in the same case, even as the percentage of noun–noun rhymes rose – i.e. variety in cases helps compensate for the heavy use of nouns in the rhyme position.
9. Cf. Valentina Polukhina, *Joseph Brodsky: A Poet for Our Time* (Cambridge University Press, 1989) pp. 97, 156, 193 *passim*.
10. 'O rifmakh odnogo stikhotvoreniia: Iosif Brodskii, "Nochnoi polet"', *Scando-Slavica*, vol. 36 (1990) pp. 69–85.
11. The care that Brodsky pays to the rhymes in his English version also hints at their importance. The English contains much more enjambment and a somewhat different rhythm, but the alternating feminine rhymes are meticulously maintained. Several key words from the Russian recur in the rhyme position (sorrow, Clio, lantern, etc.), and the approximate rhymes exhibit both wit and lively sound interplay: sorrow/swallow, sturgeon/surge on, carousing/cruisers.
12. Scherr, 'Beginning at the End', pp. 187–8.
13. Scherr, *Russian Poetry*, p. 208; cf. 'Beginning at the End', p. 185.
14. Cf. Christopher Jones, 'Rhyme and Joseph Brodsky: Making Connections', *Essays in Poetics*, vol. 18 (1993) no. 2, pp. 1–11.

15. 'Versifikatsiia v stikhotvoerenii I. Brodskogo 'Kellomäki' ', in *Poetika Brodskogo*, pp. 141–59.
16. M. L. Gasparov, *Ocherk istorii russkogo stikha: Metrika, ritmika, rifma, strofika* (Moscow: Nauka, 1984) pp. 280–1.
17. V. Polukhina, 'A New Conception of Poetry', in *Brodsky through the Eyes of his Contemporaries* (New York: St Martin's Press, 1992) p. 130.
18. Note that the English version, while evocative, seems to lose some of the 'prosaic' quality that makes the Russian so effective. Similarly, Michael Molnar ('Noetic License in Brodsky's Self-Translation', *Russian Literature*, vol. XXXVII (1995) pp. 333–7) points to some 'off-key notes' in another of Brodsky's self-translations. Whatever the quality of the English version, it is none the less valuable for pointing to important aspects of the original. Here Brodsky offers a more literal explanation of his image; at other times he explains references that remain obscure in the Russian or points to concerns that may otherwise elude notice by the reader.
19. 'The Introduction of the Prosaic into Poetry', in *Brodsky through the Eyes of his Contemporaries*, p. 65.
20. My thanks to Lev Loseff for pointing out that the image probably comes from Chingiz Aitmatov's *The Day Lasts More Than a Hundred Years* (*I dol'she veka dlitsia den'*); Brodsky liked the opening passage, which depicts a lone fox by some railroad tracks in the desert.
21. Brodsky, *Chast' rechi* (Ann Arbor: Ardis, 1977) p. 101.
22. 'Tozhdestvo dvukh variantov: zametki po povodu grafiki Iosifa Brodskogo', *Russian Literature*, vol. XXXVII (1995) p. 253.
23. Brodsky, *Konets prekrasnoi epokhi* (Ann Arbor: Ardis, 1977) p. 111.
24. M. Iu. Lotman and Iu. M. Lotman, 'Mezhdu veshch'iu i pustotoi (Iz nabliudenii nad poetikoi sbornika Iosifa Brodskogo Uraniia)', in *Uchenye zapiski Tartuskogo universiteta*, vyp. 883 (1990): *Puti razvitiia russkoi literatury*, p. 182.
25. David Bethea, *Joseph Brodsky and the Creation of Exile* (Princeton University Press, 1994) pp. 27, 165–6.
26. In her extensive commentary on the associations of this name, Josephine Roberts also provides a small bibliography of articles dealing with Urania in English poetry: Lady Mary Wroth, *The First Part of the Countess of Montgomery's 'Urania'*, ed. J. A. Roberts (Binghamton: Center for Medieval and Early Renaissance Studies, State University of New York at Binghamton, 1995) p. 715.
27. E. A. Baratynskii, *Polnoe sobranie sochinenii, Seriia Biblioteka poeta*, 3rd edn (Leningrad: Sovetskii pisatel', 1989) p. 419.
28. Kevin M. F. Platt, 'Boratynskii's *The Last Poet* and the Theme of Conflict between Poetry and Society: Dialectic and Double Bind', *Stanford Slavic Studies*, vol. 8 (1994) pp. 169–96.
29. Joseph Brodsky, *On Grief and Reason* (New York: Farrar, Straus & Giroux, 1995), p. 117.
30. Cf. W. H. Auden, *Homage to Clio* (New York: Random House, 1960). Note that Brodsky's title, 'Profile of Clio', has the same rhythmic structure as Auden's 'Homage to Clio'.
31. *On Grief and Reason*, p. 134.

32. Peter Vail, 'Prostranstvo kak metafora vremeni: stikhi Iosifa Brodskogo v zhanre puteshestviia', *Russian Literature*, vol. XXXVII (1995) p. 406.
33. On this notion, see Iakov Gordin, 'Strannik', *Russian Literature*, vol. XXXVII (1995) pp. 227–45.
34. *On Grief and Reason*, pp. 137, 252.
35. I want to thank Lev Loseff for his valuable comments on a draft of this paper; many of his remarks have found their way into my final text.

7

'Lithuanian Nocturne: To Tomas Venclova'*

Litovskii noktiurn: Tomasu Ventslova

TOMAS VENCLOVA

I

Взбаламутивший море
ветер рвется, как ругань с расквашенных губ,
в глубь холодной державы,
заурядное до-ре-
ми-фа-соль-ля-си-до извлекая из каменных труб.   5
Не-царевны-не-жабы
припадают к земле,
и сверкает звезды оловянная гривна.
И подобье лица
растекается в черном стекле,   10
как пощечина ливня.

II

Здравствуй, Томас. То – мой
призрак, бросивший тело в гостинице где-то
за морями, гребя
против северных туч, поспешает домой,   15
вырываясь из Нового Света,
и тревожит тебя.

III

Поздний вечер в Литве.
Из костелов бредут, хороня запятые

* Translated from the Russian by Andrea Sillis. The poem is translated by Tatiana Retivova.

свечек в скобках ладоней. В продрогших дворах   20
куры роются клювами в жухлой дресве.
Над жнивьем Жемайтии
вьется снег, как небесных обителей прах.
Из раскрытых дверей
пахнет рыбой. Малец полуголый   25
и старуха в платке загоняют корову в сарай.
Эапоздалый еврей
по брусчатке местечка гремит балаголой,
вожжи рвет
и кричит залихватски: ог "Герай!"   30

IV

Извини за вторженье.
Сочти появление за
возвращенье цитаты в ряды "Манифеста".
чуть картавей,
чуть выше октавой от странствий вдали.   35
Потому – не крестись,
не ломай в кулаке картуза:
сгину прежде, чем грянет с насеста
петушиное "пли".
Извини, что без спросу.   40
Не пяться от страха в чулан:
то, кордонов за счет, расширяет свой радиус
бренность.
Мстя, как камень колодцу кольцом грязевым,
над балтийской волной   45
я жужжу, точно тот моноплан –
точно Дариус и Гиренас,
но не так уязвим.

V

Поздний вечер в Империи,
в нищей провинции.   50
Вброд
перешедшее Неман еловое войско,
ощетинившись пиками, Ковно в потемки берет.
Багровеет известка
трехэтажных домов, и булыжник мерцает, как   55

пойманный лещ.
Вверх взвивается занавес в местном театре.
И выносят на улицу главую вещь,
разделенную на три
без остатка;   60
сквозняк теребит бахрому
занавески из тюля. Звезда в захолустье
светит ярче: как карта, упавшая в масть.
И впадает во тьму,
по стеклу барабаня, руки твоей устье.   65
Больше некуда впасть.

VI

В полночь всякая речь
обретает ухватки слепца;
так что даже "отчизна" на ощупь – как Леди Годива.
В паутине углов   70
микрофоны спецслужбы в квартире певца
пишут скрежет матраца и всплески мотива
общей песни без слов.
Здесь панует стыдливость. Листва, норовя
выбрать между своей лицевой стороной и изнанкой,   75
возмущает фонарь. Отменив рупора,
миру здесь о себе возвещают, на муравья
наступив ненароком, невнятной морзянкой
пульса, скрипом пера.

VII

Вот откуда твои   80
щек мучнистость, безадресность глаза,
шепелявость и волосы цвета спитой,
тусклой чайной струи.
Вот откуда вся жизнь как нетвердая честная фраза
на пути к запятой.   85
Вот откуда моей,
как ее продолжение вверх, оболочки
в твоих стеклах расплывчатость, бунт голытьбы
ивняка и.т.п., очертанья морей,
их страниц перевернутость в поисках точки,   90
горизонта, судьбы.

VIII

Наша письменность, Томас! с моим, за поля
выходящим сказуемым! с хмурым твоим
домоседством
подлежащего! Прочный, чернильный союз,   95
кружева, вензеля,
помесь литеры римской с кириллицей: цели
со средством,
как велел Макроус!
Наши оттиски! в смятых сырых простынях –   100
этих рыхлых извилинах общего мозга! –
в мягкой глине возлюбленных, в детях без нас.
Либо – просто синяк
на скуле мирозданья от взгляда подростка,
от попытки на глаз   105
расстоянье прикинуть от той ли литовской корчмы
до лица, многооко смотрящего мимо,
как раскосый монгол за земной частокол,
чтоб вложить пальцы в рот – в эту рану фомы –
и, нащупав язык, на манер серафима   110
переправить глагол.

IX

Мы похожи;
мы, в сущности, Томас, одно:
ты, коптящий окно изнутри, я смотрящий снаружи.
Друг для друга мы суть   115
обоюдное дно
амальгамовой лужи,
неспособной блеснуть.
Покривись – я отвечу ухмылкой кривой,
отзовусь на зевок немотой, раздирающей полость,   120
разольюсь в три ручья
от стоваттной слезы над твоей головой.
Мы – взаимный конвой,
проступающий в Касторе Поллукс,
в просторечье – ничья,   125
пат, подвижная тень,
приводимая в действие жаркой лучиной,
эхо возгласа, сдача с рубля.

Чем сильней жизнь испорчена, тем
    мы в ней неразличимей   130
        ока праздного для.

X

Чем питается призрак? Отбросами сна,
отрубями границ, шелухою цифири:
явь всегда норовит сохранить адреса.
Переулок сдвигает фасады, как зубы десна,   135
желтизну подворотни, как сыр простофили,
        пожирает лиса
темноты. Место, времени мстя
за свое постоянство жильцом, постояльцем,
    жизнью в нем, отпирает засов, –   140
        и, эпоху спустя,
    я тебя застаю в замусоленной пальцем
        сверхдержаве лесов
и равнин, хорошо сохраняющей мысли, черты
и особенно позу: в сырой конопляной   145
многоверстной рубахе, в гудящих стальных бигуди
    Мать–Литва засыпает над плесом,
        и ты
припадаешь к ее неприкрытой, стеклянной,
        пол–литровой груди.   150

XI

    Существуют места,
    где ничто не меняется. Это –
заменители памяти, кислый триумф фиксажа.
Там шлагбаумы на резкость наводит верста.
Там чем дальше, тем больше в тебе силуэта.   155
    Там с лица сторожа
    моложавей. Минувшее смотрит вперед
настороженным глазом подростка в шинели,
    и судьба нарушителем пятится прочь
в настоящую старость с плевком на стене,   160
с ломотой, с беск онечностью в форме панели
    либо лестницы. Ночь
    и взаправду граница, где, как татарва,
территориям прожитой жизни набегом

угрожает действительность и, наоборот,   165
где дрова переходят в деревья и снова в дрова,
где что веко ни спрячет,
      то явь печенегом
   как трофей подберет.

                    XII

Полночь. Сойка кричит   170
человеческим голосом и обвиняет природу
в преступленьях термометра против нуля.
Витовт, бросивший меч и похеривший щит,
поигружается в Балтику в поисках броду
   к шведам. Впрочем, земля   175
и сама завершается молом, погнавшимся, за,
как по плоским ступенькам, по волнам
   убежавшей свободой.
      Усилья бобра
по постройке запруды венчает слеза,   180
   расставаясь с проворным
      ручейком серебра.

                    XIII

   Полночь в лиственном крае,
   в губернии цвета пальто.
Колокольная клинопись. Облако в виде отреза   185
   на рядно сопредельной державе.
         Внизу
      пашни, скирды, плато
черепицы, кирпич, колоннада, железо,
   плюс обутый в кирзу   190
      человек государства.
      Ночной кислород
наводняют помехи, молитва, сообщенья
   о погоде, известия,
      храбрый Кощей   195
с округленными цифрами, гимны, фокстрот,
   болеро, запрещенья
      безымянных вещей.

XIV

Призрак бродит по Каунасу. Входит в собор,
выбегает наружу. Плетется по Лайсвис наллее.   200
Входит в "Тульпе", садится к столу.
           Кельнер, глядя в упор,
   видит только салфетки, огни бакалеи,
           снег, такси на углу;
   просто улицу. Бьюсь об заклад,   205
ты готов позавидовать. Ибо незримость
входит в моду с годами – как тела уступка душе,
как намек на грядущее, как масхалат
       рая, как затянувшийся минус.
           Ибо все в барыше   210
           от отсутствия, от
   бестелесности: горы и долы,
медный маятник, сильно привыкший к часам,
Бог, смотрящий на все это дело с высот,
           зеркала, коридоры,   215
           соглядатай, ты сам.

XV

Призрак бродит бесцельно по Каунасу. Он
   суть твое прибавление к воздуху мысли
           обо мне,
   суть пространство к квадрате, а не   220
   энергичная проповедь лучших времен.
           Не завидуй. Причисли
           привиденье к родне,
к свойствам воздуха – так же, как мелкий петит,
   рассыпаемый в сумраке речью картавой   225
           вроде цокота мух,
   неспособный, поди, утолить аппетит
       новой Клио, одетой заставой,
           но ласкающий слух
           обнаженной Урании.   230
           Только она,
Муза точки в пространстве и Муза утраты
очертаний, как скаред – гроши,

в состоянье сполна
оценить постоянство: как форму расплаты   235
за движенье – души.

XVI

Вот откуда пера,
Томас, к буквам привязанность.
Вот чем
объясняться должно тяготенье, не так ли?   240
Скрепя
сердце, с хриплым "пора!"
отрывая себя от родных заболоченных вотчин,
что скрывать – от тебя!
от страницы, от букв,   245
от – сказать ли! – любви
звука к смыслу, бесплотности – к массе
и свободы – прости
и лица не криви –
к рабству, данному в мясе,   250
во плоти, на кости,
эта вещь воспаряет в чернильный ночной эмпирей
мимо дремлющих в нише
местных ангелов:
выше   255
их и нетопырей.

XVII

Муза точки в пространстве! Вещей, различаемых
лишь
в телескоп! Вычитанья
без остатка! Нуля!   260
Ты, кто горлу велишь
избегать причитанья,
превышения "ля"
и советуешь сдержанность! Муза, прими
эту арию следствия, петую в ухо причине,   265
то есть песнь двойнику,
и взгляни на нее и ее до-ре-ми
там, в разреженном чине,
у себя наверху

с точки зрения воздуха.   270
Воздух и есть эпилог
для сетчатки – поскольку он необитаем.
Он суть наше "домой",
восвояси вернувшийся слог.
Сколько жаброй его ни хватаем,   275
он успешно латаем
светом взапуски с тьмой.

XVIII

У всего есть предел:
горизонт – у зрачка, у отчаянья – память,
для роста –   280
расширение плеч.
Только звук отделяться способен от тел,
вроде призрака, Томас.
Сиротство
звука, Томас, есть речь!   285
Оттолкнув абажур,
глядя прямо перед собою,
видишь воздух:
анфас
сонмы тех, кто губою   290
наследил в нем
до нас.

XIX

В царстве воздуха! В равенстве слога глотку
кислорода! В прозрачных и в сбившихся в облак
наших выдохах! В том   295
мире, где, точно сны к потолку,
к небу льнут наши "о!" где звезда обретает свой
облик,
продиктованный ртом!
Вот чем дышит вселенная. Вот   300
что петух кукарекал,
упреждая гортани великую сушь!
Воздух – вещь языка.
Небосвод –

хор согласных и гласных молекул,   305
в просторечии – душ.

XX

Оттого-то он чист.
Нет на свете вещей, безупречней
(кроме смерти самой)
          отбеляющих лист.   310
Чем белее, тем бесчеловечней.
Муза, можно домой?
Восвояси! В тот край,
где бездумный Ъорей попирает беспечно трофеи
уст. В грамматику без   315
          препинания. В рай
          алфавита, трахеи.
В твой безликий пикбез.

XXI

Над холмами Литвы
что-то вроде мольбы за весь мир   320
раздается в потемках: бубнящий, глухой, невеселый
звук плывет над селеньями в сторону Куршской
          косы.
То Святой Казимир
с Чудотворным Николой   325
          коротают часы
в ожидании зимней зари.
За пределами веры,
из свой стратосферы,
Муза, с ними призри   330
на певца тех равнин, в рукотворную тьму
погруженных по кровлю,
на певца усмиренных пейзажей.
Обнеси своей стражей
дом и сердце ему.   335
                                   (II: 322–31)

*   *   *

'Lithuanian Nocturne: To Tomas Venclova'

[I] Wind, having roughened the sea, / bursts forth like cursing from bruised lips / deep within the cold super-power, / pulling a plain do-re- / (5) mi-fa-sol-la-ti-do from chimneys. / Neither princesses, nor toads / genuflect to the ground, / and a tin dime of a star sparkles. / And the semblance of a face / (10) spreads itself through the black glass, / like the slap of downpour. / / [II] Greetings, Tomas. That is my / spectre, having abandoned the body in some / overseas hotel room, rowing / (15) against the northern clouds, it hurries home / tearing out of the New World / to bother you. / / [III] A late evening in Lithuania. / They wander from churches, burying the commas / (20) of candles in the brackets of [their] palms. In the freezing courtyards / hens dig with their beaks in the dry-rotted sawdust. / Over the stubble of Zhemaitiia / snow weaves like celestial cloisters' ashes. / From the doors flung open – / (25) the smell of fish. A half naked boy / and an old kerchiefed woman chase a cow into the barn. / A Jewish cabby in a cart, hurries late / drumming the village's cobblestones, / yanks the reins / (30) and roars 'Gerai!' ['O.K.']/ / [IV] Pardon this invasion. / Consider this sighting as / the return of a quote back to the rows of the 'Manifesto': / a bit more burred / (35) and with higher pitch thanks to distant wanderings. / So don't cross yourself, / don't tear at the tassel: / I'll be off before the cock's 'fire!' bursts from the roost. / (40) Pardon such an intrusion. / Don't back off in fright into the pantry: / it's merely one's mortality expanding its radius at the expense of borders. / Avenging myself, like the pebble – the well with its muddy ring / (45) over the Baltic wave, / I buzz just like a monoplane, / like some Darius and Girenas, / though not as vulnerable. / / [V] Late evening in the Empire / (50) in a destitute province. / Having waded across the Neman, / an army of conifers bristling with lances / takes Kaunas into the darkness. / The stucco of three-storied houses / (55) turns scarlet, and cobblestones glisten / like bream in a net. / Up soar the curtains of some local theatre. / And the most important thing gets brought out / to be divided by three / (60) down to the last drop. / A draft worries the fringe of / a tulle curtain. A star in the middle of nowhere / shines brighter, like a card following suit. / And river-like, your hand / falls drumming the glass into darkness. / (65) Nowhere

else to fall. // [VI] At midnight [any] speech / acquires the ways
of the blind. / So that even 'homeland' to the touch is like
Lady Godiva. / (70) In the web of corners / of the bard's room,
the microphones of the special service / tape the screeching
mattress and the splash of / a common song without words. /
Here shame is in charge. Leaves / (75) torn between turning
heads or tails / irritate a lamppost. Having no use for
loudspeakers, / one informs the world of oneself by inadvertently
stepping on an ant, / in the indecipherable morse of one's pulse,
/ the scratch of one's pen. // [VII] (80) Hence the mealiness of
/ your cheeks, your stare aimed nowhere, / the lisp and the
hair dull like the colour / of a stream of old tea. / Hence all of
life like some soft honest phrase / (85) moving comma-ward. /
Hence the upward continuation of my membrane / washed
out in your windows, / the mutiny of the masses of willow
twigs, etc. outlines of seas, / (90) their upside down pages in
search of a full stop, / the horizon, fate. // [VIII] Our writing,
Tomas! With my predicates / [spilling] beyond margins! With
your dour, homebody / (95) subjects! A sturdy alliance of ink,
/ lace, monograms, / the mixtures of Roman typeset with Cyrillic,
ends with means, / as per 'Macrowhisker'! [Stalin] / (100) Our
imprints, in damp wrinkled sheets, / the dumpy convolutions
of our common brain, / in the soft clay of the beloved, in the
children without us. / Or else, a mere bruise / on the cheekbone
of the universe from the glance of the adolescent, / (105) from
the attempt to determine at a glance / the distance between
this one, is it? Lithuanian inn / and the face, multi-eyed, looking
past / like some squint-eyed Mongolian at the palisade, / so
that he might stick his fingers into his mouth, that wound of
Thomas, / (110) and feeling his tongue, in the manner of some
Seraphim / redirect the verb. // [IX] We're alike. / We, in essence,
Tomas, are one; / you, smoking the window from within, while
I looking in from the outside. / (115) We're for each other / the
common floor / of the amalgamated puddle / incapable of
sparkling. / Make a wry face, I'll respond with a smirk. / (120)
I'll respond to your yawn with a gut-tearing speechlessness, /
I'll spill into three forked rivers / from the hundred watt tear
[shape] / over your head. / We're a mutual convoy, / Pollux
seeping through Castor, / (125) or put simply, we're a draw, /
a stalemate, a moveable shadow / rendered active by a hot
flicker of light, / the echo of a cry, change from a ruble. / The

more broken the life, the more / (130) we are indistinguishable
in it / to the idle eye. / / [X] What feeds a spectre? The refuse
of dreams, / the husks of borders, the chaff of numerics: / reality
always tries to hold on to its addresses. / (135) A side street
moves house fronts, like gums moving teeth, / the sallow bottom
of the courtyard gate, like some simpleton's cheese, / gets gulped
down by the fox of / darkness. Place begrudging time / its
permanence with a dweller, a lodger, / (140) life therein, opens
the latch, / and an epoch later / I find you in the [fingered]
slobbered / super-power of forests / and plains, so good at
preserving thoughts, features, / (145) and above all the pose:
in its damp multiversted / shirt of hemp, in its droning steel
curlers, / Mother Lithuania falls asleep along the river, / and
you / fall to her uncovered, glass / (150) half-litre breast. / / [XI]
There are places / where nothing changes. These / are memory
substitutes, the acid triumph of fixing solutions. / The barriers
are brought into focus by versts. / (155) There, the further you
go, the more of what is left of you is a silhouette. / There the
guards appear / younger. What has just come to pass looks
ahead / with the guarded eye of a teen in an overcoat, / and
fate, the trespasser, backs away / (160) into deep old age with
spit upon wall[s], / rheumatic aches, and infinity in the form
of a sidewalk / or a staircase. Night / is indeed the border,
where like a horde / (165) reality threatens to raid the territories
of spent life, and vice versa, / where firewood joins tree and
becomes firewood again. / Where whatever the eyelid covers, /
reality, Pecheneg-like, / will plunder as spoils. / / [XII] (170)
Midnight. A [blue]-jay / screams / in a human voice blaming
nature / for the crimes of a thermometer against zero. / Prince
Vytautas, having flung his sword and crossed out his shield, /
penetrates the Baltic in search of the shoal way / (175) toward
the Swedes. While earth / itself ends in a pier, racing after / as
if along flat steps, on the waves / of runaway freedom. / All
attempts of a beaver / (180) in building a dam are crowned by
a tear, / parting with the quick stream of silver. / / [XIII] Midnight
in a deciduous region, / in a province the colour of topcoats. /
(185) The cuneiform of a belfry. A cloud, a scrap of material, /
of burlap for a contiguous nation. / Below / ploughed fields,
haystacks, plateaux of / roof tiles, bricks, colonnades, cast-iron,
/ (190) plus a shod-in-ersatz leather / man of the state. / Evening's
oxygen / gets flooded with static, prayers, weather / reports,

announcements, / (195) the brave Koshchey / with rounded numbers, hymns, foxtrot, / bolero, the forbidding / of nameless things. / / [XIV] A spectre wanders in Kaunas. Enters a cathedral, / (200) runs out. Winds its way down Laisves avenue. / Enters 'Tulpe', takes a seat. / The headwaiter looking straight through it, / sees only the napkins, the grocery's lights, / snow, the taxicab on the corner, / (205) the street itself. I bet you anything / you're envious. Since invisibility / has become *'de rigeur'* with the years, as the body's concession to soul, / as a hint of what's to come, as the masked robe of / Heaven, like a drawn-out minus. / (210) Since everyone profits / from absence, from / incorporeality: hill and dale, / the brass pendulum, relying heavily on the clock, / God looking at all of this from up high, / (215) mirrors, corridors, / your tail [spy] and yourself. / / [XV] A spectre wanders aimlessly in Kaunas. It / is your addition to the air of thought / about me, / (220) is space in a square / and not / the energetic sermon of better days. / Don't be envious. Rank this ghost / as one of kin, / the properties of air – the same as some fine brevier / (225) scattered in the twilight by burred speech / sort of like the buzzing of flies, / that cannot, go figure, appeal to the appetite / of a new Clio, adorned in an outpost, / but is music / (230) to naked Urania's ears. / Only she, / Muse of a point in space, Muse of loss / of features, like a miser appreciates his pennies, / can fully / (235) appreciate constancy as a form of retribution / for the movement of the soul. / / [XVI] That's where Tomas, the pen's / attachment to letters is from. / That's how / (240) one should explain gravitation, shouldn't one? / Grudgingly, with a hoarse 'it's time!' / tearing oneself away from patrimonial marshlands, / and, frankly, from you! / (245) From the page, from the letters, from – do I dare say it – the love / felt by sound – for sense, by the incorporeal – for mass, / and by freedom – forgive me, / don't make a face – / (250) for slavery, given its flesh form, / meat on the bones, / this thing soars in the inky darkness of empyrean / past the dreaming local angels in niches / (255) above them / and bats. / / [XVII] The Muse of a point in space! Of things visible / only / through a telescope! Of subtraction / (260) with nothing left over! Of zero! / You who order the throat / to avoid lamentation / or resist going higher than 'la', / and recommend being reserved! Oh Muse, accept / (265) this aria of effect, sung to the ear of cause, / in other words to one's double, / and observe it and its do-re-mi,

/ there in its rarefied ranks / , up there, / (270) from air's point of view. / Air is indeed the epilogue / for the retina, since it's uninhabitable. / It is our 'go home', / the syllable returning to its place. / (275) No matter how much of it we grasp with our gills, / it is well patched / with light racing darkness. / / [XVIII] Everything has a limit: / the horizon – for [the eye's] pupil, for despair – memory, / (280) for growth – / the widening shoulders. / Only sound is able to separate from body, / like a spectre, Tomas. The orphan / (285) of sound, Tomas, is speech! / Pushing aside the lampshade, / one looks straight ahead of oneself / and sees – air: in full view / (290) the swarms of those / who with their lips / have left their prints in it / before us. / / [XIX] In the kingdom of air! In the equality of a syllable to a gulp of / oxygen! In our transparent whipped into cloud / (295) exhalations! In that / world where like dreams floating to the ceiling / our 'o's!' cling to the palate, where a star acquires its shape / as dictated by the mouth! / (300) That is what the universe breathes by. / That the cock crowed, / forestalling the great drought for the larynx. / Air is a thing of the tongue. / Heaven's vault is / (305) a molecular chorus of consonants and vowels, / in common parlance – souls. / / [XX] That is why it is pure. / There is no other thing more flawless / (other than death itself) / (310) when it comes to bleaching the page. / The whiter, the less human. / Muse, can we go home? / To our place! To that land / where thoughtless Boreas keeps carelessly trampling / the trophies of / (315) the mouth. Into that grammar without / punctuation. Into the paradise of / the alphabet, the trachea. / Into your faceless 'likbez'. ['liquidation of illiteracy'] / / [XXI] Over Lithuania's hillocks / (320) something like supplication for all of mankind / is uttered in the darkness: the droning, muffled, cheerless / sound floats above settlements toward Curonian Spit. / That's St Casimir and / (325) St Nicholas the Miraclemaker / whiling time away / in anticipation of winter's dawn. / Beyond creed, / from its stratosphere, / (330) O Muse! Take in with these two / the singer of these plains, into the manmade darkness / sunk up to the roof, / the singer of pacified landscapes. / Cover with your guard for him / his home and his heart. / /*

*   *   *

The present work may be seen as a continuation of, or companion work to a previous article on 'Lithuanian Divertissement'.[1] In that article I touched on questions relating to the unusual position of the researcher, who is analysing a text which is dedicated to him personally (although it is true to say that he is appearing in another role, as a poet and not as a literary scholar). The brief comments made on that occasion still hold true. I am aware that my choice of an object of research not only transgresses the rules of rigorous scientific etiquette, but may also lead to a distortion of perspective. It is difficult (although interesting) to deal with a text while one is being situated at one and the same time both inside and outside it. Incidentally, this difficulty is even more pronounced in the case of 'Lithuanian Nocturne' than in that of 'Lithuanian Divertissement'. While in the latter the addressee of the poem is present only implicitly, here he is presented as a partner in the dialogue (although not as an active participant: the poem remains a monologue throughout). Nevertheless, the loss is possibly outweighed by the gain. The concrete circumstances and details associated with Brodsky's poems – and even with the epoch itself – soon fade from the memory of his contemporaries. Those who remember them have a duty to record them. And generally speaking, the opinion of someone who has witnessed events, or participated in them, be that in a limited or even biased way, can contribute towards understanding a poet.

One could refer to a 'Lithuanian cycle' in Brodsky's works.[2] Included in it would be not only the two poems already mentioned, but also 'Kon'iak v grafine – tsveta iantaria' [Cognac in a Decanter – the Colours of Amber], and several others. For example, 'Anno Domini', written in Palanga, transforms the Lithuanian surroundings (including events in the lives of his circle of friends), into defamiliarized ancient, or, rather, medieval forms. 'Otkrytka iz goroda K.' [Postcard from the Town K.] is dedicated to Königsberg (which was renamed Kaliningrad – a name starting with the same letter);[3] but this poem is clearly linked with conversations which took place in Lithuania. It is difficult to establish the boundaries of the cycle. Impressions of Lithuania run through many poems; for example, in 'Elegiia' [Elegy]: 'Podruga milaia, kabak vse tot zhe . . .' [My dearest, the tavern is still the same], 'pilot pochtovoi linii' [a pilot of a postal line] – refers to a Russian aviator Brodsky met in Palanga, in the restaurant of the hotel 'Pajúris', and the restaurant itself is the *kabak* [tavern] mentioned in the first line. As a whole, Lithuania, which Brodsky often visited from 1966 right up to his emigration,[4] thoroughly influenced his ideas about 'empire' and 'province' – in 'Pis'ma rimskomu drugu' [Letters to a Roman Friend] for example: 'esli vypalo v Imperii rodit'sia, / luchshe zhit' v glukhoi provintsii, u moria' [If you happen to be born in an Empire, / it is better to live in a remote province, by the sea' – II: 285).[5] 'Lithuanian Nocturne', written after he had emigrated, is like a completion of the cycle. It is a farewell to Lithuania, which the poet would never see again.

The poem was first published in *Kontinent* (1984, no. 40, pp. 7–18). It was included in *Uraniia* (Ann Arbor: Ardis, 1987, pp. 55–65) and has since been reprinted many times. It is more difficult to establish when it was written. Neither in *Kontinent* nor in *Uraniia* is there any indication of its date of composition. Later the date was usually fixed at 1973[6] or 1974.[7] Both dates are inaccurate. It is possible to establish this from my diary, in which many conversations with Brodsky are recorded.

'Lithuanian Nocturne' was indeed started either in 1973 or 1974, that is to say, soon after Brodsky's departure from Leningrad. At that time I was still living in Lithuania, and the poem was conceived as an epistle to Vilnius: in it are reflected several personal events occurring at that time, with which Brodsky was familiar from my letters. Incidentally, Brodsky said that he wrote the poem in the 'Wales' hotel in New York (cf. ll. 12–14: 'To – moi / prizrak, brosivshii telo v gostinitse gde-to / za moriami . . .' [That is my / spectre, having abandoned the body in some / overseas hotel room . . .]). However, shortly afterwards the unfinished poem was, according to him, abandoned. Brodsky only came back to it at the end of 1983, when I myself had already long-since emigrated to New Haven, and the subject of the poem – an 'other-worldly' meeting of the *émigré* and *non-émigré* – had, so to speak, become purely historical. I will now cite the corresponding extracts from my diary:

11 [December 1983]. [. . .] Brodsky is already home. 'Tell me, did Darius and Girenas have a monoplane or a biplane?' He had been intending to write about them for a long time. I said that it was a monoplane, although who knows. [. . .]
19.   Brodsky was asking a lot of questions about Vilnius, its towers etc. etc. – for a poem. 'At the end there you have to

scale a high mountain – I don't know if I'll manage it; I am already rather weary of this poem.'

I remember very well that at that particular time Brodsky was questioning me about Saint Casimir (the patron saint of Lithuania) and about Nikolas the Miraclemaker: it follows that at precisely that point he was putting together the last part of the poem (and elaborating the beginning). Thus work on 'Lithuanian Nocturne' was drawn out over a whole decade, and the date of composition of the poem should consequently be given as 1973/4(?)–83.

The time-lapse between 'Lithuanian Divertissement', which was written in 1971, and the start of work on 'Lithuanian Nocturne' is slight – either two or three years. Addressed to one and the same addressee and thematically linked, these poems are essentially like the introduction and coda of a single work. Their common theme may be defined as meditations on fate and poetry, and was aroused on visiting a small country, which had been enslaved by a powerful empire. That said, 'Lithuanian Divertissement' focuses on fate, played out in different variations and in different registers, 'Lithuanian Nocturne', on poetry, which here, as in all Brodsky's mature work, is completely coincident with fate. Between the poems there lies an important biographical caesura. The poems also employ contrasting poetics. 'Lithuanian Divertissement' is, as I have said previously, generically light-hearted, but with a serious theme breaking through the unconstrainedly comical tone. 'Lithuanian Nocturne' is also stuffed with elements of parody and *risqué* jokes, but on the whole it involves poetry 'of a high style', emotionally intense and even sombre. The first poem is, in fact, a cycle. It is a series of sketches, diverse in theme, intonation and rhythm. As I tried to show in my earlier article, they are arranged on the principle of a compositional ring. The second poem is, from beginning to end, a sustained dramatic monologue. It develops against the background of a monotonous landscape. It is also permeated by a single intonational–rhythmical pressure, and possesses plot, development and denouement.

Strictly speaking, this difference is already emphasized in the titles of the poems, which define them as belonging to 'musical genres'. While the divertissement is a strict musical form basically linked to Baroque and the eighteenth century, the nocturne does not have such well-defined formal characteristics and harks back rather to the age of romanticism. Its sources are sometimes found in the Italian *notturno* – a collection of light pieces for a chamber ensemble, which were usually performed at night outdoors. However, the typical nocturne differs considerably from the *notturno*. It is most often simply a meditative composition for the piano, which is loosely defined as being 'inspired by night', or 'creating a sense of night'. It takes its beginnings in the teens of the nineteenth century and is linked above all with Chopin, Schumann and Liszt (and in Russia with Glinka, Tchaikovsky and Skriabin). In the modernist era the nocturne genre was significantly revived by Debussy and, in particular, Bartok. This modernized nocturne is not confined to the piano and often has dark, 'other-worldly' nuances: it frequently contains imitations of the calls of nocturnal creatures, birds and so on. It is not dificult to observe that Brodsky's poem corresponds to the musical nocturne, although it is only possible to describe this correspondence in the most general terms: it is a 'nocturnal', 'pensive', 'shadowy' work in theme and colouring, not devoid of a romantic element (although on the whole this is re-interpreted through parody).

Let us consider 'Lithuanian Nocturne' in more detail – first on a purely formal, then a thematic level.[8]

The poem, as is often the case with Brodsky's mature work, is divided into parts, which are typographically demarcated and numbered (with Roman numerals). In all there are twenty-one of these parts. Each of them is self-contained: nothing is carried over from one to another, although, generally speaking, such enjambments would be entirely possible for Brodsky. It is difficult to call the parts stanzas, owing to the diversity in their construction. The term 'chapter' would be more suitable; following Barry Sherr, I will call them sections.[9]

All the sections are written using anapaest of different feet. The number of feet (from rhyme to rhyme) fluctuates within very wide limits – from one (l. 219: 'obo mne' [about me]) to eight (ll. 157–8: 'molozhavei. Minuvshee smotrit vpered / nastorozhennym glazom podrostka v shineli' [younger. What has just come to pass looks ahead / with the guarded eye of a teen in an overcoat];[10] ll. 160–1: 'v nastoiashchuiu starost' s plevkom na stene, / c lomotoi, s beskonechnost'iu v forme paneli' [into deep old age with spit upon the wall(s), / rheumatic aches, and infinity in the form of a sidewalk]). Lines of two feet predominate (there are 118 of them), followed by lines of four feet (of which there are 92). There are two lines of eight feet, one of six feet, forty-three of five feet, thirty of three feet, one of one foot. In six cases (always in the second half of the section) the metrical scheme of the anapaest is infringed: 'tochno Darius i Girenas' [like some Darius and Girenas] (l. 47); 'miru zdes' o sebe vozveshchaiut, na murav'ia' [one informs the world of oneself by inadvertently stepping on an ant] (l. 77); 'ugrozhaet deistvitel'nost' i, naoborot,' [reality threatens, and vice versa,] (l. 165); 'navodniaiut pomekhi, molitva, soobshchen'ia' [gets flooded with static, prayers, weather / reports], (l. 193); 'Ottolknuv abazhur, / gliadia priamo pered soboiu' [Pushing aside the lampshade, / look straight ahead of you] (ll. 286–7); 'pogruzhennykh po krovliu, / na pevtsa usmirennykh peizazhei' 'sunk up to the roof, / the singer of pacified landscapes] (ll. 332–3).

In some cases this infringement becomes less evident when reading aloud: *naoborot* may be pronounced as *navborot*, *soobshchen'ia* as *sobshchen'ia*, restoring the anapaestic scheme.

Additional stress often falls on the initial foot of an anapaestic line, usually on the first syllable. Compare, for example, the beginnings of sections I and II (ll. 1–3, 12–13):

Взбаламутивший море
ветер рвется, как ругань с расквашенных губ
в *глубь* холодной державы . . .

Wind, having roughened the sea, / bursts forth like cursing from bruised lips / deep within the cold super-power...

*Здра*вствуй, Томас. То – мой
*при*зрак, бросивший тело в гостинице где–то . . .

Greetings, Tomas. That was my / spectre, having abandoned the body in some / overseas hotel room...

In all there are 93 of these instances (not including arguable ones), which constitutes 31.7 per cent of the total number of metrical lines. The occurrence of supplementary stress on other feet is much rarer – there are around ten instances (compare, for example, l. 109: 'chtob vlozhit' **pal**'tsy v rot – v etu ranu Fomy' [so that he might stick his fingers into his mouth, that wound of Thomas]).[11] In six cases the stress fails to fall in a strong position: 'my v nei nerazlichimei' [we are the indistinguishable] (l. 130); 'chelovecheskim golosom i obviniaet prirodu' [in a human voice blaming nature] (l. 171); 'Raia, **kak** zatianuvshiisia minus' [Heaven, like a drawn-out minus] (l. 209); 'ikh i **ne**topyrei' [and bats] (l. 256); 'dlia setchatki – poskol'ku on **ne**obitaem' [for the retina, since it's uninhabitable] (l. 272); 'Chem belee, tem **bes**chelovechnei' [The whiter, the less human] (l. 311).

The rhythmical variations described here diversify the anapaest, although on the whole – and this is charateristic of tri-syllabic metres – anapaest creates an impression of monotony. This is all the more perceptible given that 'Lithuanian Nocturne' is a long poem, which could even be described as deliberately drawn out. Let us note, incidentally, that it consists, to a considerable extent, of extended narrative phrases and is saturated with long words – often of five syllables with the stress falling on the third syllable (for example, *amal'gamovoi, beskonechnost'iu, bestelesnosti, vzbalamutivshii, zabolochennykh, zavershaetsia, zatianuvshiisia, kolokol'naia, oloviannaia, otbeliaiushchikh, oshchetinivshis', perevernutost', razdelennuiu, rastekaetsia, rasshirenie*, and many more).[12] During the period of his emigration, Brodsky consciously strove for a monotonous 'neutral' intonation, which is indeed evident in 'Lithuanian Nocturne'. However, the monotony is broken by various devices which give rise to an inner tension within the poem.

Above all the sections of 'Lithuanian Nocturne' differ sharply in length,[13] and their construction is very varied. Eight of them (III, IV, VI, VII, XII, XIII, XIX, XX) are made up of two sets of sextets.[14] They are constructed according to the scheme aBcaBc dEfdEf (upper-case letters denoting a feminine rhyme, lower-case a masculine rhyme). Three sections (VIII, X, XIV) consist of three sets of sextets, rhyming in an analogous way. One section (II) consists of a single set of six, again rhyming on the same principle. In all the remaining sections this basic versification and rhyme scheme is violated, moreover, in a different way each time:

I:	AbCAbC dEdE
V:	aBaB cDcD efgeFg
IX:	aBcaBc dEfddEf ghigHi
XI:	aBcaBc DeDe fGhGh[15]
XV:	aBccaBc dEfdEf ghigHi
XVI:	aBcaBc dEfdEf gHHg

XVII: aBcaBc dEfdEf gHigHHi
XVIII: aBcaBc DeDe
XXI: aBcaBc dEEd fGGf

The rhyming lines, as a rule, have an uneven number of feet. The complexity, intricacy and diversity of the rhyme scheme is also heightened by the fact that at times there are internal rhymes. See, for example, ll. 34–5:

> чуть **картавей,**
> чуть выше **октавой** от странствий вдали . . .

a bit more burred / and with a higher pitch thanks to distant wanderings . . .

The lack of correspondence between the metrical scheme and the graphic layout is also evident. The anapaestic line is nearly always divided into two, sometimes three parts, distributed over several adjacent lines, as, for example: 'I podob'e litsa / rastekaetsia v chernom stekle . . .' [And the semblance of a face / spreads itself through the black glass . . .] (ll. 9–10); 'vozhzhi rvet / i krichit zalikhvatski "Gerai!"' [yanks the reins / and roars 'Gerai!'] (ll. 29–30); 'Pozdnii vecher v Imperii, / v nishchei provintsii. / Vbrod . . .' [Late evening in the Empire / in a destitute province. / Across . . .] (ll. 49–51).

The number of graphic lines (335) proves to be appreciably greater than the number of metrical lines (293). This device is not uncommon in Russian poetry written in multi-foot anapaest (compare, for example, Pasternak's 'Nine Hundred and Fifth Year'), but Brodsky emphasizes it through his specific arrangement of lines on the page, about which we will speak in more detail below.

A constant feature of Brodsky's poetry is an exceptionally severe conflict between rhythm and syntax, expressed through enjambments, inversions, breaks in syntagmatic links and so on. This feature is fully evident in 'Lithuanian Nocturne', although here, perhaps, less extremely than in several other poems of the emigration period. Because of the enjambments and inversions in the poem, the rhyme often falls on auxiliary words (it has been noted that this device – peculiar to English poetry, but until Brodsky very rare in Russian poetry – is one of the resources of defamiliarization[16]). Compare: 'Izvini za vtorzhen'e. / Sochti poiavlenie **za**' [Pardon this invasion. / Consider this sighting as] (ll. 31–2); 'Chem sil'nei zhizn' isporchena, **tem** . . .' [The more broken the life, the more . . .] (l. 129); 'oka prazdnogo **dlia**.' [for the idle eye.] (l. 131); 'i sama zavershaetsia molom, pognavshimsia **za** . . .' [itself ends in a pier, racing after . . .] (l. 176); 'ot otsutstviia, **ot** . . .' ['from absence, from . . .] (l. 211); 'sut' prostranstvo v kvadrate, a **ne** . . .' [the space in a square / and not . . .] (l. 220); 'Muza tochki v prostranstve! Veshchei, razlichaemykh / **lish**" [The Muse of a point in space! Of things visible / only . . .] (ll. 257–8); 'Vot chem dyshit vselennaia. **Vot** . . .' [That is what the universe breathes by. / That . . .') (l. 300); 'ust. V grammatiku **bez** . . . [of the mouth. / Into that grammar without] (l. 315).

There is an interesting and typical case, where a word (incidentally, a non-standard, nonce-word) is split in the rhyme position: 'zauriadnoe **do-re-** / **mi-fa-sol'-lia-si-do** izvlekaia iz kamennykh trub.' [pulling a plain do-re- / mi-fa-sol-la-ti-do from [concrete] pipes] (ll. 4–5).

As Efim Etkind correctly observed, in Brodsky's poetry 'a composed, prosaic sentence, eruditely ramified, moves forward, without looking at the metrico-strophic hurdles, as if it existed in its own right and were not taking part in any 'poetic game'. But this is not true – it not only takes part in the game, but is, strictly speaking, the very flesh of the poetry, that which gives it form, entering into a paradoxical, or, more precisely, ironical relationship with it'.[17] Later on, this contradiction is described by the critic as 'a conflict between reason and open emotion, or between the cosmos of consciousness and the chaos of the subconscious, harmony and the elements'.[18]

One could say that in 'Lithuanian Nocturne', as in many other poetic works by Brodsky – in almost all of them – two tendencies come sharply into conflict. On the one hand, the poem moves as if in a single seamless flow, approaching prose. Rhyme becomes less evident, being placed unexpectedly; rhythm is partly eroded, an effect which is, paradoxically, promoted by its very monotony. On the other hand, there are multi-dimensional and multi-levelled articulations in the poem, which go beyond the bounds of traditional poetics of the nineteenth and twentieth centuries. Rhythm and rhyme are defamiliarized, striving towards greater perceptibility. In particular, there is a strict, refined graphic organization which, from the first glance, says to the reader of 'Lithuanian Nocturne' that what he/she has before him/her is by no means prose.[19]

The graphic organization of the poem, evidently, dates back

to the genre of *carmen figuratum*, which was common during late
antiquity, the Renaissance and baroque.

It features in Brodsky's
favourite English metaphysical poets, in Dylan Thomas and others;
in Russian literature instances of it can be found in Simeon
Polotskii, some of the experimental poets of the Silver Age and
in Voznesenskii (though, in the last case, in a vulgarized form).
The lines of a poem in the genre of *carmen figuratum* are distributed in such a way that the poem takes on the form of the subject which it describes (a pitcher, a star, even a car in Apollinaire).
Sometimes the lines of a poem form a geometric figure. The comical
'Stikhi na butylke, podarennoi Andreiu Sergeevu' [Poem on a
Bottle, Given to Andrei Sergeev] (1966), is an early experiment
of this type by Brodsky. But such exercises in 'applied versification' soon give way to serious poetry, where only the special
symmetry of the graphic construction[20] refers back to the genre
of *carmen figuratum*. For example, see: 'Fontan' [Fountain] (1967);
'Razgovor s nebozhitelem' [Conversation with a Celestial Being]
(1970); 'Osen' vygoniaet menia iz parka . . .' [Autumn Drives Me
out of the Park] (1970–1); 'Babochka' [Butterfly] (1972); and others.
'Lithuanian Nocturne' also belongs to these, and is the most extensive poem of this type.

Incidentally, in the graphic form of 'Lithuanian Nocturne' – as
in that of 'Fontan' and 'Babochka' – one can also see a certain
iconicity. 'Fontan' brings to mind the image of a gushing stream
of water extending up into the air, while the stanzas of 'Babochka'
are reminiscent of the unfolded wings of a butterfly; in a similar
way, the sections of 'Lithuanian Nocturne' bear a distant similarity to a human body seen from *en face* – reflected in a mirror,
for example (and indeed, itself having mirror symmetry).[21] Its
outline is indistinct (see ll. 86–8: 'Vot otkuda moei, / kak ee
prodolzhenie vverkh, obolochki / v tvoikh steklakh
rasplyvchatost' . . .' [Hence the upward continuation of my membrane / washed out in your window . . .]. It is easy to relate all
this to the themes of the *apparition* and the *mirror*, which are
essential to the structure of the poem.

At a lexical and grammatical level, the attention is drawn in
'Lithuanian Nocturne' to the quantity and diversity of nouns.
Brodsky is, in general, a poet of the noun rather than the verb:
in this, as in many other respects, he is linked with the line of
Mandelshtam, rather than Pasternak.[22] The 'poetics lesson', which
he received from Evgenii Rein, is well-known and has already

been mentioned in the literature on Brodsky: 'A good poem is such that should you apply to it a blotter, which removes the adjectives and verbs, when it is lifted away the page would still nonetheless be black, since the nouns will remain: table, chair, horse, dog, wall-paper, couch. . . .'[23] Out of the 1386 words in the poem 595 (42.9%) are nouns, 107 (7.7%) are adjectives, 141 (10.2%) are verbs, 45 (3.2%) are participles. Moreover, 401 of the nouns occur only once each. We find among them colloquialisms and foreign words, archaisms, sovietisms and neologisms, geographic, historical and mythological names; besides ordinary words, signifying parts of the body, objects from everyday life, atmospheric and meteorological phenomena, temporal categories or, let us say, religious concepts, 'Lithuanian Nocturne' is chock-full of abstract nouns and also philosophical, mathematical, linguistic, literary, musical, architectural and biological terms, terms from physics and chemistry, right down to military and chess terminology ('camouflage cloak' and 'stalemate', respectively). Words which are linked with language, speech and especially writing (for example, 'alphabet', 'letter', 'monogram', 'comma', 'Cyrillic alphabet', 'cuneiform', 'type', 'pen', 'brevier', 'written language', 'punctuation marks', 'brackets', 'page', 'full stop', 'quotation', 'cypher') occupy a significant amount of space.

The syntactical construction of the work, about which we have already spoken in part, is no less characteristic of Brodsky. One's attention is arrested by long, involved sentences with co-ordinate and subordinate clauses, stuffed with adverbial phrases, parenthetic constructions and so on. On the other hand, parts of sentences often split off into independent sentences. Their dimensions range between one word, such as *Nulia!* [Of zero!] (l. 260), up to 62 words. Such a sentence takes up 16 lines, almost the whole of section XVI (ll. 241–56). The rhetorical and logical complexity, interminable digressions, elaborations and enumerations, compel the reader to concentrate on the semantics of the poems (although at times the opposite effect is achieved – one of inarticulateness, 'rambling speech', ravings). In any case, the syntax of 'Lithuanian Nocturne', as in most of Brodsky's poems, is defamiliarized and deautomatized although, as has already been said, the poet steers clear of experimental extremes: side-by-side with intricately constructed – or, on the contrary, fragmented – sentences there are (especially in the first half) rapid, comparatively simple sentences, which are nominative or descriptive.

On the thematic level, the poem develops the topos of the meeting of two poets, which is as well known in classical as in romantic poetry – and in particular, in Pushkin.[24] It is interesting that Brodsky retains, while indeed transforming, many of the motifs entailed by this topos in the work of Pushkin. Here a very early example of the exploitation of this theme by Pushkin is especially brought to mind – the Kishinev poems, in which Ovid is discussed: 'Iz pis'ma k Gnedichu' [From a Letter to Gnedich] (1821); 'Chaadaevu' [To Chaadaev] (1821); 'K Ovidiiu [To Ovid] (1821); 'Baratynskomu. Iz Bessarabii' [To Baratynsky. From Bessarabia] (1822). Just like Brodsky's poem, these take the form of apostrophes, addresses to friends (or to an ancient poet), a fact which is also reflected in their titles. The subject is a meeting of exiled poets in a 'desert country'. This country lies on the very edge of an empire – or rather, of two empires: once a remote province of Rome, many centuries later it became a remote province of Russia. In Brodsky, Bessarabia is replaced by another imperial province – Lithuania. There are still other traits of the Kishinev cycle, which are repeated in 'Lithuanian Nocturne':[25] in the description of the meeting-place sombre colours prevail, the meeting itself is conducted at night and the senior poet appears as a shade.

Brodsky felt a deep and constant interest both in the Roman empire and in Pushkin's era. They both took on archetypal characteristics for him, serving as both criterion and explanation of the present. The theme of Ovid's – just as the theme of Pushkin's exile – is easily projected on to his own biography.[26] In 'Lithuanian Nocturne' Brodsky takes on both roles, Ovid and Pushkin. He takes the form of an apparition – not in the same way, it is true to say, as the ghost of Ovid in the Kishinev cycle, not from a temporal, but a spatial distance, from the New World (which is almost identified with the kingdom of the dead). If Ovid in the Kishinev poems remains a 'desert neighbour' and a silent partner of the dialogue, Brodsky (like Pushkin) speaks in the first person, leaving silence to the addressee.[27] All the same, the theme of the 'two exiles' is retained. The addressee of the poem is also described as an exile in his own country, the mirror double of the author – perhaps that very author in the past.

A section by section summary of 'Lithuanian Nocturne' may be presented in the following form:

I. Introduction. Maritime landscape; the appearance of the apparition at the window.
II. Appeal to the addressee.
III. Landscape of the Lithuanian countryside.
IV. Appeal to the addressee; development of the theme of the apparition; account of his flight.
V. Lithuanian townscape (Kaunas).
VI. Description of the addressee's flat.
VII. Portrait of the addressee; attempt to provide a 'portrait' of the apparition.
VIII. Meditation on written language; similarities and differences between the apparition and the addressee.
IX. Identification of the apparition and the addressee.
X. Habits of the apparition; meditation on space and time; addressee against the background of the Lithuanian landscape.
XI. Meditation on borders.
XII. Countryside; continuation of the meditation on borders and overcoming them.
XIII. Countryside; motif of the border; speech, sounding in the air (ether).
XIV. Apparition in Kaunas; meditation on air immateriality.
XV. Apparition in Kaunas; meditation on air and speech.
XVI. Meditation on speech (poetry).
XVII. Appeal to the Muse; meditation on speech and air.
XVIII. Meditation on speech, air, immortality.
XIX. Meditation on air and immortality.
XX. Appeal to a muse; reversion of speech into air.
XXI. Coda. Saints Casimir and Nicholas; appeal to the Muse; prayer for the addressee.

As we can see, the poem can be divided in two at the central section XI, which is devoted to the theme of the border (the strictly guarded border of a totalitarian empire, but also the border between the past and the present). The first part could be called 'descriptive', the second 'philosophical'. Up to the central section, scenes of the country predominate, of its miserable poverty-stricken life, of the everyday way of life of the addressee, which is equally miserable; after this section there follows a vast and complex meta-literary monologue, dedicated to the kinship of

poetic speech and the air. It goes without saying that this division
is, to some extent, theoretical: one can speak only of a certain
prevailing tonality; just as descriptions run through the second
half of the poem, discourse – including the metaliterary – is to
be found in the first. Let us trace the development of the principal poetic themes.

The beginning of the poem introduces the theme of the sea
(as a border separating the author and addressee). The situation
which was foreseen in 'Lithuanian Divertissement' has become
reality: the poet 'stupil na vody' [walked on the water] and found
himself in the New World. His spirit, having abandoned his body
while still alive, flies above the ocean, home. Here, home still
means the empire, from which the poet was exiled. This word,
one of the most frequently occurring in the poem,[28] changes
through accumulating new meanings. From the first lines the theme
is that of dismal customs of the empire.[29] From the very beginning we are given the motifs which run right through the poem
– cold, darkness, flight, and also music (incidentally, music appears
as a simple, but fragmented gamut). It is worth noting in this
connection the emphasized acoustic organization of ll. 1–3:

Взбаламутивший море
ветер рвется, как ругань с расквашенных губ,
в глубь холодной державы . . .

Wind, having roughened up the sea, / bursts like cursing
from bruised lips / deep within the cold super-power . . .

The ghost appears at the very end of the section: it presses itself
against the window of a familiar flat, looking in.[30] The glass of
the window pane – a new embodiment of the border – proves to
be a mirror as well. Only speech is capable of crossing the surface of the mirror, and connecting a space (and time) which have
broken in two. Direct speech also begins from the next section;
it goes on for the duration of the poem, and the descriptive passages, continuing from the introduction, as well as the overtly
expressed philosophical monologue, are contained within it.

The theme of the apparition goes back not only to Pushkin,
but also to the tradition of early Romanticism (Zhukovsky), and
further back to folklore. The word *apparition*, itself almost automatically draws on numerous connotations and micro-motifs, which

are also present in 'Lithuanian Nocturne': it is usually linked with winter[31] (Christmas Eve), midnight,[32] water; it is compelled to roam,[33] it cracks jokes, one cannot speak to it,[34] it is only seen by those to whom it appears, remaining invisible to others,[35] and finally, it disappears at cock-crow. This last micro-motif to some extent determines the composition of the work. At the beginning of his monologue the apparition makes the following assurance (ll. 38–9): 'sginu prezhde, chem grianet s nasesta / petushinoe "pli!".' [I'll be off before the cock's 'fire' / bursts from the roost.] At the end this prophecy is fulfilled. After section XV, the apparition ceases to refer to himself: he gradually merges with his 'natural medium' – the air and the void. Significantly later (in past time) the discourse turns to the promised cock's crow (ll. 300–2): 'Vot chem dyshit vselennaia. Vot / chto petukh kukarekal, / uprezhdaia gortani velikuiu sush'!' [That is what the universe breathes by. / That is what the cock crowed, / forestalling the great drought for the larynx.]

The topos of the apparition undergoes diverse modifications. Having abandoned its body if only for a time, the apparition predicts his future death ('gortani velikuiu sush'' [the great drought for the larynx]) – it talks about its gradual approach, about a certain slipping away of individuality,[36] of a build-up of 'invisibility' and 'absence'. The poet looks at himself from within (coinciding with the apparition) and simultaneously from outside, as though belonging to two different temporal and spatial worlds. This is one of the devices Brodsky uses constantly; in 'Lithuanian Nocturne' it is emphasized by the coincidence–non-coincidence of the addresser and addressee. Moreover, the theme appears in an ironic key. For a person who has grown up in the USSR, the word *prizrak* [apparition] automatically correlates with the first sentence of the 'Communist Party Manifesto', which in the Soviet Empire was not only hammered into the brains of school children and students, but also served as the subject of indecent jokes. Hence the humorous nuances of the beginnings of sections XIV and XV: 'Prizrak brodit po Kaunasu. Vkhodit v sobor . . .' [A spectre wanders in Kaunas. Enters a cathedral . . .] (199);

Призрак бродит бесцельно по Каунасу. Он
суть твое прибавление к воздуху мысли
обо мне,

суть пространство в квадрате, а не
энергичная проповедь лучших времен.

A spectre wanders aimlessly in Kaunas. It / is your addition
to the air of thought / about me, the space in a square / and
not / the energetic sermon of better days. (ll. 217–21)

The incidental word *Makrous* [Macrowhisker] (99)[37] refers to
'propoved' luchshikh vremen' [sermon of better days]. It is interesting, though, that the identification of the author with a quotation from the 'Manifesto' (l. 33) corresponds to a serious moment
in the poem – the identification of apparition and text.[38]

Another important theme of 'Lithuanian Nocturne' is the theme
of the border, which is also modulated in various forms from
the beginning to the end of the work.[39] We have noted that the
border between 'the space of the addresser' and 'the space of
the addressee' at first appears as the sea, then as glass (a mirror).[40]
The theme of the mirror leads on to the theme of the double;
section IX is given over to an elaboration of this theme. Compare
ll. 112–14:

Мы похожи;
мы, в сущности, Томас, одно:
ты, коптящий окно изнутри, я, смотрящий снаружи . . .

We're alike. / We, in essence, Thomas, are one. / You, smoking the window from within, while I look in from the outside.

The 'myth of the twins', which is developed in the poem has
its origins in 'Lithuanian Divertissement'. There the subject of
the Gemini sign of the zodiac had already been raised. On the
observatory of Vilnius university there is a bas-relief series depicting
the signs of the zodiac; the most memorable of these is, namely,
the Twins (Castor and Pollux). Here, 'prostupaiushchii v Kastore
Polluks' [Pollux seeping through Castor] (l. 124) corresponds to
the addresser and the addressee. Brodsky refers not only (and
not so much) to the fact that the addressee is similar to the author
in line of work and fate. The author is, in fact, meeting himself,
but in another temporal dimension before his emigration – and,
perhaps, in a state of prescience of his emigration. The border

proves to be a boundary not only in space, but also in time. The distance between the mirror doubles is insurmountable: Lithuania, the homeland and past life is described as 'through the looking glass'.[41]

Let us look more closely at this description of Lithuania. It is saturated, or even over-saturated with facts and details of Lithuanian everyday life, but appears strangely dual and flickering. In the words of Mikhail Lotman, 'the poet celebrates not an empirically real country, but some mental form, which is deposited in his memory'.[42] I should add that in this mental image different chronologic strata unite – time spreads out, becomes indistinct. At the beginning the poor countryside of Zhemaitiia is depicted (this is a westerly, coastal area of Lithuania, speaking its own dialect, always more stubbornly resistant than most to imperial attempts to suppress its distinct religion and culture). However, this is not the Zhemaitiia of collective farms during the seventies and eighties, but Zhemaitiia before the Second World War: 'zapozdalyi evrei' [A Jewish cabby in a cart, hurr[ying] late] who 'po bruschatke mestechka gremit balagoloi' [drum[s] the village's cobblestones] (ll. 27–8), would be an absolutely unthinkable figure in Lithuania after the Holocaust. In this same section yet another theme which is of great importance right through 'Lithuanian Nocturne' makes its first appearance – the theme of the written word (writing), which is linked to the theme of religion: 'Iz kostelov bredut, khoronia zapiatye / svechek v skobkakh ladonei' [They wander from churches, burying the commas / of candles in the brackets of [their] palms.] (ll. 19–20).[43] For the reader who is familiar with the history of Lithuania, this point in the poem is associated with an even earlier epoch – that is to say the period of 'the fight for the written language' (1865–1904), when books – above all prayer-books – printed in the Roman alphabet were smuggled into Lithuania from abroad.

In section IV the theme of the border crossing changes once again. In l. 47 the lost pilots Darius and Girenas are mentioned.[44] Along with this reference to them, the motif of the border between states[45] appears for the first time – moreover, this is a border of the kind it is impossible (or in any case extremely dangerous) to cross. The border of the Empire insurmountably divides the author and his silent interlocutor, the present and the past, the New World and Lithuania. Without delay (in the first line of the next section) the very word 'Empire' appears. Note the contrast: 'Pozdnii vecher v Litve' [A late evening in Lithuania] (18) – 'Pozdnii vecher v Imperii, / v nishchei provintsii' [Late evening in the Empire / in a destitute province.] (ll. 49–50). At the beginning we are given a hint of the border of tsarist Russia, which passed through the Neman [Nemunas]. Crossing that river, Napoleon once took Kovno [Kaunas], an act which started the 1812 war (in 1915 Kaiser Wilhelm II did the very same thing). Compare ll. 51–3:

> Вброд
> перешедшее Неман еловое войско,
> ощетинившись пиками, Ковно в потемки берет.

Having waded across the Neman, / an army of conifers bristling with lances / takes Kaunas into the darkness.

But almost straight away there follows a detail which unmistakably indicates the post-Stalinist Soviet Union – a bottle of vodka 'divided in three' (ll. 58–60).

> И выносят на улицу главную вещь,
> разделенную на три
> без остатка . . .

And the most important thing gets brought out / to be divided by three / down to the last drop.[46]

Further on, Lithuania is discussed in a totally concrete epoch – that in which the poem is written. The timeless, rural landscape gives way to a sovietized, urban setting. Some 'doubling' and temporal and spatial erosion none the less remains. There are hints at tsarist Russia; for example, these characteristic pre-revolutionary words: 'v *gubernii* tsveta pal'to' [in a *province* the colour of topcoats] (l. 184); 'na pevtsa *usmirennykh* peizazhei' [the singer of *pacified* landscapes] (l. 333). The contemporary restaurant turns out to be the 'litovskoi korchmoi' [Lithuanian inn] of l. 106 – that is to say, the inn on the Lithuanian border from Pushkin's 'Boris Godunov'. A medieval ruler of Lithuania, Prince Vytautas' appears (he was also mentioned in 'Lithuanian Divertissement'); moreover, he tries to cross the border 'k shvedam' [towards Sweden] (ll. 174–5) – a situation referring to much more recent times.[47] The addressee's flat is in Vilnius, but the apparition, while talking to him, wanders around Kaunas.[48] However, the impenetrable boundary separating Lithuania from the world and the past poet from the present is described unambiguously (ll. 154–9, 189–91):

> Там шлагбаумы на резкость наводит верста.
> Там чем дальше, тем больше в тебе силуэта.
> Там с лица сторожа
> моложавей. Минувшее смотрит вперед
> настороженным взглядом подростка в шинели
> и судьба нарушителем пятится прочь . . .
> [. . .]
> . . . железо,
> плюс обутый в кирзу
> человек государства.

The railroad crossings are brought into focus by versts. / There, the further you go, the more of what is left of you is a silhouette. / There the guards appear / younger. What has just come to pass looks ahead / with the guarded eye of a teen in an overcoat, / and fate, the trespasser, backs away [. . .] / / [. . .] cast-iron, / plus a shod-in-ersatz leather / man of the state.

This is the border of a totalitarian 'superpower' (l. 143), of a world 'where nothing changes' (l. 152) – of a world of which the Berlin Wall was all but the main symbol. Even a description of a starry sky (ll. 107–8) or the relationship of the addresser and the addressee (l. 123) is given in terms which stem from the experience of life in the Soviet empire: 'do litsa, mnogooko smotriashchego mimo / kak raskosyi mongol za zemnoi chastokol'[49] [and the face, multi-eyed, looking past / like some squint-eyed Mongolian at the palisade]; 'My – vzaimnyi konvoi . . .'[50] [We're a mutual convoy].

It would be a flagrant over-simplification to interpret all these images only politically (although this level of interpretation is also vital). The issue, as usual for Brodsky, is above all about loneliness, despair, loss of a link with the world in its entirety, existence in the face of death, the 'boundary situation', as an existentialist philosopher would say.[51]

At this point there arises the characteristic opposition of two Muses – 'novoi Klio, odetoi zastavoi' [of a new Clio, adorned in an outpost] (l. 228) and 'obnazhennoi Uranii' [to naked Urania]

(l. 230),[52] that is to say, of history which equals slavery and death, and poetry which is linked to the void of the world; this void is, however, overcome by the creative act.[53] This returns us to the third basic theme in 'Lithuanian Nocturne', which is introduced from sections II and III on – the theme of speech, and also writing. This theme is developed in sections VI–VIII. Here, in particular, the addresser and the addressee are both described – and contrasted – in terms of writing and grammar (ll. 84–97):

> Вот откуда вся жизнь как нетвердая честная фраза
> на пути к запятой.
> Вот откуда моей
> как ее продолжение вверх, оболочки
> в твоих стеклах расплывчатость, бунт голытьбы
> ивняка и т. п., очертанья морей,
> их страниц перевернутость в поисках точки,
> горизонта, судьбы.
>
> Наша письменность, Томас! с моим, за поля
> выходящим сказуемым! с хмурым твоим
> домоседством
> подлежащего! Прочный, чернильный союз,
> кружева, вензеля,
> помесь литеры римской с кириллицей . . .

Hence all of life – / like some soft honest phrase / moving comma-ward. / Hence the upward continuation of my membrane / washed out in your windows, / the mutiny of the masses of willow twigs, etc. outlines of seas, / their upside down pages in search of a full stop, / the horizon, fate. / / Our writing, Tomas! With my predicates / [spilling] beyond margins! With your dour, homebody / subjects! A sturdy alliance of ink, / lace, monograms, / the mixtures of Roman typeset with Cyrillic . . .[54]

The words relating to Roman type and the Cyrillic alphabet, evidently refer not only to the fact that the author and the addressee are primarily participants in different cultural worlds – East and West (Brodsky crossed the border which separated them when he travelled out of the Soviet Union and became a bi-lingual writer). This is, perhaps, yet another allusion to the Lithuanian 'fight for its written language', for its own cultural tradition, for the Roman alphabet rather than Cyrillic – that is to say, it is the development of the motif which we saw in section III. After a long break, the second half of section XIII is devoted to the theme of speech, and here for the first time speech is linked with air. 'Nochnoi kislorod' [Evening's oxygen] (l. 192) – this is the ether in which meaningless snatches of words, melodies and sounds float as if extending the daily life of the superpower. Or, rather, it is precisely in the air that it is possible to cross the imperial border. In it are audible not only forbidden things/prohibitions, but also prayers (ll. 193, 197). The theme takes yet another, rather unexpected turn. Almost everyone who lived in the Soviet Union and contiguous countries, remembers the Western radio broadcasts, which were most clearly audible at night. On these, poetry could often be heard, including Brodsky's poems. (Lines 42–4 evidently refer to the radio-waves.) Is not the apparition, crossing the ocean, identical with these poems?

The identification of the apparition with speech (written language) and the air grows closer towards the end of the poem (ll. 222–6):

> Не завидуй. Причисли
> привиденье к родне,
> к свойствам воздуха – так же, как мелкий петит,
> рассыпаемый в воздухе речью картавой
> вроде цокота мух . . .

Don't be envious. Rank this ghost / as one of kin, / the properties of air – the same as some fine brevier / falling apart in the twilight as burred speech / sort of like the buzzing of flies . . .

Right after this point the apparition is lost from sight. As we said, he goes off into his 'natural medium', tearing himself 'away from patrimonial marshlands' (l. 243), he melts into the air and emptiness. The sentence which describes his disappearance, or rather transformation (ll. 241–56) is a key one in 'Lithuanian Nocturne'. This fact is emphasized by different means. It has already been mentioned that it is the longest sentence of all in the poem, regardless of whether one counts the words or the lines; it has convulsive, writhing syntax broken up by parentheses; the punctuation is over-saturated with dashes; finally, at the end of the sentence the anapaestic scheme is abruptly disrupted.

The apparition coincides with the poem, which dwells in the very same medium – namely the air, in which it sounds, the ether, permeated with voices on the radio waves, a nocturnal emptiness of non-existence. The apparition already had a distinctive 'ontological status' in Zhukovsky's poetry: it was both an creature and a sign, a participant in communication and a symbol of it, a messenger from another world and the testimony of its existence.[55] Brodsky takes up what seems, at first glance, to be a distant tradition, and characteristically transforms it: the apparition is the text of 'Lithuanian Nocturne' – that is to say, the trace of the poetic impulse.[56] What is more, it is pure meaning, disengaged from the sign (ll. 245–7):

> от страницы, от букв,
> от – сказать ли! – любви
> звука к смыслу, бесплотности – к массе

From the page, from the letter, / from – do I dare say it – the love / felt by sound – for sense, by the incorporeal – for mass . . .

It is precisely this which proves to be the supreme value, the only alternative form of existence available to humanity. Incidentally, the traditional forms of good and evil appear here – the statues of angels on the Lithuanian Catholic churches and bats, which are latently linked with demons (ll. 252–6):

> . . . эта вещь воспаряет в чернильный ночной эмпирей
> мимо дремлющих в нише
> местных ангелов:
> выше
> их и нетопырей.

. . . this thing soars in the inky darkness of empyrean / past the dreaming local angels in niches / above them / and bats.

The following sections are, indeed, 'a hymn to the air'. Air is the most frequent noun (and the most frequent significant word) in 'Lithuanian Nocturne': it occurs seven times in the poem.[57] It acquires many layers of meaning – not least, religious. The air is a universal void, the dwelling-place of Urania (ll. 257–60):

Муза точки в пространстве! Вещей, различаемых
лишь
в телескоп! Вычитанья
без остатка! Нуля!

The Muse of a point in space! Of things visible only / through
a telescope! Of subtraction / with nothing left over! Of zero!

The air is associated with a white sheet of paper, just as the
hopeless Vilnius night is associated with ink: 'Net na svete veshchei,
bezuprechnei / (krome smerti samoi) / otbeliaiushchikh list' [There
is no other thing more flawless / (other than death itself) / when
it comes to bleaching the page.] (ll. 308–10). Air is a celestial kingdom, dwelling-place of souls, or, rather, of voices, which have
survived the body: 'Nebosvod – / khor soglasnykh i glasnykh
molekul, / v prostorechii – dush' [Heaven's vault is / a molecular
chorus of consonants and vowels, / in common parlance – souls']
(ll. 304–6). Air is the place where the orphanhood of the poet is
overcome through breathing – that is, through speech: 'Muza,
mozhno domoi?' [Muse, can we go home?] (l. 312); 'Sirotstvo /
zvuka, Tomas, est' rech'!' [The orphan / of sound, Tomas, is speech!]
(ll. 284–5).

It is, precisely, in the air – or in the ether, or in the heavens,
or on a sheet of paper – that the last scheme of 'Lithuanian
Nocturne' plays itself out. The earthly twins – the author and
the addressee – are replaced by the heavenly twins. These are
the patrons of Lithuania and of Russia, of two countries, whose
fates are antithetical but none the less close – one might say
unmerged yet inseparable. The poem ends with a prayer addressed
to both saints and to the third, 'poetic saint' – Urania. The meaning
of *home* and *border* is transformed for the last time: *home for the
poet is poetry*; that is the meaning guarded by the lines: 'V kontse
tam nado vlezt' na vysokuiu gory . . .' [At the end there you have
to scale a high mountain . . .].

Notes

1. 'Joseph Brodsky "Lithuanian Divertissement"', in *The Third Wave:
   Russian Literature in Emigration* (Ann Arbor: Ardis, 1984) pp. 191–
   201). For another version of this article see Tomas Venclova, in

Neustoichivoe ravnovesie: Vosem' russkikh poeticheskikh tekstov [Unsteady Equilibrium: Eight Russian Poetic Texts] (New Haven: Yale Center for International and Area Studies, 1986) pp. 165–78.

2. 'Lithuania for a Russian person is always a step in the right direction', Brodsky loved to say. Together with many Russians of his generation, he perceived Lithuania as a 'half-western' country (and, incidentally, as an experience of 'emigration which stopped just short of emigrating').

3. Brodsky wrote about Konigsberg even before visiting Lithuania: 'Einem alten Architekten in Rom' [To an Old Architect in Rome].

4. On this subject see: Ramunas Katilius, 'Iosif Brodskii i Litva' [Joseph Brodsky and Lithuania], *Zvezda* (1997) no. 1, pp. 151–4; Evgenii Rein, 'Litva i Brodskii, Brodskii i Litva . . .' [Lithuania and Brodsky. Brodsky and Lithuania . . .], *Vil'nius* (1997) no. 2, pp. 112–21; Andrei Sergeev, 'O Brodskom' [About Brodsky], *Znamia* (1997) no. 4, pp. 139–58.

5. Brodsky said to me that 'for the main part, Lithuania' also served as a model for the play 'Democracy'.

6. See *Sochineniia Iosifa Brodskogo* [Works of Joseph Brodsky], vol. 2 (St Petersburg: Pushkinskii Fond, 1992) p. 331.

7. See, for example, Joseph Brodsky, *Bog sokhraniaet vse* [God preserves everything] (Moscow: Mif, 1992) p. 107.

8. We will use the text of 'Lithuanian Nocturne', which was published while the poet was still alive in the second volume of *Sochineniia Iosifa Brodskogo*, as indicated above, pp. 322–31. There are comparatively few variations from the form in which the poem was first published, and from the version in *Uraniia*. On the whole they amount to a few differently arranged verses and punctuation, which affect the length of the poem (313 verses in *Kontinent* [Continent], 327 in *Uraniia*, 335 in *Sochineniia*, and its syntactical construction. In the last line of chapter (section) IX in *To Uraniia*, a misprint crept in ('oka prazdnogo dnia' instead of 'oka prazdnogo dlia'), which was carried forward into *Sochineniia* and several other (although not all) publications; it has been corrected in our text. In *Sochineniia* there is a more precise transcription of the surname 'Girenas', although inaccuracies remain in the transcription of other Lithuanian names (which have similarly been corrected here).

9. Barry Scherr, 'Strofika Brodskogo' [Brodsky's Versification], in *Poetika Brodskogo: Sbornik statei*, ed. L. Loseff [The Poetics of Brodsky: A Collection of Articles Edited by L. V. Loseff] (Tenafly, NJ: Hermitage, 1986) p. 98.

10. However, it is possible to divide this metrical line into two of four feet, if you consider that the word *vpered* rhymes with the words *naoborot* and *podberet*, which are situated far away from it in the text.

11. This conforms with the general laws of Russian trisyllabic metre. See M. L. Gasparov, *Sovremennyi russkii stikh: Metrika i ritmika* (Moscow: Nauka, 1974) p. 186: 'the distribution of stresses which occur outside the normal scheme in a metrical line displays a clear tendency towards being increased at the beginning of the line and

decreased at the end of the line'. It follows that as regards 'weighti-ness of the line' (its saturation with stresses over and above the normal scheme) Brodsky is affiliated with Fet and Pasternak, rather than with his contemporaries, who in general steer clear of stress falling outside the normal pattern.

12. In all there are 1386 words in 'Lithuanian Nocturne' (including prepo-sitions and conjunctions); there are 861 different words (discarding repetition); there are 50 words with five syllables.

13. The longest section (XVII) consists of 21 lines, the shortest (II) of six lines in all. As regards the number of feet, the most extensive sec-tions are VIII, X and XI (in each of these there are 65 feet; moreover in section XI the metre in one foot is infringed by an additional syllable). The most compact section is II (17 feet). As we can see, the size of the sections fluctuates within a very wide range (1: 3.5–1: 3.8).

14. Let us note that these sections are distributed in pairs, and are also symmetrically arranged around the centre of the poem (on mirror symmetry in the poem see n. 41).

15. An alternative reading (see n. 10): aBcaBc dEfEfgHdgHd.

16. See, for example, 'Pis'mo o russkoi poezii' [A Letter on Russian Poetry], in *Poetika Brodskogo*, pp. 25–6; Scherr, 'Strofika Brodskogo', pp. 105, 107.

17. E. Etkind, *Materiia stikha* [The Stuff of Poetry] (Paris: Institut d'études slaves, 1978) p. 114.

18. Ibid., p. 119.

19. The first tendency, incidentally, strives for dominance with respect to acoustic perception of the poem, the second, visual perception.

20. Such poems, the successors, as it were, of the *carmen figuratum* genre, are well-known in the poetry of different countries and ages.

21. Icons of this type are to be found in the poetry of the Polish poet Aleksander Wat, whom Brodsky valued highly and translated. See Tomas Venclova, *Aleksander Wat: Life and Art of an Iconoclast* (New Haven and London: Yale University Press, 1996) pp. 224, 300.

22. See Mikhail Lotman, 'Mandel'shtam i Pasternak (opyt kontrastivnoi poetiki)', [Mandelshtam and Pasternak (Towards a Contrastive Poetics)] in *Literary Tradition and Practice in Russian Culture*, eds V. Polukhina, J. Andrew and R. Reid (Amsterdam: Rodopi, 1993) pp. 123–62.

23. An interview with Brodsky in *Russkaia mysl'* [Russian Thought] no. 3450 (3 February 1983) p. 9.

24. See Boris Gasparov, 'Encounter of Two Poets in the Desert: Pushkin's Myth', in *Myth in Literature*, eds A. Kodjak, K. Pomorska and S. Rudy (Columbus, OH: Slavica, 1985) pp. 124–53.

25. Cf. ibid., p. 125.

26. Compare Brodsky's very interesting comments about Ovid in one of his last essays; 'Letter to Horace' (1995). On several intertextual links between these two poets, see, for example, Leon Burnett, 'The Complicity of the Real: Affinities in the Poetics of Brodsky and Mandelstam', in *Brodsky's Poetics and Aesthetics*, eds L. Loseff and V. Polukhina (Basingstoke: Macmillan Press, 1990) pp. 23–5. See K. Ichin,

146   *Joseph Brodsky*

'Brodskii i Ovidii', *Novoe literaturnoe obozrenie*, no. 19 (1996) pp. 227–49.

27. At several points in 'Lithuanian Nocturne' one might suspect links with the addressee's poetry, which was known to Brodsky in word-for-word translation. Compare: ll. 42–3, 'rasshiriaet svoi radius / brennost' [It's merely one's mortality expanding its radius] with 'memory, like a pair of compasses, expands its diameter' ('Sutema pasitiko šalčiu'); ll. 55–6: 'bulyzhnik mertsaet, kak / poimannyi leshch' ('cobblestones glisten / like bream in a net') with 'under the net of a heavy cloud, the narrow squares gleam, like fish' ('Pašnekesys Žiema'); ll. 64–5: 'vpadaet vo t'mu . . . ruki tvoei ust'e' [And river-like your hand / falls . . . into darkness] with 'the rivers' estuaries find the dark sea' ('Poeto atminimui. Variantas'); l. 122: 'ot stovattnoi slezy nad tvoei golovoi' [from the hundred watt tear [shape] over your head] with 'where onto a blind brick wall falls the hundred watt, intricate ray of light' ('Sutema pasitiko šalčiu'); l. 314: 'bezdumnyi Borei' [thoughtless Boreas] with 'senseless Boreas behind a nameless hill' ('Ode miestui'). It would be inappropriate to speak about 'influence' here: in referring to a motif from another poet's text, Brodsky demonstrates how it should be developed.

28. The word *dom/domoi* [home] occurs five times in 'Lithuanian Nocturne', *domosedstvo* [stay-at home] once. These words usually appear in marked places (for example, in the rhyme position); the last line begins with the word *dom* [home] (l. 335: 'dom i serdtse emu' [his home and his heart]).

29. Compare: 'Ia, pasynok derzhavy dikoi / s razbitoi mordoi, / drugoi, ne menee velikoi, / priemysh gordyi . . .' [I, the stepson of a wild power / with a broken snout, / of another, no less great, / am the proud adopted child . . .] ('P'iatstsa Mattei' [Piazza Mattei] 1981).

30. The flat (or, rather, attic) in question is in Vilnius, the one in which the addressee lived from the end of 1970 through to 1973. Brodsky visited this flat and even lived in it for a while; with it are linked events which served as an impetus for 'Lithuanian Divertissement'. Beneath the attic, on the second floor of the building, there was some sort of establishment, officially linked with the radio. We suspected (without particular grounds and not entirely seriously), that it was the eavesdropping centre of the Vilnius KGB, and that everything which happened in the attic was automatically recorded. Hence, ll. 71–3: 'mikrofony spetssluzhby v kvartire pevtsa / pishut skrezhet matratsa i vspleski motiva / obshchei pesni bez slov.' [In [. . .] / [. . .] the bard's room, the microphones of the special service / tape the screeching mattress and the splash of / a common song without words.]

31. Cf. ll. 22–3, 'Nad zhniv'em Zhemaitii / v'etsia sneg, kak nebesnykh obitelei prakh' [Over the stubble of Zhemaitiia / snow weaves like celestial cloisters' ashes]; ll. 202–4, 'Kel'ner, gliadia v upor, / vidit tol'ko salfetki, ogni bakalei, / sneg, taksi na uglu,' [The headwaiter looking straight through it, / sees only napkins, the grocery's lights, / snow, the taxicab on the corner,]; ll. 324–7, 'To Sviatoi Kazimir / s Chudotvornym Nikoloi / korotaiut chasy / v ozhidanii zimnei zari.'

[That's St. Casimir and / St. Nicholas the Miraclemaker / whiling time away / in anticipation of winter's dawn.].

32. Cf. ll. 67–8, 'V polnoch' visakaia rech' / obretaet ukhvatki sleptsa;' [At midnight speech / acquires the ways of the blind]; l. 170, 'Polnoch'. Soika krichit' [Midnight. A [blue]-jay screams]; l. 183, 'Polnoch' v listvennom krae,' [Midnight in a deciduous region,].

33. At the level of syntax and narrative this is reflected in the involved composition of the monologue with its numerous 'loops', recurrences of previous themes and so on.

34. As we have already noted, dialogue never even arises in 'Lithuanian Nocturne'.

35. See section XIV, which is entirely devoted to this theme.

36. Compare a line which is characteristic for Brodsky: 'Tam chem dal'she, tem bol'she v tebe silueta.' [There, the further you go, the greater your silhouette.] (l. 155).

37. In this untranslatable joke, in which great play is made with the notion of 'a large, (damp?) moustache', and the sound of the name 'Marx', the moustached Marx and the moustached Stalin – two prophets of the maxim 'the end justifies the means' (cf. ll. 97–8) – are, evidently, conflated.

38. On this subject see the end of this article.

39. We have already touched upon the fact that the category of the border in Brodsky is almost always also emphasized at the purely structural level. Compare in this respect Aleksandr Zholkovsky, 'Brodsky's "Ia vas liubil . . ." ("I loved you . . ."): intertexts, invariants, thematics and structure', in Poetika Brodskogo, pp. 39ff.

40. Incidentally, what appear to be neutral details at first glance – 'zanaves v mestnom teatre' ('the curtains of some local theatre') (57) and 'zanaveski iz tiulia.' ('the fringe of / a tulle curtain.') (62) – are in fact related to this theme. The theatre in section V is one of the numerous hints at the day-to-day circumstances of the addressee, who at that time worked as a literary consultant at a theatre in the provincial town of Siauliai.

41. The 'mirror factor' in the poem is also present at the formal level. Apart from the mirror symmetry of the sections which has already been mentioned, the attention is also drawn by the fact that many of them are formed in sets of two, both starting in a similar or identical way. Compare III and V ('Pozdnii vecher v Litve' – 'Pozdnii vecher v Imperii'), XII and XIII ('Polnoch'. Soika krichit' – 'Polnoch' v listvennom krae'), XIV and XV ('Prizrak brodit po Kaunasu' – 'Prizrak brodit bestsel'no po Kaunasu'), and similarly VII and XVI ('Vot otkuda tvoi' – 'Vot otkuda pera'). Let us note in addition that the syllabic palindrome 'bezlikii likbez' [Into your faceless 'likbez'] (318) is like a mirror set into a line.

42. M. Iu. Lotman, 'Baltiiskaia tema v poezii Iosifa Brodskogo' [The Baltic Theme in the Poetry of Joseph Brodsky], in Slavica Helsingiensia 11: Studia Russica Helsingiensia et Tartuensia III: Problemy russkoi literatury i kul'tury, eds L. Biukling and P. Pesonen (Helsinki, 1992) p. 238.

43. It was precisely these lines which were quoted as being especially

characteristic of Brodsky by the Secretary of the Swedish Academy Sture Allen in his speech when Brodsky was presented with the Nobel Prize, 10 December 1987.

44. Steponas Darius and Stasys Girenas were American aviators of Lithuanian ancestry who, in July 1933, crossed the Atlantic Ocean in a small and ill-equipped aeroplane; they set out from New York for Kaunas, but were lost over what was then German territory. The legend is doggedly upheld (probably in error) that they were killed by the Nazis. Darius and Girenas became national heroes in Lithuania (in fact they are not forgotten in the USA either). The remains of their plane are kept in the war museum in Kaunas. This story made a considerable impression in Brodsky – at one time he was even intending to write a long narrative poem about the flight of the two Lithuanians.

45. Compare the word *kordonov* [borders] (42).

46. Alcoholism is yet another of the themes which runs through 'Lithuanian Nocturne'. It is set out in a humorously blasphemous key. Religious motifs (the wound, into which the celestial patron of the addressee, the apostle Thomas, laid his fingers; the Mother of God with her child; the prophet Isaiah), are refracted through cultural texts (Lithuanian folk sculpture; Pushkin's 'Prophet'): they are presented – as is often the case with Brodsky – in a parodying and shocking form. See ll. 109–11: 'chtob vlozhit' pal'tsy v rot – v etu ranu Fomy – / i, nashchupav iazyk, na maner serafima / perepravit' glagol' [so that he might stick his fingers into his mouth, that wound of Thomas, / and feeling his tongue, in the manner of some Seraphim / redirect the verb.]; ll. 145–50: 'v syroi konoplianoi / mnogoverstnoi rubakhe, v gudiashchikh stal'nykh bigudi / Mat'-Litva zasypaet nad plesom, / i ty / pripadaesh' k ee neprikrytoi, stekliannoi, / pol-litrovoi grudi.' [in its multi-versted / shirt of hemp, in its droning steel curlers, / Mother Lithuania falls asleep along the river, / and you / fall to her uncovered, glass / half-litre breast.] (It is worth noting that the identification of the bottle with the maternal breast stems from Freud.)

47. The theme is used to good effect in one more respect: 'Vitovt, brosivshii mech i pokherivshii shchit' [Prince Vytautas, having flung his sword and crossed out his shield,] (l. 173) is a humorous allusion to the 'sword and shield' emblem of the KGB.

48. 'Classical' features of Kaunas, such as the cathedral and the café 'Tulpe', which are situated on the town's central street, Laisves aleia [Freedom Avenue], appear in the poem; these were as well known to the author as to the addressee

49. Compare the same 'Eurasian' theme: *tatarva* [a horde] (l. 163); *pechenegom* [Pecheneg-like] (l. 169).

50. Compare *sogliadatai'* [your tail] (l. 216).

51. Incidentally, the apparition is linked with the theme of the border by virtue of the fact that it is situated on the border between life and death, dream and reality, night and day (cf. ll. 132–4 and 162–9).

52. It is developed in 1982 in the poem 'To Urania', which gave its

name to Brodsky's collection of poems entitled *Uraniia* (1987) in
Russian and *To Urania* in the English translation: 'Because of that
Urania is older than Clio.' Compare also the echo between ll. 278–9
of 'Lithuanian Nocturne' and the first line of 'To Urania': 'U vsevo
est' predel: / gorizont – u zrachka, u otchaian'ia – pamiat' . . .' [Every-
thing has its limit: / for the pupil its the horizon, for despair –
memory . . .]; 'U vsego est' predel: v tom chisle u pechali' [Every-
thing has its limit; including sorrow].

53. In this, one is justified in perceiving Brodsky's links with the acmeists
(above all Mandelshtam), although Brodsky emphasizes nihilism more.
54. Compare further on: 'Nashi ottiski' [Our imprints] (l. 100).
55. On this subject see S. Senderovich, 'Mir mimoletnykh videnii' [The
World of Fleeting Visions], in Marena Senderovich and Savelii
Senderovich, *Penaty* [Penates] (East Lansing, MI.: Russian Language
Journal) p. 21.
56. It has been pointed out that it is characteristic of Brodsky to identify himself with the word, existence with writing (and, let us add,
with the uttering of words). See, for example, Valentina Polukhina,
'Grammatika metafory i khudozhestvennyi smysl' [The grammar of
metaphor and artistic meaning], in *Poetika Brodskogo*, p. 91.
57. The next most frequent words are: *thing, Muse* and the name of the
addressee, *Tomas* (each of which occurs six times).

8

'Galatea Encore'

LEON BURNETT

As though the mercury's under its tongue, it won't
talk. As though with the mercury in its sphincter,
immobile, by a leaf-coated pond
a statue stands white like a blight of winter.
After such snow, there is nothing indeed: the ins
and outs of centuries, pestered heather.
That's what coming full circle means –
when your countenance starts to resemble weather,
when Pygmalion's vanished. And you are free
to cloud your folds, to bare the navel.
Future at last! That is, bleached debris
of a glacier amid the five-lettered "never."
Hence the routine of a goddess, née
alabaster, that lets roving pupils gorge on
the heart of the color and temperature of the knee.
That's what it looks like inside a virgin.

(III: 382)

*   *   *

GALATHÉE [avec un soupir]:
Ah! encore moi.
JEAN-JACQUES ROUSSEAU

Microsoft Encarta 97 is in no doubt. Under the entry 'Brodsky,
Joseph', it announces definitively: *Russian-born American poet*.[1]
Dictionaries decimate and encyclopaedias truncate the lives and
works of poets, but poets, like statues, invent procedures to avoid

the reduction to less than one by time or tome. Poets are changed, not by academic definitions, but (as Mallarmé said of Poe) by eternity. Into themselves. Joseph Brodsky's exploration of the resources of the English language in his own poetry and prose, from the early, and not entirely auspicious, attempt at an 'Elegy to W. H. Auden' (1974) to the more assured reflections in the Venetian *Watermark* (1992), was as much an act of self efface-ment as it was of self assertion.[2] Or, rather, it was, to employ one of Brodsky's own favourite concepts, an *amalgam* of efface-ment and assertion; in other words, an unrelenting process of self-discovery, in which the individual poems and prose pieces were the products. Few would disagree with the view that Brodsky, when he died, had still to achieve a mastery of his adopted language equal to that of fellow Nobel prize-winners and friends, Seamus Heaney and Derek Walcott, both of whom came at it from the margins. No less an achievement would have satisfied Brodsky that he had earned the right to be called an 'American poet'. 'Russian-born', while it cannot be gainsaid, is also prob-lematic in its equivocation. If 'American poet' is too assertive in its declaration of independence, then 'Russian-born' effaces too much in its failure to acknowledge the gravamina and bafflements of a poet so deeply immersed in the culture, and yet so peremp-torily exiled from the soil, of his homeland. His was the dilemma of an author inhabiting the *Zwischenraum* of 'the two cultures to which fate has willed me to belong' (as Brodsky described him-self in his Nobel Prize acceptance speech) and experiencing it as a constructive principle for the poetry of the last two decades of his life. This sense of duality is at the root of 'Galatea Encore', one of five poems that Brodsky composed in English in 1983 and included in his collection, *To Urania*.[3] Structurally, it is a matter of interest that all of the English poems composed in 1983 are sixteen lines long.[4] Yet, although they may be said to start from the same formal imperative (to write a sixteen-line poem), the-matically and compositionally each one pursues its objective dif-ferently, while still retaining some memory of, or contact with, the originating impulse. Biographically, these five poems are situ-ated mid-way between the poet's moment of exile (in July 1972) and the moment of his death (in January 1996).

Brodsky stated at the end of his Nobel lecture that 'that which is being created today in Russian or in English, for instance, secures the existence of these languages in the course of the next millennium'. The poet is instrumental in that he carries the literary 'chromosomes' of language, and language represents the best guarantee for the survival of the human species, since it has a greater capacity for 'mutation':

> The poet . . . is language's means for existence. . . . I who write these lines will cease to be, as will you who read them. But the language in which they are written and in which you read them will remain not merely because language is more lasting than man, but because it is more capable of mutation.[5]

Poets, of course, have always known this. Shakespeare expressed the same idea in the language of his time when he ended Sonnet No. 63 with the couplet: 'His beauty shall in these black lines be seen, / And they shall live, and he in them still green'. Dostoevsky gave voice to a related conviction, when he stated (through a fictional character) that 'Beauty will save the world'. Brodsky's rejoinder, in the Nobel lecture, to his Russian precursor was that 'It is probably too late for the world, but for the individual man, there always remains a chance' (*BPA*, p. 5). In that same speech, he restated his own belief in the primacy of language and aesthetics:

> Art is an unrecoiling weapon, and its development is determined not by the individuality of the artist but by the dynamics and the logic of the material itself, by the previous fate of the means that each time demand (or suggest) a qualitatively new aesthetic solution. Possessing its own genealogy, dynamics, logic, and future, art is not synonymous with, but, at best, parallel to history; and the manner by which it exists continually reinvents aesthetic reality. (*BPA*, p. 4)

Since language shares with myth the dynamics and logic to which Brodsky refers, it is not at all surprising to find that he employed the shorthand of mythological reference to 'reinvent aesthetic reality'. The source – or canonical – text for the Pygmalion and Galatea material, upon which Brodsky's poem draws, is the Tenth Book of Ovid's *Metamorphoses*, ll. 243–97, although other Classical versions exist. The theme of the animated statue also occurs in the works of the national poets of England and Russia – in Shakespeare (at the end of *The Winter's Tale*, 1610–11) and in

Pushkin (most notably in *The Bronze Horseman*, 1833).[6] The 'Romantic' Pygmalion and Galatea saw the light of day in Rousseau's 'lyrical scene' *Pygmalion* (1762).[7] It was subsequently taken up by Hazlitt, in his confessional novel, *Liber Amoris, or The New Pygmalion* (1823), in the wake of Mary Shelley's *Frankenstein, or The Modern Prometheus* (1818), although Hazlitt's composition lacked the range and vision of Mary Shelley's fantasia. William Morris included the Pygmalion story in *Earthly Paradise* (1868–70), and Shaw gave it a new, twentieth-century twist in *Pygmalion* (1914), only for it to be turned into the musical, *My Fair Lady*. Each age has its versions of Pygmalion.[8] Ours includes the application of the 'Galatea Principle' to the design of computer programmes, at which stage it could be said effectively to have become so altered as to have camouflaged its connections with Ovid.[9] This, then, would seem to confirm the truth – for poetry as much as for genes – that 'the life of the inherited message is separate from that of its carriers'.[10]

Language seeks out and finds its own agents. If, on the one hand, Brodsky's poem, 'Galatea Encore', is indicative of how attenuated the filament of fable has become at the end of the twentieth century, in that it is only the solitary mention of Pygmalion, within the poem, that provides any clue as to the statue's identity and circumstance, then, on the other hand, the 'genetic coding' of language ensures the preservation of the myth's trace. Language, as Brodsky has claimed, dictates the next line (*BPA*, p. 11). Naming *Galatea* explicitly in the title offers a clue as to the theme of the poem, but ideas of preservation, continuation and survival are also implicit in the word that follows the mythological reference: *encore*. To entitle a late twentieth-century poem simply 'Galatea' would, in itself, amount to reverting to Galatea *again*. But Brodsky does not entitle his poem 'Galatea Again' or 'Galatea Once More', thereby eschewing the accents of irony or apology.[11] Belonging to two cultures, the poet chooses for his title two words that occupy the *Zwischenraum* between Russian and English. *Galatea* is part of a Mediterranean myth and *encore*, in travelling across from the French to the English (or Russian) language, undergoes a metamorphosis to become a theatrical call for repetition, at once a doubling and a recalling into existence of that which has passed. It is the vulgar echo of Goethe's *Verweile doch, du bist so schön*.[12] Or to allow *encore* another 'encore', it is one of the last words attributed to Madame Dubarry, as quoted subtextually by Dostoevsky: *Encore un moment, monsieur le bourreau, encore un moment!*[13]

When Rousseau turned to the Galatea mythologem in 1762, he dramatized the moment of awakening of the statue in the following exchange:

> *He returns and sees the statue move and descend by herself from the pedestal down the same steps that he mounted up to her. He drops to his knees and lifts his hands and eyes to heaven:*
> Immortal gods! Venus! Galathée! O triumph of fanatic love.
> GALATHÉE [*touches herself and says*]:
>   Me.
> PYGMALION [*enraptured*]:
>   Me!
> GALATHÉE [*touches herself again*]:
>   This is me.

There follows a moment of doubt, when she touches a marble, and cries out: 'This is no longer me' ('Ce n'est plus moi'). It is only with the touch of Pygmalion that she is reassured and utters her last line in the 'lyrical scene': 'Ah! me again.' ('Ah! encore moi.').[14] Whether uttered at the moment life terminates (Madame Dubarry), or at the moment life commences (Galathée), *encore* signifies the moment of change, or transition, which cannot be arrested (Goethe), and yet is arrested – or preserved – in language.

Brodsky had made frequent use of classical and mythological motifs in his poetry before he composed 'Galatea Encore', but the introduction of the Pygmalion mythologem marks a shift in emphasis from his earlier work, most notably in the rejection of his preference in classical statuary for bust or torso and in the inversion of his more usual 'reductive' practice of figurative deanimation. This shift in emphasis coincides with a shift in language from Russian to English. The reason that Brodsky gave for 'resort[ing] to a language other than his mother tongue', was 'a desire to please a shadow'.[15] The *shadow* to which the poet referred was that of W. H. Auden, who had died in 1973:

> My desire to write in English had nothing to do with any sense of confidence, contentment, or comfort; it was simply a desire to please a shadow. Of course, where he was by then, linguistic barriers hardly mattered, but somehow I thought that he

might like it better if I made myself clear to him in English.
(*LTO*, p. 358)

In this passage, Brodsky speaks of two desires: to write in English and to please a shadow. At one level, taking the second of
these desires as constituting the main motivation, we might regard
'Galatea Encore' as a homage to the memory of Auden, less direct
than the two elegies that he had already composed by 1983, but
a mark of respect all the same.[16] To please a shadow, Brodsky
breathed new life into a statue.[17] At a second level, we might
read 'Galatea Encore' as a meta-commentary on writing poetry
in English, that is to say, on a literary activity that goes beyond
'the process of composition' to encompass what Brodsky referred
to at the start of his 1987 Nobel Lecture as 'the creative process
itself'. In that acceptance speech, he went on to recall the name
of one of his Russian precursors.[18]

The great Baratynsky, speaking of his Muse, characterised her
as possessing an 'uncommon visage'. It's in acquiring this single
'uncommon visage' that the meaning of the human existence
seems to lie, since it is for this uncommonness that we are, as
it were, prepared genetically. (*BPA*, p. 3)

It is a critical commonplace to note that poets who invoke the
Muse will also, in one way or another, register her presence in
the poetry that she inspires. This is as true for Brodsky as it was
for his Romantic and Classical predecessors.[19] After all, the collection which contains 'Galatea Encore' bears the title: *To Urania*.
Galatea, in this respect, is a fitting choice, for a prominent motif
in the mythologem is that Pygmalion modelled her on his 'muse',
Venus. Thomas Lovell Beddoes makes this the point of Pygmalion's
impassioned plea in his remarkable, but much neglected 231-line
poem, 'Pygmalion: The Cyprian Statuary':

'Goddess, that made me, save thy son, and save
The man, that made thee goddess, from the grave.'[20]

Galatea may be regarded as an incarnation of the creative principle in art, which male poets have traditionally associated with
the Muse of composition. For Brodsky, the shaping of her 'uncommon visage' in 'Galatea Encore' is equivalent to the production

of meta-poetry. It is not without significance, therefore, that he takes up the hybrid figure of the 'sweet woman-statue' or 'she-rock' (as Beddoes designates his Galatea) at a time when exile was leading him to the acquisition of a second, literary language which, according to certain authorities, marked his transition from the 'Russian-born' to the 'American poet'.[21]

*   *   *

> ... *if the Coyn be good, it will pass from one hand to*
> *another. I Trade both with the Living and the Dead,*
> *for the enrichment of our Native Language*
>   JOHN DRYDEN

Brodsky keeps Pygmalion and Galatea apart. The male artist is not destined to enjoy the woman he creates. The Ovidian consummation celebrated in Dryden's couplet –

> He kisses her white lips, renews the bliss,
> And looks, and thinks they redden at the kiss

– is a world and at least two poetic revolutions away.[22] The promise of an immortal plenitude that T. S. Eliot, *sotto voce*, called 'pneumatic' has been replaced in 'Galatea Encore' by a vision of deprivation that may or may not 'keep our metaphysics warm'.[23] In Brodsky's minimalist retelling of the story, the thermometer has replaced the sculptor's chisel mentioned in the Romantic versions,[24] for it is the 'temperature of the knee', not sexual desire, that is being measured:

> As though with the mercury in its sphincter,
> immobile, by a leaf-coated pond
> a statue stands white like a blight of winter.

This is a poem about Galatea's freedom from Pygmalion. The second half of the poem commences with the line:

> when Pygmalion's vanished. And you are free

Pygmalion's disappearance is symptomatic of a more drastic, and at the same time more discreet, withdrawal, or effacement, in Brodsky's five English poems of 1983, namely, that of the poet himself. It is an arresting fact that Brodsky entirely avoids using the first-person singular pronoun in any of the five, sixteen-line poems composed in English in that year and subsequently included in *To Urania*, although all five poems assume a vocative 'you'. Indeed, the disappearance of the self (or, conversely, the donning of a lyrical mask) is one of the more remarkable aspects of Brodsky's English poetry in this collection.[25] Apart from the long poem 'Gorbunov and Gorchakov' and the translation of the 3000-year-old Sumerian text, 'The Dialogue of Pessimism' (see n. 3), 44 poems are included in *To Urania*, of which exactly half (22) are translated into English by the author and one quarter (11) are written by him originally in English.[26] In the 11 English poems, the pronoun 'I' appears on only four occasions and in only two poems.[27] No such inhibition affects the other poems in *To Urania*, which have been translated by the poet himself into English.[28] The scale of the difference may be indicated by observing that the first poem in the volume, 'May 24, 1980' (1980), twenty lines long and translated by the author, begins with 'I' and includes five other instances of the pronoun, more in total than in all the English poems put together. It is as if, as Brodsky writes at the end of 'Venetian Stanzas II', the landscape is 'quite happy/here without me'.[29] The poet, we might conjecture, is not yet ready to introduce himself *in propria persona* as an American poet.[30]

Instead, he asserts himself in his mastery of the verse structure. Barry Scherr has written on rhyme and enjambment in Brodsky's poetry as complementary devices, noting that they 'work in harmony'.[31] This, as Scherr points out, is something that Brodsky had learnt from the English verse tradition. When he comes to write in English, therefore, it is natural that he should exploit the formal potentialities of the native tradition. Thus, whereas Dryden employs a strong Augustan couplet to intensify the conjunction of *bliss* and *kiss*, Brodsky's looser construction suggests a discordance, a resistance to union that is reinforced by the *alternation* of the *abab* rhyme scheme. Yet the superficial impression given by the 'irregular' devices of enjambments and inexact rhymes that 'Galatea Encore' is more casual in its composition than Dryden's verse is contradicted by an analysis which discloses a studied concern for pattern and symmetry, as Table 1 (setting

TABLE 1

Rhyme words	Kind	Type	Enjambment[32]
won't/pond	inexact	masculine	enj. + enj.
sphincter,/winter.	inexact	feminine	stop + stop
ins/means –	inexact	masculine	enj. + enj.
heather./weather,	exact	feminine	stop + stop
free/debris	exact	masculine	enj. + enj.
navel./'never'.	inexact	feminine	stop + stop
née/knee.	inexact	masculine	enj. + stop
gorge on/virgin.	inexact	feminine	enj. + stop

out the sequence of rhymes and enjambments) demonstrates. Brodsky's art, as Ovid said of Pygmalion's, is one that 'conceals art' (*ars adeo latet arte sua*).

The only two pairs of exact rhymes occur in the middle of the poem, that is to say, the rhymes appear most stable at the very moment that 'Galatea' is most unstable, when the transformation of statue into virgin is taking place. What is more, the middle two lines of the poem (which, given the alternating rhyme-scheme, cannot rhyme with each other) are, as it were, yoked together by a repetition of the temporal marker ('when') at the start of each line, creating a dynamic sense of conflicting forces at play and culminating in the release that is communicated in the last word of the ninth line: *free.*

> when your countenance starts to resemble weather,
> when Pygmalion's vanished. And you are free

The least inventive rhyme of the whole poem – *weather* – occurs a line earlier. It not only rhymes fully with *heather*, but it also matches it in part of speech (noun) and in field of reference (natural world).[33] These two lines record a wonderful transformation, yet the marvel of the statue's incarnation, as it becomes organic ('starts to resemble weather') and is first addressed vocatively ('*your* countenance' as opposed to the earlier 'it' and 'its'), is deliberately downplayed, diminished by the banality of the rhyme. Metamorphosis is redefined as the 'routine of a goddess', just as the making of a poem might be considered no more than the natural reflex of a poet, his trade with both the living and the dead.

The structural repetition noted above ('when . . . when') is one of three prominent syntactic parallelisms in the poem, which have the effect of foregrounding the 'prosaic' rhythm of the sentence as unit (as against that of the 'poetic' line). The first parallelism ('As though . . . As though') occurs at the outset of the poem, linking the first two sentences, and the last, somewhat less obvious in that it is delayed, concludes the composition ('That's what . . . That's what'). It is only here, at the end of the poem, that line length and sentence length coincide to establish a resolution of the two countervailing rhythms.

What, in effect, the poem is 'about' is this resolution of distinctly sensed antinomies: statue and virgin, prose rhythm and poetic rhythm, the richness of the past (mythological and literary) and the impoverishment of the present, eternity and the moment. In short, the antinomy of Galatea and her *encore* – the 'bleached debris / of a glacier amid the five-lettered "never"'. The resolution, when it comes, is sensed not as a synthesis or fusion, but as an amalgam, one layer pressed down upon another.

In a cogent reading of what he designates as Brodsky's 'Ironic Journey into Antiquity', George Nivat has described Brodsky's *ars poetica* as containing two elements: 'life seized in moments of eternity and the impersonality of the world, and of the man made solid, made into statue in this world'.[34] Nivat refers to the 'bleached vision' of statuary, the 'bleached immortality' of the antique statue (white on white, like Malevich's square) and the 'passage of debris into eternity away from the present' (*BPA*, p. 94) that one finds in the Roman Elegies.[35] It would appear that this *ars poetica* has undergone some revision in 'Galatea Encore', for what we are presented with is eternity – the statue – seized in the moment of life (the world as personality), and statue made flesh in this world, where the passage is not to, but from, eternity. Part of the explanation for this inversion, I would suggest, is to be sought for in the cultural and linguistic 'passage' into a different 'native' tradition. 'Galatea Encore' charts the poet's journey into a modernity that is American, though not entirely without its ironies, as he carves out his niche in a newly acquired, or 'virginal' [*nesozdannyi*], world. As Brodsky, who had a fondness for catachresis, might have said, the minimalism that has always been a feature of his poetic perspective is accommodated here in the niche of time.

At the start of the poem, Galatea possesses all the attributes of the 'bleached immortality' of Brodsky's antique, Russian statues.

She is silent, immobile, white, cold, dilapidated and alone. Hers, however, is no Immaculate Conception, no wet dream of Adam for an Eve trapped 'amid the five-lettered "never"', although the birth is a virgin one.[36] It would seem that Galatea's virginity is a paradise regained, rather than a paradise lost, for the 'full circles' of Brodsky's universe run counter-clockwise, back to their origins.[37]

The meaning and orientation of Brodsky's 'full circle' is explicated through reference to the disintegration of fabric in *Watermark*:

> They were shedding, those curtains, and some of their folds exposed, broad, bald, threadbare patches, as though the fabric felt it had come full circle and was now reverting to its pre-loom state. Our breath was perhaps too great an intimacy also; still, it was better than fresh oxygen, which, like history, the drapes didn't need. This was neither decay nor decomposition; this was dissipation back into time, where color and texture don't matter, where perhaps having learned what may happen to them, they will regroup and return, here or elsewhere, in a different guise. (p. 54)

What is said of the fabric of curtains in this extract may be extended to the fabric of language. Brodsky's poetic idiom is distinctive, but it draws upon the words of earlier writers, who may thus be said to 'regroup and return . . . in a different guise'. Indeed, one might say that one of the main achievements of his idiom is that it draws upon, and revitalizes, the writings of others. This is one of its main resources, 'better than fresh oxygen'. Thus, we might juxtapose 'Galatea Encore' and 'The Statue' (by John Berryman – another JB), to account for the revisionary swerve in Brodsky's iconography.[38] The accoutrements of Brodsky's poem are to be found at the beginning of Berryman's poem, a memorable restatement of the American Dream *c.* 1950, telescoped in the words that end the first five lines: *weather* (l. 1), *look* (l. 2), *pallor* (l. 3), '*colour*' (l. 4) and *alone* (l. 5); the dominant statement or theme is enunciated in the middle stanza of the same poem ('Disfigurement is general.'); and a prototype for his Pygmalion is presented at the end ('an insignificant dreamer', who 'wasted so much skill, such faith, / And salvaged less than the intolerable statue').

The statue of Berryman's poem is that of a European: Humboldt.

Since graduating from its years of flesh
The name has faded in the public mind
Or doubled: which is this? the elder? younger?
The statesman or the traveller?

If we add that the 'elder' Humboldt was also a philologist, then
we might venture the proposition that Brodsky, acutely conscious
of his 'doubling' (*BPA*, p. 2) personates the Humboldt of our time,
a kind of Humboldt amalgam, a traveller *in* language.

For Brodsky, Venice was the most important stage on the journey
from Russia to the United States. Venice, which became a city of
annual renewal for the poet, is also, of course, the location for
poems that he originally wrote in Russian, in which he chroni-
cled the 'pallid marble' of its virginal statuary.[39] Marble statues
abound in Brodsky's work and their symbolic significance has
received detailed attention in the critical literature.[40] Yet he chose
to identify the Galatea of the poem under discussion not with
marble (or ivory as Ovid had done), but with alabaster. Neither
the exigencies of rhyme nor any other structural consideration is
sufficient to motivate the choice of substance or the location of
the word in the poem (although one may wish to point out how
Brodsky, in placing 'alabaster' at the start of l. 14, exploits the
internal off-rhyme with 'of a glacier' at the start of l. 12 in order
to emphasize the contrast between the two substances). The choice
of 'alabaster' seems, rather, to be determined by a semantic preference. Marble has its own connotations in Brodsky, and the refusal
to 'marmorize' Galatea has certain implications, one of which is
to distance it from the 'Russian' Venetian stereotype. (His 'English' Venice was not properly composed until 1989 when he wrote
Watermark, and then it turned out to be a prose version of the
city.) Alabaster allows light to shine through. It is translucent
and 'warm' to the eye. It 'lets roving pupils gorge on / the heart
of the color'. The 'soft' light that English poets have seen shining through alabaster lamps have ranged from Mary Tighe's 'milky'
to Soame Jenyns' 'ruby'.[41] Dryden's imagery of 'white lips' that
seem to 'redden at the kiss' moves from the one to the other
end of this colour spectrum, though it lacks the Renaissance lus-
tre and lustiness of Sandys's rendition of Ovid: 'It seem'd a virgin, full of living flame' or, yet more succulently, 'A perfect Virgin
full of iuyce and heat'![42]

Brodsky's Galatea is not Venetian, nor is the statue's location

'by a leaf-coated pond'. Nevertheless, 'Galatea Encore' reveals a
trace of Venice refracted through the English language. One hint
as to the subtext is supplied in a punning reference in the first
stanza of 'Venetian Stanzas I'.[43] In English literature, before Byron
and Browning laid claim to the city, Venice was canonized by
Shakespeare in two of his most famous plays: *The Merchant of
Venice* (1596–7) and *Othello* (1602–3). It is surely no coincidence
that both plays contain monologues that allude to alabaster. In
the opening scene of *The Merchant of Venice* (ll. 83–4), Gratiano
asks: 'Why should a man, whose blood is warm within, / Sit like
his grandsire cut in alabaster?' 'There are', he goes on to say (ll.
88–90), 'a sort of men, whose visages / Do cream and mantle like
a standing pond; / and do a wilful stillness entertain'. Although
these lines provide one source for the third line of Brodsky's
poem ('immobile, by a leaf-coated pond'), it is the other Shakespearean passage that is better known, though perhaps (in the
nature of subtexts) less significant for Brodsky's poem.[44] What
the combination of the two Shakespearean passages does under-
line, however, is a dynamic relation between alabaster and death.
Desdemona, if not a virgin, is innocent of blame, pure, and yet
slain by a husband who wields the power of life or death over
her. She has her counterpart in Hermione, who enacts the role
of a statue come to life at the end of *The Winter's Tale* (Act V,
Scene iii). For Leontes, the husband who had wronged her, what
distinguishes a living woman from a statue are speech and
movement:

> What you can make her do,
> I am content to look on, what to speak,
> I am content to hear; for 'tis as easy
> To make her speak as move.

Alabaster, as the inorganic material of the artist, stands in simple
opposition to the glacier and the snow, formed by nature, which
belong to the field of meteorology. A more complex opposition,
however, is the structurally foregrounded one between alabaster
and mercury. Mercury is twice mentioned in the first two lines
of the poem as part of the object (*comparant*) of a simile, whose
subject (*comparé*) is the inanimate statue ('it'), not named in the
poem, but assumed, on the basis of the title, to be Galatea.[45]
Brodsky's similes focus upon the two qualities that distinguish

woman from statue in the lines (quoted above) from *The Winter's Tale*: speech and movement. A third simile, employing the most common term for figurative comparison ('like'), establishes the association of this 'tale' with winter. The conclusion of the introductory phase of 'Galatea Encore', signalled by the standard poetic effects of alliteration and assonance, is reached when line ending and full stop coincide (for the first time in the poem):

As though the mercury's under its tongue, it won't
talk. As though with the mercury in its sphincter,
immobile, by a leaf-coated pond
a statue stands white like a blight of winter.

Mercury, which in the Ovidian context carries intimations of the god who presided over various kinds of intertraffic and exchange (including that between the living and the dead, and across languages), is metonymic for the thermometer, an instrument never mentioned explicitly in the poem.[46] Brodsky's similes 'animate' the statue by assuming that its physical condition may be measured in the same way as the 'virgin', which it eventually becomes, can. What is less immediately apparent, but of significance in the light of the *ars poetica* that Nivat and other have elucidated, is that this statue is neither bust nor torso. A torso has no tongue and a bust has no sphincter to accommodate the immobilizing thermometer (a metamorphosis of 'Hermes' rod' into medical instrument). Unlike the earlier statues of Tiberius and others, Galatea is not *dis*membered, but *re*membered, as the *encore* implies. She is, to employ a forensic term used of virgins, intact.

Brodsky has another reason for starting his poem with a reference to mercury. He is responding to the opening stanza of Auden's poem 'In Memory of W. B. Yeats':

He disappeared in the dead of winter:
The brooks were frozen, the airports almost deserted,
And snow disfigured the public statues;
The mercury sank in the mouth of the dying day.
What instruments we have agree
The day of his death was a dark cold day.

Disfigurement is general, but Brodsky reconfigures the imagery in this stanza (of winter, snow, statues, mercury, mouth) and reverses the passage from life to death that Auden records. The thematic inversion finds its justification in Yeats's 'The Statues' (1938), a late poem called to mind by Auden's reference to 'statues'. In the first stanza of this poem, Yeats had invoked the Pygmalion motif in alluding to 'boys and girls, pale from the imagined love / Of solitary bed', who:

> pressed at midnight in some public place
> Live lips upon a plummet-measured face.

He ends the poem with the same 'plummet-measured face', rhyming it, on the second occasion, with 'trace', the vestige of what remains present of the past.

Valentina Polukhina, who has examined Brodsky's debt to Auden in detail, refers to the Russian poet's 'deliberate self-effacement' and his 'use of quotations and allusions to the poets of foreign traditions as a mask for personal experience and inner feelings'.[47] She concludes her analysis with some remarks upon Brodsky's 'multi-faceted', 'intertextual links with English poetry'. They are, she notes 'by no means entirely unobscure':

> Even when they go back to a common source, they are reworked differently, as if they are subject to different thematic demands and a different linguistic frame of mind. And for all the many similarities, the differences are no less fundamental. . . . Auden was not caught by an *idée fixe* – the search for a poetic mythology of time or the creation of a teleology of language – to the extent that is characteristic of Brodsky. (p. 100)

Brodsky's announcement, then, that 'Pygmalion's vanished', which takes up the theme from Auden's line, 'He disappeared in the dead of night', and which could refer either to Auden or to Yeats, might apply, equally well, to himself. Disappearance may thus be understood as a radical form of a general disfigurement. Pygmalion is a mask that all male poets may put on, figuratively speaking.

*   *   *

beauty at low temperatures is beauty
JOSEPH BRODSKY

The first half of 'Galatea Encore' is dominated by the figure/dis-figurement of the simile. In addition to the three instances in the first four lines, discussed above, there is also the comparison of the countenance to 'weather'. These similes are supplemented by 'weak' metaphors, that is to say, those that are either expressed in a single epithet ('leaf-coated', 'pestered') or else have been diluted in potency to become an idiomatic phrase ('the ins / and outs of centuries', 'coming full circle'). The ninth line, where the second half of the poem commences, is the only line containing no figures of speech. It is also the crux of the poem in that it marks the necessary conditions for the metamorphosis of statue into virgin (disappearance of the male, freedom of the female). From l. 10 onwards, in the absence of any further similes, the metaphors become more complex or unusual ('to cloud your folds', 'bleached debris / of a glacier amid the five-lettered "never"', 'née / alabaster', 'roving pupils gorge on', 'the heart of the color'). The complexity or unusualness in several of these instances, how-ever, may be elucidated contextually by reference to imagery found elsewhere in Brodsky's writings. The line 'to cloud your folds, to bare the navel', for example, recalls the declarative utterance in the first stanza of 'Roman Elegies': 'The world's made of naked-ness and of foldings.'[48] The *glacier* is to be associated, directly or indirectly, with the North (and its perspectives) in Brodsky's poetry;[49] the phrase 'roving pupils' is picked up again in *Water-mark*;[50] and the interiorized perspective implicit in the expres-sion 'the heart of the color' has been a characteristic of the poet's way of seeing since his earliest poetry.[51] Finally, 'Galatea Encore' ends with an analogy of discovery or recognition ('That's what it looks like inside a virgin'). This may be read either as a com-ment on the preceding sentence or as a summation of the 'meaning' of the whole poem, which has moved in its focus from the exter-nal to the internal.[52] Thus, taking the poem as a unit, the simile is considered a more appropriate figurative device for dealing with surfaces and the metaphor for that which lies within.

This is what Brodsky was later to write of surfaces in *Watermark*:

Surfaces – which is what the eye registers first – are often more telling than their contents, which are provisional by definition,

except, of course, in the afterlife.... On my first sojourns [in
Venice] I often felt surprised, catching my own frame, dressed
or naked, in [the mirror of] the open wardrobe; after a while I
began to wonder about the place's edenic or after-life effects
upon one's self-awareness. Somewhere along the line, I even
developed a theory of excessive redundancy, of the mirror
absorbing the body absorbing the city. The net result is, obviously, mutual negation. A reflection cannot possibly care for a
reflection. The city is narcissistic enough to turn your mind
into an amalgam, unburdening it of its depths.   (pp. 21–2)

The transformations are not too radical to mistake the resemblance of the Venetian traveller depicted in this passage to the
figure represented in 'Galatea Encore': 'dressed or naked' is the
prose equivalent of 'to cloud your folds, to bare the navel', and
the 'afterlife' replaces the 'future' that, like tomorrow, 'never'
comes.[53] Pygmalion's vanished, but Narcissus stands in his place.

In a city of mirrors such as Venice (or Petersburg), the mind
becomes an 'amalgam', unburdened of its depths. According to
Brodsky's 'theory of excessive redundancy', the outer world (city)
is absorbed into the physical being (body) which, in turn, is
absorbed into the *amalgam* of the mirror, so that epistemic depth
becomes, as it were, the surface of a multi-dimensional reality.
Reality collapses. Into itself. As a metal, mercury absorbs other
metals to form amalgams, in much the same way as Mercury,
the Roman psychopomp, 'absorbed' (or extinguished) life in carrying souls to the realm of the dead. The mirror is a *Zwischenraum*,
which resists the imperative of dimensionality: space.[54]

When Brodsky introduces the *amalgam* into his poetry, it is as
a key aspect of his symbolism of the mirror.[55] The word is chosen with an eye to philological accuracy, for it is defined quite
explicitly as 'An alloy of mercury with another metal or metals;
fig. a mixture or combination' (*New Webster's Dictionary of the English
Language*). There are, perhaps, two qualities of the amalgam in
Brodsky's poetics that need to be extracted from the 'opaque'
symbolic complex in which it is embedded: (i) the amalgam,
whether it absorbs or reflects, has the power to 'contain' the world
outside; and (ii) it contains not 'for a time', temporarily, but for
all eternity. This is no two-way mirror. Entry into the inner world
of the amalgam is an irreversible process. Given the omnipres-
ence of mirrors, especially in Petersburg and Venice, and the

plenitude of time, everything will eventually end up 'contained' in the mirror, as part of the amalgam. This is the basis for Brodsky's theory of excessive redundancy. All that is outside the mirror is surplus, existing only to be absorbed (or reflected). Understood in this way, the theory is, of course, symbolically, an account, or better, a recognition, of what happens when we die.

When, in 'Galatea Encore', Brodsky employs mercury metonymically to designate the thermometer, the mirror has, in effect, turned measure, and its inner quicksilver shines with a different intensity from that of the rosy, interior light of the alabaster lamp which, like Desdemona's life (*Othello* V, ii), once put out cannot be re-lit.

> I know not where is that Promethean heat
> That can thy light relume. When I have pluck'd the rose
> I cannot give it vital growth again,
> It needs must wither.

One consequence of Brodsky's shifting the location of the statue, from artificial city (Venice or Petersburg) to natural landscape ('leaf-coated pond', 'pestered heather'), is to transfer some of the emphasis from the visual, associated with the mirror and the eye, to the 'Promethean heat' (or cold) of body temperature and climate, from theme to therm.

Brodsky returned to the Pygmalion–Galatea mythologem in his essay 'On Grief and Reason', presenting Pygmalion in a predatory role.[56] When he did so, he made it clear that Galatea repudiated her creator's sexual advances: '"Don't, don't, don't, don't" . . . That's what the story of Pygmalion and his model is all about.'[57] In the light of this remark, it is tempting to read Brodsky's poem as constructed upon an opposition, or dual perspective: cold outside, warm inside (Galatea 'née / alabaster') versus warm outside, cold inside (Galatea as 'virgin'). The warmth of alabaster seems to come from within. The internal 'color' of the statue glows through and softens the mineral surface. In contrast, quicksilver has the appearance of a congealed liquid. It 'looks' cold, and this coldness radiates outwards in confirmation of the declaration that beauty at low temperatures *is* beauty, not desire.[58] The integument of the thermometer is transparent, of the lamp translucent, but they share a common symbolic function. As mementoes, they speak of death, but they speak also of the survival that the poet's language guarantees.[59]

The mercury, used in taking the temperature of the 'knee', is associated with the flesh-and-blood Galatea of the poem's 'future', whereas the alabaster is associated with the statue of the petrified past, a temporality proclaimed in the participial 'née' which is one of only two past-tense verbal forms found in the whole poem.[60] Indirectly, the opposition between mercury and alabaster is reconciled in Brodsky's 'theory of excessive redundancy'. In adumbrating his 'theory' in relation to the physical reality of Venice in *Watermark*, Brodsky lists mirror, body and city as progressively larger entities. The mirror, we might say, is a two-dimensional surface, the body is three-dimensional (with a consciousness that exists in and for the present), and the city four-dimensional (with a temporality, or story, that extends along another axis, beyond the reach of any human life-time). In an alabaster world, the entities corresponding to 'body' and 'city' are already indicated in the title of the poem, for they are represented, respectively, by the statue in its animated presentness (Galatea)[61] and by its story, the mythologem that is told and retold (*encore*). Now, if mercury is to the mirror (or, displaced, to the thermometer) as alabaster is to the surface or exterior of the statue, then what remains to be identified is the 'principle' of alabaster that functions, like amalgam, as an index of transformation and which is capable of negating, or collapsing, the 'excessive redundancy' of the superfluous dimensions. This principle, I would suggest, is that of the mask. The mask of time, the mask of a name, the mask of metaphor. It is the mask that moulds the face in life and in death.

The making of such a mask is, quite literally, a *prosopopoeia*, a figure of speech which J. Hillis Miller associates with the story of Pygmalion. He writes:

If most of the metamorphoses in the *Metamorphoses* go from human to inhuman, life to death, animate to inanimate, the coming alive of Galatea goes the other way. The name for the figure of speech of which this metamorphosis is the literalizing allegory is *prosopopoeia*. . . . Prosopopoeia is the ascription to entities that are not really alive first of a *name*, then of a face, and finally, in a return to language, of a voice.[62]

The sequence that Hillis Miller establishes is precisely the one that we encounter in reading 'Galatea Encore'. The name of the beloved female is included in the title of the poem and sets up its own expectations for a reader at the end of the twentieth century. The face, first glimpsed partially in the reference to the mercury 'under the tongue' and then fully 'when your countenance starts to resemble weather', becomes the focus of the reader's attention in the process of animation within the first half of the poem.[63] And, finally, as the reader comes to recognize, the voice heard in the 'return to language' is one that is superimposed upon the poem, for Galatea remains silent and the lyric persona, as I have already argued, creates *in absentia*.[64] The poem's utterance is an acoustic amalgam of artist and artifact: *Future at last!* The phrase is accorded the only exclamation mark in the entire composition, but it is left unattributed, that is to say, not placed in quotation marks (although the poem acknowledges in the following line that such a form of punctuation exists).

As a prosopopoeic utterance, *Future at last!* is to be interpreted as a cry of the exile confronting a world not yet made (or, as Brodsky put it in his Nobel speech, 'that which is being created today'), an exultant cry of self-discovery whose full import must embrace ('contain') language itself, in that it is conceived in the *Zwischenraum* between the 'Russian-born' and the fully-fledged 'American poet', and in that, since the double-facing month of January 1996, it occupies the aperture between life and death. If, in a poet's 'return to language' every figure of speech is also a disfigurement, then the making of the mask in this poem is tantamount to an unmasking, and its closure to a form of disclosure.

That's what coming full circle means!
That's what it looks like inside a virgin.

Notes

1. An identical description is employed by the anonymous contributor of the entry for 'Brodsky, Joseph' in *The Cambridge Guide to Literature in English*, ed. Ian Ousby (Cambridge University Press, 1993) p. 117.
2. For Brodsky's own response to a negative view of the 'Elegy to W. H. Auden', see Valentina Polukhina, *Joseph Brodsky: A Poet for Our Time* (Cambridge University Press, 1989) pp. 88–90. His prose meditation, *Watermark* (dated 1989) was published by Hamish Hamilton (London).
3. Joseph Brodsky, *To Urania: Selected Poems 1965–1985* (London: Penguin, 1988). This volume is to be differentiated from his collection of Russian poems, *Uraniia* (Ann Arbor: Ardis, 1987). In their selection

of poems, the two volumes overlap, but do not coincide. The majority of the poems in *To Urania* belong to the 1980s. Although the sequence is not arranged chronologically, dates of composition – and name of translator(s) for poems written originally in Russian – are given in square brackets at the end of each poem. It would appear from this information that composition of the poems does not correspond entirely with the time-span mentioned in the book's title. The earliest date is 1968 ('October Tune', p. 6) and the latest 1987 ('"Slave, Come to My Service"', pp. 122–5, an English 'translation', based upon 'two interlinear renditions', of a Sumerian text, *c*.1000 BC). Three other poems, placed in sequence (pp. 107–18), one composed in English and two translations, are dated 1986. The last poem, 'Gorbunov and Gorchakov' (pp. 131–70), clearly marked off as separate from the rest of the volume, is dated 1968.

4. Four of them – 'Seaward' (p. 96), 'Galatea Encore' (p. 97), 'Letter to an Archaeologist' (p. 99) and 'Ex Voto' (p. 105) – have no stanzaic divisions, whereas the fifth – 'variation in V' (p. 98) is split into four quatrains.

5. Quoted from the translation by Barry Rubin, in *Brodsky's Poetics and Aesthetics*, eds L. Loseff and V. Polukhina (Basingstoke: Macmillan, 1990) pp. 1–11 (10–11). In subsequent references this volume will be identified as *BPA*.

6. See Roman Jakobson, 'The Statue in Pushkin's Poetic Mythology', in *Pushkin and His Sculptural Myth*, trans. [from the Czech] and ed. John Burbank (The Hague: Mouton, 1975) pp. 1–44, for a fuller analysis of Pushkin's treatment of the theme.

7. In its compression and unity of focus, Rousseau's work may be considered as a possible source for Pushkin's 'little tragedies'.

8. See J. Hillis Miller, *Versions of Pygmalion* (Cambridge, MA: Harvard University Press, 1990), for a close reading of some of the 'versions' that fall between the Romantic and the Computer ages.

9. See Julian Hilton, 'The Galatea Principle: learning machines', *Comparative Criticism*, vol. 11 (1989) pp. 111–35. A variation – on the theme of artificial intelligence and neural networks – appears in Richard Powers' novel *Galatea 2.2* (London: Abacus, 1996).

10. 'The most elusive, but most important, truth about genetics is that the life of the inherited message is separate from that of its carriers.' Steve Jones, *In the Blood: Gods, Genes and Destiny* (London: HarperCollins, 1996) p. 16.

11. Irony is saved for the poem, where *encore* is glossed as *routine* rather than return: 'That's what coming full circle means' (l. 7).

12. Compare Polukhina, *Joseph Brodsky*, p. 186.

13. Quoted in *The Idiot* (1868) and in 'Vlas', *A Writer's Diary* (1873).

14. The translation is from Hilton, 'The Galatea Principle', pp. 125–6 (French original on p. 134. 'Pygmalion, scène lyrique' is included in *Oeuvres de J. J. Rousseau, Citoyen de Genève; tome neuvième* (Paris: P. Didot l'aîné, AN IX [1801]) pp. 297–306.

15. See Joseph Brodsky, 'To Please a Shadow', in *Less than One: Selected Essays* (London: Penguin, 1987) pp. 357–83 (357–8). Subsequently LTO.

16. At one level, we can speak of traces (or transformations) of Auden in 'Galatea Encore', which revive, by pleasing, the shadow of the dead poet. Thus, the 'pestered heather' takes up the image of 'Yorkshire heather' in 'York', Brodsky's second elegy to Auden, and the description of the 'countenance' that 'starts to resemble weather' could be said to allude to the familiar folds in the face of the English poet in his later life.

17. For a contrast in the semiotic significance of 'shadow' [ten'] and 'statue' in Pushkin, see Michael Shapiro, 'Pushkin's Modus Significandi: A Semiotic Exploration', in Russian Romanticism: Studies in the Poetic Codes, ed. Nils Åke Nilsson (Stockholm: Almqvist & Wiksell, 1979) pp. 110–32 (117).

18. Evgeny Baratynsky, another shadow in the gathering throng of dead poets that Brodsky has commemorated by name, provides an additional subtext for 'Galatea Encore' in his 18-line lyric poem 'The Sculptor' (1841). See E. A. Baratynskii, Polnoe sobranie sochinenii (Leningrad, 1957) pp. 187–8.

19. '[U]nlike anyone else, a poet always knows that what in the vernacular is called the voice of the Muse is, in reality, the dictate of the language' (BPA, p. 10).

20. 'Pygmalion', ll. 157–8. Earlier in the poem, Beddoes had described 'Lonely Pygmalion' as one 'who made gods who make men' (l. 38). See Thomas Lovell Beddoes, The Works, ed. H. W. Donner (London: Oxford University Press, 1935) pp. 78–83.

21. The choice of subject is reinforced by the fact that the source-text for 'Galatea Encore' was written by an earlier literary exile, banished for a 'political' offence – Ovid.

22. John Dryden's lines are a translation of Ovid's Metamorphoses, Book X, ll. 334–5.

23. The allusions in this sentence are to Eliot's poem 'Whispers of Immortality'.

24. Baratynsky: 'Rezets s bogini sokrovennoi / Koru snimaet za koroi' ('Skul'ptor', ll. 8–9); Rousseau: 'Dieux! je sens la chair palpitante repousser le ciseau!' ('Pygmalion', Oeuvres IX, p. 302); Beddoes: 'The magic chisel thrust and gashed and swept / Flying and manifold' ('Pygmalion', ll. 110–11).

25. The absence of the 'I' form is all the more unusual in the light of Polukhina's observation that '[i]n all Brodsky's collections man is represented first of all by the lyrical "I" and the addressee "you"' (BPA, p. 161).

26. Of the remaining 11, eight are translated by Brodsky in collaboration with another person and three are translated by someone other than Brodsky.

27. The English poems date from 1980 to 1986. 'Café Trieste: San Francisco' (1980), a 40-line poem, contains three uses of the first-person pronoun, and 'Belfast Tune' (1986), another 16-line poem, one. The 48-line 'A Martial Law Carol' (1980) has two occurrences of the possessive form ('my', 'mine'), the second strongly marked through a rhyming with its homonym ('mine'). 'Allenby Road' (1981) is an earlier

172   *Joseph Brodsky*

English composition of 16 lines, with a specific but unidentified addressee (compare, 'your throat'), in which the first-person pronoun is avoided. Thus, seven of the 11 poems composed in English and included in *To Urania*, are 16-lines long.

28. Yet the very act of translation, even self-translation, may be construed as the donning of a mask, of a *persona*.

29. *To Urania*, p. 95. The positioning of 'Venetian Stanzas II', immediately before the five English poems of 1983, lends its last word a meta-textual significance, that is, 'without "me"'. The eclipse of the self ('I', 'me') is a prerogative of Pygmalion, who casts himself as female Other. If Brodsky's title – Galatea *encore* – constructs a mirror image for *encore moi* – the last words uttered by Rousseau's Galathée – then 'Galatea' becomes the equivalent of 'moi'. It is worth recording the fact that, in the play of pronouns, the last word spoken by Rousseau's Pygmalion (which marks the end of the lyrical scene) is 'toi': 'je ne vivrai plus que par toi'. These words are followed in the French text by the words: FIN DE PYGMALION. This announcement may be taken in two contrasting ways.

30. Brodsky's precursor, Osip Mandelshtam, wrote in *Kamen*, his first collection of poems: 'I, nesozdannyi mir, leleia, / Ia zabyl nenuzhnoe "ia"'. ['As I cherished a world not yet made / I relinquished the useless 'I'.] Original and translation in *Osip Mandelstam's Stone*, trans. and introduced by Robert Tracy (Princeton University Press, 1981) pp. 90–1. Brodsky's second poetical language – in the American dialect – may also be represented as 'nesozdannyi mir', a world still in the process of being created.

31. 'Enjambement, especially when it leads to innovative rhymes, does not necessarily efface line boundaries but can just as well emphasize them' (*BPA*, p. 177).

32. The line-endings in the last column of the table are identified according to whether they manifest run-on (enj.) or rest (stop), that is, the 'strong' punctuation of comma or full stop. Line 7, which ends with a 'weak' punctuation, a dash, is taken to be equivalent in effect to enjambment.

33. This contrasts with 'free /debris', the only other aurally exact rhyme-pair in the poem, in which part of speech, field of reference and the 'look' of the two words are distinct.

34. George Nivat, 'The Ironic Journey into Antiquity', *BPA*, pp. 89–97 (89).

35. 'Bleaching', for Brodsky, is a function of marble. In 'Flight from Byzantium', he states that the Bosporus belongs to Urania 'no matter how hard Clio tries to put it on', and that 'in the form of a deep current, [it] escapes back [from the Black Sea] into Marmara – the Marble Sea – presumably to get itself bleached'. The modern bridge over the Bosporus, Brodsky also notes, is named 'Galata'. See *LTO*, p. 441.

36. I suspect that the enclosure of 'never' in quotation marks points to an elaborate, but disguised, multi-lingual word-play, which would be consistent with the hybrid status of the poem as a whole. The key to this is the lexical item: *nix*. In American idiom it means a

refusal ('nothing doing', 'never in a million years'), equivalent to a rejection issuing from a statue-virgin; in Teutonic folklore it is a female water-sprite (virginal); and in Latin it means 'snow' (which may also be virginal). The Latin noun declines *nix, nivis* to generate the English technical term *névé*, halfway between 'never' and *née*, defined by the dictionary as snow 'compacted into glacial ice'. In such a constellation, the pronunciation common in America for the river Neva (that is, *nee*-va) would play its part. For the claim that 'Brodsky's letters and, in his view, the letters of any language, stand in eternal expectation of meaning' and that (in his own words) a poet 'repeats the development of language; he begins with some sort of childish babble, then moves to maturity, and to greater maturity and, finally, to language itself', see Polukhina, *Joseph Brodsky*, pp. 180–1.

37. I associate the idea of virginity with paradise, since Brodsky does not leave much else: 'I'd like to assert that, Northerner though I am, my notion of Eden hinges on neither weather nor temperature. For that matter, I'd just as soon discard its dwellers, and eternity as well.' (*Watermark*, p. 20). It is significant, in this argument, that Brodsky also uses the phrase 'empty circle' in the last stanza of his poem, 'Folk Tune' (*To Urania*, p. 63), where it serves as an image of self-effacement: 'Draw an empty circle on your yellow pad. / This will be me: no insides in thrall. / Stare at it awhile, then erase the scrawl.' For a more schematic reference to the 'closed circle' as a *return to the origin*, see *LTO*, pp. 401–2.

38. The juxtaposition is not entirely adventitious, for Berryman alludes to Brodsky in *Dream Songs* 180 and 181 ('The Translator – I' and 'The Translator – II'). The occasion of these two poems is Brodsky's trial in Leningrad for 'parasitism'. See John Berryman, *The Dream Songs* (New York: Farrar, Straus & Giroux, 1969) pp. 199–200. 'The Statue' is included in John Berryman, *Homage to Mistress Bradstreet and Other Poems* (London: Faber & Faber, 1959) pp. 36–7.

39. The reference is to the 'new Susannah' in the second stanza of 'Venetian Stanzas II' (*To Urania*, p. 93).

40. In addition to the works listed elsewhere in the notes, mention should be made of Dan Ungurianu's 'The Wandering Greek: Images of Antiquity in Joseph Brodsky', in *Russian Literature and the Classics*, eds P. I. Barta, D. H. J. Larmour and P. A. Miller (Amsterdam: Harvard Academic Publishers, 1996) pp. 161–91.

41. Mary Tighe's 'Psyche' has the line: 'While alabaster lamps a milky light disclose' (Canto I, l. 441), and we find the contrast, 'Without is alabaster white, / And ruby all within', in Jenyns's 'The Temple of Venus' (ll. 7–8). Compare the simile in R. W. Buchanan's 'Pygmalion the Sculptor': 'And the live blood show'd brightlier, as wine / Gleams thro' a curd-white cup of porcelain' (ll. 278–9). Poetic etymology would lead one to expect *Gala*tea to be *milky* white.

42. George Sandys, *Ovid's Metamorphosis Englished, Mythologized and Represented in Figures* (Oxford: Lichfield, 1632) Book 10, ll. 289, 334.

43. 'As the Moor grows more trusting, words turn the paper darker . . .' (*To Urania*, p. 90).

44. 'It is the cause, it is the cause, my soul; / Let me not name it to you, you chaste stars! / It is the cause. Yet I'll not shed her blood, / Nor scar that whiter skin of hers than snow, / And smooth as monumental alabaster. / Yet she must die, else she'll betray more men. / Put out the light, and then put out the light . . .' (*Othello*, V, ii, 1–7).

45. For a comment on the use of terminology (*comparé /comparant* or subject /object) in identifying parts of the simile, see Polukhina, *BPA*, p. 172, n. 1. In the opening similes of 'Galatea Encore', Brodsky opts for the 'as though' form (with its 'trace' of the Russian 'kak budto' construction) in preference to the more frequently used English alternative, 'as if'. Compare Polukhina, *BPA*, p. 152.

46. The link between mercury and thermometer is made explicit in the ninth stanza of 'Eclogue IV: Winter' (1977): 'In February, the later it is, the lower / the mercury. More time means more cold. Stars, scattered / like a smashed thermometer, turn remotest / regions of night into a strep marvel' (IX, 1–4). The poem is dedicated to Derek Walcott, who responded with his 'winter' poem, 'Forest of Europe' (*Collected Poems, 1948–1984* [New York: Farrar, Straus & Giroux, 1986] pp. 375–8).

47. See the section entitled 'Elegies to the admired dead: John Donne, T. S. Eliot, W. H. Auden', in Polukhina, *Joseph Brodsky*, pp. 72–101 (100).

48. Earlier in the same stanza, Brodsky links the actions of clouding and folding when he refers to 'the nebulous and the ironed' (*To Urania*, p. 64).

49. See, for example, 'May 24, 1980', ll. 5–6, 'Roman Elegies', vii, ll. 9–11, and 'Eclogue IV: Winter', x, 7–12 (*To Urania*, pp. 3, 67, 79). See also the reference in his prose in *LTO*, p. 430. Structurally, the metaphor of the 'bleached debris / of a glacier amid the five-lettered "never"' resembles the complex figure in 'Allenby Road' (1981): 'for no matter what size a lump / melts in your throat, the future snowballs each "no" / to coin a profile by the burning lamp' (*To Urania*, p. 31).

50. Beauty is where the 'roving' eye rests. See *Watermark*, pp. 108–9. Polukhina comments: 'The pupil, the eye in Brodsky's poetry, substitutes metaphorically for poetic vision, the imagination of the poet . . .' (*Joseph Brodsky*, p. 181).

51. The most-quoted of Brodsky's early poems – the 'black horse' poem – employs this perspective ('I think: inside our bodies we are black', *Poets of Modern Russia*, trans. Peter France [Cambridge University Press: 1982] pp. 199–200). Compare the metaphor (translated from the Russian): 'The marble is blond, / like a coal turned inside out', which Polukhina (*BPA*, 165) classes – questionably – under oxymoron.

52. Brodsky constructs the analogy in such a way as to amalgamate the declarative showing of a metaphor ('That's what') and the partial resemblance of a simile ('looks like') to achieve a resolution of the figurative dichotomy between inside and outside.

53. The transformation of statue into virgin as a temporal process involving the future can be seen as a reversal (or mirror image) of the one proposed in 'Roman Elegies': 'Setting a naked foot on the rosy marble, / the body steps toward its future' (*To Urania*, p. 64).

54. I have taken the word *Zwischenraum* from Rilke's *Sonnets to Orpheus*, in which he refers to the *Zwischenräume der Zeit* ('interstices of time') that define the mirror's essence. Rilke's mirror, like Brodsky's, is capable of absorbing or reflecting (that is, of accepting or rejecting the image), at whim. See the third sonnet in Part Two of the *Sonnets to Orpheus*. My emphasis, however, is different. Rilke uses the plural form (*Zwischenräume*) to suggest the metaphorical resemblance of the mirror to a sieve, full of holes, whereas I employ the singular noun (*Zwischenraum*) in order to signify a non-spatial 'location' for a poet who moves between languages. See my article 'Neither Nomos nor Polis: Locating the Translator', *Translation and Literature*, vol. 5 (1996) pp. 149–66, for a fuller exposition of the idea of 'living between languages'.

55. Brodsky's concept of the amalgam is discussed by Gerald Smith ('Polden' v komnate', in *BPA*, pp. 124–34 [130–2]), who concludes that it constitutes 'a version of the immortality theme, expressed with formidable opacity'. In Brodsky's poem 'Polden' v komnate', Petersburg is the city of Narcissus.

56. Joseph Brodsky, *On Grief and Reason: Essays* (New York: Farrar Straus & Giroux, 1995) pp. 223–66. The collection of essays was published in England by Hamish Hamilton in 1996 while this article was in preparation. I should like to thank Valentina Polukhina for drawing my attention to the Pygmalion and Galatea references in 'On Grief and Reason' and for her generous help in response to a number of questions that I e-mailed to her in the preparation of this article.

57. *On Grief and Reason*, p. 247. Brodsky has been anticipated, to a certain extent, in defining Pygmalion as a hunter by Beddoes's punning allusion to Galatea as 'quarry' in 'Pygmalion' (l. 96). Earlier in his essay, Brodsky writes that 'the lack of cooperation here *is* cooperation. The less you cooperate, the more you are a Galatea'. This is explained by the fact that she represents man's self-projection: 'He ascribes it to her. So by turning him down she only enhances his fantasy.' (p. 239). This aspect of Brodsky's subsequent re-working of the myth is latent in the 'five-lettered "never"' of 'Galatea Encore'.

58. In a Finnish variant of the 'animated statue' motif ('Ilmarinen's Gold and Silver Bride', Runo 37 of the *Kalevala*), Ilmarinen, the craftsman, fails to bring his female creation to life. The runo concludes with the poet Väinämöinen's warning: 'Do not . . . / Ever woo a woman of gold / Or succumb to lures of silver. / "Frozen is the gleam of gold, / Icy is the shine of silver"'. Earlier, he advises Ilmarinen to forge the statue into 'useful tools / Or . . . take it off to Russia . . .'. *The Kalevala: Epic of the Finnish People*, trans. Eino Friberg (Helsinki: Otava, 1988) pp. 290–1.

59. In this contrast, Brodsky, it might be noted, succeeds not only in breathing new life into Galatea, but also in reminding us of the antithesis between mirror and lamp that M. H. Abrams brought to prominence some 40 years ago in his critical exposition of two modes of aesthetic representation, *The Mirror and the Lamp: Romantic Theory and the Critical Tradition* (Oxford University Press, 1953).

60. The other is 'vanished'. Pygmalion's disappearance and the meta-
    morphosis announced by the word *née* (an ironic choice, since the
    word is normally employed to denote a *married* woman's former
    'maidenly' status) are the minimal requirements to ensure that Galatea
    is created – and remains – the 'virgin' identified in the final word
    of the poem. *Née* also picks up the motif of the 'naturalized' foreign
    expression initiated in the word *encore*.
61. Compare the way in which the bust is presented in 'The Bust of
    Tiberius' (*To Urania*, pp. 71–3). Ungureanu ('The Wandering Greek')
    discusses what he regards as the repeated animation of Tiberius's
    bust in the course of the poem (pp. 181–2).
62. Miller, *Versions of Pygmalion*, pp. 3–5.
63. Compare Brodsky's later, Bakhtinian interpretation of Pygmalion's
    double-bind: 'He invests her with mystery and then rushes to uncloak
    it: this rapacity is always Pygmalion's double-bind. It is as though
    the sculptor found himself puzzled by the facial expression of his
    model: she "sees" what he does not "see". So he has to climb to the
    pedestal himself, to put himself in her position' (*On Grief and Reason*,
    p. 239). As noted earlier in the article, this is what Rousseau's
    Pygmalion does: *He returns and sees the statue move and descend by
    herself from the pedestal down the same steps that he mounted up to her.*
    The poem, 'Home Burial', by Robert Frost, which Brodsky analyses
    in the essay 'On Grief and Reason' is also constructed upon the
    interplay between the ascent of the male and the descent of the
    female.
64. Galatea's virginal silence is, in part, determined by one of the con-
    straints of the genre, which requires that she remains an 'unravish'd
    bride of quietness'. This convention, however, allows oracular pro-
    nouncements such as 'Beauty is truth, truth beauty', provided they
    are once-and-for-all utterances. Thus, Keats's Grecian urn can still
    be described as a 'silent form' even when the ode's closing aes-
    thetic aphorism is attributed to it. William Morris was acknowledged
    (by George Barlow in 'The Singers of the Nineteenth Century', l.
    105) as the poet, who 'Made us feel with Galatea what the glory of
    passion ought to be / Made her break time's marble silence once,
    and then reseek eternity'. Rousseau's Galathée, in contrast, when
    she came to life, was rather too inquisitive for Brodsky, who took
    the word 'encore' out of her mouth, for use in his title, and in-
    serted a thermometer in its place.

9

'The Thought of You Is Going Away...'

Mysl' o tebe udaliaetsia, kak razzhalovannaia prisluga...

WILLEM G. WESTSTEIJN

Мысль о тебе удаляется, как разжалованная прислуга,
нет! как платформа с вывеской "Вырица" или "Тарту."
Но надвигаются лица, не знающие друг друга,
местности, нанесенные точно вчера на карту,
и заполняют вакуум. Видимо, никому из
нас не сделаться памятником. Видимо, в наших венах
недостаточно извести. "В нашей семье – волнуясь,
ты бы вставила – не было ни военных,
ни великих мыслителей". Правильно: невским струям
отраженье еще одной вещи невыносимо.
Где там матери и ее кастрюлям
уцелеть в перспективе, удлиняемой жизнью сына!
То–то же снег, этот мрамор для бедных, за неименьем тела
тает, ссылаясь на неспособность клеток –
то есть, извилин! – вспомнить, как ты хотела,
пудря щеку, выглядеть напоследок.
Остается, затылок от взгляда прикрыв руками,
бормотать на ходу "умерла, умерла", покуда
города рвут сырую сетчатку из грубой ткани,
дребезжа, как сдаваемая посуда.

(III: 142)

* * *

177

Joseph Brodsky

'The Thought of You Is Going Away Like a Maid-Servant Who Has Been Dismissed . . .'

The thought of you is going away like a maid-servant who has been dismissed, / no! like a railway platform with the signboards Vyritsa or Tartu. / But persons are approaching, who do not know each other, / places, as if they were only yesterday put on the map, / and fill up the vacuum. Apparently, for none of us / will be erected a statue. Apparently, in our veins / is not enough lime. 'In our family', you would have said, in agitation, / 'their have neither been military people, / nor great thinkers.' Right: for the streams of the Neva / the reflection of still another thing is unbearable. / Where is there a place for a mother with her pans / to remain whole in the perspective, made longer by her son's life! / That is why snow, that marble for poor people, because it has no body, / melts, hinting at the incapacity of brain cells – / that is to say windings! – to remember how you wanted, / powdering your cheeks, to look forever. / What only remains is, burying your head in your hands, / to mutter on the way 'she has died, she has died', whereas / the cities tear up the humid retina made of course fabric, /clanging, like utensils being returned.

*   *   *

'Mysl' o tebe . . .' is the last poem of the collection *Urania* (1987). In the English translation of this collection, *To Urania* (1988), to which Brodsky himself contributed with translations of his own poems, among which 'Mysl' o tebe . . .', the poem appeared under the title 'In Memoriam'. As no name is mentioned, it does not become clear, at least not from the title, who is commemorated or to whom the poem is dedicated.

In several of his books[1] Ricoeur has pointed out that in written discourse the question of reference to a context is always more or less problematic. Owing to its textuality, the text itself is 'decontextualized', although it may contain a number of features (deictics) which indicate a particular context. On the basis of these features, the reader will connect the text with its context, relate it to a situation outside the text.

One of the principal differences between a non-literary text and a literary text is that a non-literary text refers to a context which is already given (the world as it 'objectively' exists, if one may say so for simplicity's sake), whereas a literary text creates, or in any case has the possibility to create its own context. Deictics in a literary text (adverbs of time and place, personal pronouns etc.) do not refer to a situation and to persons in the actual world, but indicate their own situation. This situation, which is constructed from the linguistic material of the text, is in principle not connected with 'real' persons and 'real' time and place.

The difference on the situational level between non-literary and literary texts is closely related to the different realities both text-types represent. Whereas a non-literary text refers to the empirical, actual world, a literary text creates its own reality: a fictional world, which exists autonomously and is only secondarily connected with the real world (we may interpret features of the fictional world through the real world as we know and understand it).

The decontextualization of the literary text has as its consequence that the intratextual sender is not to be automatically identified with a 'real' sender outside the text, the empirical author. Each narrative text has its own narrator, which belongs only to that particular text. As regards poetic discourse, the empirical author is represented in the text by the speaker, who often manifests himself as the 'persona' (lyric subject, lyric 'I'). The poem generally being a monologue by the persona, the latter can be considered the main, usually only, participant of the situation. As regards this situation there are various possibilities, ranging from the presence of two participants in one spatio-temporally defined place[2] to an unspecified and not explicitly referred to persona without any spatio-temporal context.[3] Each poem has its own persona. Although a poet's personae tend to resemble each other, a poet can create various 'masks', for instance when introducing historical figures or mythological heroes as speakers. On the other hand, the mask becomes very flimsy when the poem is clearly based on autobiographical facts.

The poem 'Mysl' o tebe . . .' creates a situation which is rather usual, even conventional for a lyric poem: a speaker who addresses an addressee who is not present in the immediate surroundings of the speaker at the moment of speaking. We do not receive any information about these surroundings, so that we can say that the point of departure of the poem ('osnovnaia tochka otscheta', according to Tamara Sil'man's terminology)[4] is an un-specified place at an unspecified moment. This point of depar-ture, a fixed though unspecified point in time and place, does not change in the course of the poem. There is no interval of time and there are no events. The only real event is that a speaker addresses an absent 'you', but because of the absence of the 'you' the addressing takes place only in the mind of the speaker. The moment of addressing coincides with the point of departure of the poem. Everything which 'happens' in the poem is concen-trated in this one moment. Instead of a real plot a so-called 'lyri-cal plot' (Sil'man, 'liricheskii siuzhet', 1977; pp. 8–9) develops, which manifests itself as a succesion of thoughts, wishes, remembrances and observations of the speaker. In this lyrical plot, which is confined to the experience of the speaker, past, present and future alternate.

In the first words of the poem: 'mysl' o tebe udaliaetsia', the situation of the poem becomes clear: a speaker addresses a 'you' whose absence, according to poetic convention (and, if we take into consideration the poet's own translation, according to the title of the poem in English), is supposed. The relation between addresser and addressee, however, becomes clear only gradually, in the course of the poem: a son thinks of his mother who has (recently) died. The family relation son–mother is not explicitly indicated, but can be deduced from the text of the poem. The first hint we find in ll. 7 and 8, in which the speaker, remember-ing a statement by the female (*ty by vstavila*) addressee, quotes it in his thoughts. The statement contains the words *nasha sem'ia*. Decisive are ll. 11 and 12, in which the words *mat'* and *syn* occur in an emotional utterance (exlamation marks) of the speaker. The still more emotional l. 19, with the repeated *umerla* indicates that the mother has died.

In which way does the lyrical plot develop? It begins in the present, the speaker saying to a 'you' that the thought he has of her is gradually disappearing. To express the image of the disap-pearing thought he uses two highly different similes ('kak razzhalovannia prisluga', 'kak platforma s vyveskoi Vyritsa ili Tartu'), which are separated from each other by an emphatic '*net*!' at the beginning of the second line. The word *net* denies the first simile, which is probably based on an association the speaker has when he thinks of the 'you' and replaces it with another simile (based on another association). At the same time, *net* can be read as a denial of the statement that l. 1 contains: the thought of the 'you' does not disappear at all. In fact, the entire poem, being dedicated to the memory of the 'you', testifies to that. The third line is, in a sense, again a denial of the second one. Instead of thoughts of the you and instead of concrete images, the mind of the speaker is occupied by vague figures and nondescript places without any history. Although these lines are in the present and refer to what happens 'now' in the mind of the speaker, they can also be read in a wider perspective: the death of the 'you', the mother, has created a vacuum, which has gradually been filled up with persons and places, with which the speaker does not have any close relationship. This explains the word 'no' at the beginning of l. 3. If the poet only wanted to say that one thought was suppressed by another, he would have used the word 'i'.

In ll. 5 and 6 the speaker makes two observations which follow from the negative situation described in the first lines of the poem. He concludes that neither he himself, nor the 'you', will be granted to become a statue: the mother does not remain in the memory of the son, the latter has surrounded himself with people 'who do not know each other'. The second observation, that 'there is too little lime in our veins' anticipates the explication of the family-relation, 'our veins' suggesting a hereditary tie. As indicated already, the family-relation between the speaker and the 'you' becomes clear from the direct speech of the 'you' in l. 7.

Whereas the observation about the impossibility of becoming a statue points towards the future, in quoting the words of the mother, who has already died, the lyrical plot makes a sudden leap to the past. The son remembers what his mother said when they were still living together: there were no important people in the family. In his reaction at the remembered words of the mother the son returns to the present. The word *pravil'no* can be explained in two ways: the son agrees with his mother – it is a fact that great figures did not occur in his family. Moreover, it is rather fortunate that they did not occur: it would be unbearable for the Neva to have to reflect still more statues. The topographical designation 'nevskie strui' suggests that the city of the family of the speaker and probably the birthplace of the son and /or his mother is Petersburg.

If Petersburg refuses to accept another statue, how can the image of the mother remain intact in the memory of the son who becomes older. In ll. 10 and 11, which end with an exclamation mark, the mother–son relation becomes explicit and the image of the mother becomes somewhat more concrete. Just as she said herself, she is not a famous personality, but turns out to be 'a woman with pans', which places her in domestic surroundings. This domestic image concurs with the image of the *prisluga* in l. 1. The exclamation mark is a sign of the speaker's emotional involvement: although the thought of his mother gradually disappears, he remembers her and calls to mind not her entire image perhaps, but in any case some details (which are enough to bring her back to him). This contrast in the poem, a receding image which nevertheless, through some remembered details, comes back again and causes a strong emotion, is elaborated in the next lines. After a general statement, which contains the image of melting snow (ll. 14–15), and mention is made of the inability of brain cells to remember things (blurring of the image), the speaker turns again to the past by describing his mother who puts powder on her cheek to look 'durable'.

In the last lines the thoughts of the speaker are directed at the future, whereas at the same time something which happened in the (recent) past becomes clear: the mother is dead. The emotion becomes very strong here. The only thing left for the speaker is to mutter to himself 'she has died', while covering his head with his hands (mourning, guilt, shame that he so little remembers of his mother, shame because of the fact that he weeps [*syruiu setchatku*, l. 20]) and protecting himself from the eyes of strangers in apparently hostile (*rvut*) and noisy (*drebezzha*) cities.

In the lyrical plot, which develops in the mind of the speaker, we find some information about the two protagonists of the poem, the son and his mother. In former days the family lived in Petersburg; the son, however, has left his native city and has gone to other places. The new impressions of these places and from the people living in these places has shut out the image of his mother. The message that his mother has died (or in any case the realization that she, probably rather recently, has died) moves him deeply. His pain is all the greater, because he realizes that he could not keep the image of his mother intact and will not be able to do so in the future. His memory is, after all, rather weak and a statue has not been erected for her.

As many of the empirical facts mentioned in the poem correspond with those of Brodsky's own life (he wrote the poem approximately two years after the death of his mother, whom he, since his emigration to America, had never seen again), it is tempting and even seems to be obvious to identify the speaker in the poem with Brodsky himself and to read the poem as an autobiographical text. However, the 'decontextualization' of the literary text does not allow such an identification. Just because of the fact that the literary text creates its own context there has to be drawn a distinction between the author outside and the speaker inside the text, between the actual world and the world of the text. It is exactly this distinction that raises the literary text above the mere autobiographical and makes the strictly personal universal. In the actual world Brodsky mourned the death of his mother, in the world of the text it is 'the' son who grieves for his mother's death or, still more generally, a human being who grieves for the death of a person who is very dear to him and realizes that the memory of this person will irrevocably fade away.[5]

The actual world and the world of the text being separated from each other (both are autonomous) does not mean that they have no relation with each other. The latter cannot do without the former; the reader will always connect the world of the text with the actual world and use (his knowledge of) the actual world to interpret certain phenomena, events, relations and situations in the world of the text.

For the interpetation of 'Mysl' o tebe . . .' the most relevant aspects of the extratextual context are, of course, Brodsky's life and his other work. 'Mysl' o tebe . . .' can be read as a poem about the painful inadequacy of the memory, but is, secondarily, also a poem by Brodsky in memory of his mother. In this connection it is useful to confront the text of the poem with Brodsky's essay 'In a Room and a Half' (1985) in the collection *Less than One*,[6] in which Brodsky recalls to memory his parents and his youth in his parental home.

As mentioned above, the comparisons in the first lines of the poem might have been suggested by associations the speaker has when he thinks of his mother. In 'In a Room and a Half' Brodsky describes his mother as someone who is always mending clothes and whose task it is to clean up the apartment (when it is their turn to do so in the communal flat they are living in). 'Which meant scrubbing and washing the floors in the corridors and the kitchen, as well as cleaning the bathroom and the john' (*LTO*, p. 487). Moreover, she is an excellent cook. 'I recall her most frequently in the kitchen, in her apron, face reddened and eye-glasses a bit steamy . . .' (*LTO*, p. 456). This cleaning woman and cook is not free, she lives in 'captivity' (*LTO*, p. 479), being the 'slave' of a tyrannous regime (*LTO*, p. 479). The description can easily be connected with the negative image of a chambermaid given notice in the first line of the poem. The image of 'the mother with her pans' in l. 11 echoes the mental picture on p. 456 of *Less than One*: 'Nor shall I see the door opening (how did she do it with both her hands holding a casserole or two big pans? By lowering them onto the latch and applying their weight to it?) and her sailing in with our dinner /supper /tea /dessert.'

The comparison in l. 2, the platform with the signposts Vyritsa (the name of a place near Petersburg) and Tartu (a university city in Estonia) can also be connected with the mother on the basis of 'In a Room and a Half'. Brodsky writes that his mother was born in the Baltic states. He has in his possession a photo-graph on which she, as a young woman, is shown 'on a foot-board of a railroad carriage, demurely waving her kid-gloved hand' (*LTO*, p. 500). The thought of his mother calls up flashes in the memory about how she was: the first, rather negative image, is emphatically superseded by the second.

The images /associations in the first lines are inadequate in the sense that they only bring forward some aspects of the remem-bered person. This anticipates what Brodsky later in the poem says about the son's inability to remember his mother 'completely' and about the general inability of brain cells to remember things. In 'In a Room and a Half', written in the same year (1985) as 'Mysl' o tebe . . .', Brodsky extensively discusses memory's defi-ciency. After having quoted a number of remarks his parents would make he writes:

I hear these admonitions and instructions, but they are frag-ments, details. Memory betrays everybody, especially those whom we know best. It is an ally of oblivion, it is an ally of death. It is a fishnet with a very small catch, and with the water gone. You can't use it to reconstruct anybody, even on paper.
   What's the matter with those reputed millions of cells in our brain? (*LTO*, p. 492)

And a page further:

And one can use those prudently saved brain cells for pondering whether failures of memory are not just a mute voice of one's suspicion that we are all but strangers to one another. That our sense of autonomy is far stronger than that of unity, let alone that of causality. That a child doesn't remember his parents because he is always outbound, poised for the future. He, too, presumably, saves his brain cells for future use.   (*LTO*, p. 493)

Before these passages he compared memory to art: both do not create the entire image, but select, have a 'taste for detail' (*LTO*, p. 489).

What is said, or suggested, about memory in 'Mysl' o tebe . . .' can be seen as a continuation of Brodsky's remarks about memory in 'In a Room and a Half'. He considers memory a traitor; this can be related to the feeling of shame or guilt which is called forth by the image of l. 17 of the son who covers his head with his hands. ' . . .We are all but strangers to one another' echoes l. 3 of the poem 'ne znaiushchie drug druga' and the comparison of memory with a fishnet comes back in the last but one line of the poem, in which the retina is presented as made of a course fabric. The word *syruiu* suggests tears, which in the context of 'In a Room and a Half' acquires a special meaning. 'Tears were infrequent in our family', Brodsky writes, adding to his observation a statement of his mother: ' "Keep your tears for more grave occasions", she would tell me when I was small. And I'm afraid I've succeeded more than she wanted me to' (*LTO*, p. 480).[7] The fact that the speaker in the poem cries indicates a really very strong emotion (apart from shame or guilt another reason to hide himself from the eyes of others).

The observation in ll. 9–10: the Neva cannot bear the reflection of still another thing can also be elucidated by *Less than One*. In the essay 'A Guide to a Renamed City' Brodsky writes about the dominating role of the water (Neva) in Petersburg.

The twelve-mile-long Neva branching right in the center of the town, with its twenty-five large and small coiling canals, provides this city with such a quantity of mirrors that narcism becomes inevitable.[. . .] No wonder that sometimes this city gives the impression of an utter egoist preoccupied solely with its own appearance. It is true that in such places you pay more attention to façades than to faces; but the stone is incapable of self-procreation. The inexhaustible, maddening preoccupation of all these pilasters, colonnades, porticoes hints at the nature of this urban narcism, hints at the possibility that at least in the inanimate world water may be regarded as a condensed form of time. (*LTO*, p. 77)

In this 'urban narcism' there is no room for statues of people. 'Mysl' o tebe . . .' has to be read not only in the context of Brodsky's autobiographical writings, but also in the context of his other poetry.[8] Brodsky has written a relatively great number of 'in memoriam' poems, dedicated to famous persons, in particular poets admired by him ('Bol'shaia elegiia Dzhonu Donnu', 'Stikhi na smert' T. S. Eliota', 'York' – the last poem is dedicated to Auden), as well as to unknown people (in many of Brodsky's elegies the addressee is only referred to as 'you', in some cases, for instance in the poem 'Pamjati T.B.', we learn only the addressee's initials). Many of these poems have motifs which also occur in 'Mysl' o tebe . . .'.

Brodsky's predilection for 'in memoriam' poems has a clear relation to his main themes. In her study about Brodsky,[9] Valentina Polukhina discusses the fact that in Brodsky's work death is often associated with time and that 'in opposition to them we find faith, love, memory, poetry and language'. These latter elements together form a 'force which is able to withstand time' (*Joseph Brodsky*, p. 87).[10] That the poem can be considered a stronghold against time becomes clear from Brodsky's own statements about poetry as an important protector and defender of culture. In one of these statements he explicitly connects poetry, culture and memory:

There is no love without memory, no memory without culture, no culture without love. Therefore every poem is a fact of culture as well as an act of love and a flash of memory – and, I would add, of faith.[11]

The 'act of love' and 'flash of memory' is in 'Mysl' o tebe . . .' much more personal than in other poems of Brodsky, but in this poem too, despite memory's deficiency, it is capable of calling up the mother and erecting a 'statue' (in language) for her. The son's memory is weak, he knows that he can only evoke some details of his mother's image, including some of her utterances. This metonymical description of a person recalls some lines of the poem ' . . . i pri slove "griadushchee" iz russkogo iazyka . . .' from the collection *Chast' rechi*.

От всего человека вам остается часть
речи. Часть речи вообще. Часть речи.   (II: 415)

From the entire man remains only a part / of speech. Not more than a part of speech. A part of speech.

'Mysl' o tebe . . .', which as an in memoriam poem in two ways, is 'brought into action' against death, as a poem in itself and as a poem which raises someone from the dead,[12] contains many typical Brodskian words and motifs. Words such as *pamjatnik* (l. 6) and the directly related *mramor* (mark the sound-equivalence with 'memoriam') are relatively frequent and the same holds true for snow in its combination with death (as regards the latter motif see, for instance, the poems to commemorate John Donne and T. S. Eliot) and for that reason with time as well.[13] The image of melting snow can be read as victory over coldness/death and at the same time, also in its combination with 'mramor dlia bednych' as something which is not permanent. In this double, positive as well as negative meaning, the image excellently fits in the poem, in which, on the one hand, the poet complains about the weakness of memory and its inability to create an entire picture of a person, whereas, on the other hand, that person is called to mind and wrested from the past.

The combination of cold, death, memory, statue, we often find in Brodsky's poetry. In the last lines of 'Primechanie k prognozam pogody' these motifs are connected with the word 'vacuum' ('i gde snezhinki medlenno kruzhat'sia, kak primer / povedeniia v vakuume'); in the 'in memoriam' poem 'Pamjati Klifforda Brauna' we find apart from the motifs cold and ice that of the retina (and as a kind of fabric that of brocade). At the end of the much earlier poem 'Bol'shaiia elegiia Dzhonu Donnu' (1965) there is the image of torn fabric with a hole in it.

Ведь если можно с кем-то жизнь делить
то кто же с нами нашу смерть разделит?
Дыра в сей ткани. Всяк, кто хочет, рвет.[14]   (I: 251)

For if it is possible to share one's life with someone, / who
will share our death with us? / Holes in the entire fabric.
Anybody can tear it up.

Until now, the analysis has been particularly directed at the
semantic aspects of the poem, these being apparently more important than the formal ones. This does not mean, of course, that
formal aspects do not play a part in 'Mysl' o tebe . . .' Specific
nuances Brodsky makes, for instance, with his use of words. The
slightly archaic *razzhalovannaia* in l. 1 fits the image of the mother,
who is not integrated in Soviet society, but belongs more to the
pre-revolutionary period. The mother is introduced with direct
speech, but her words do not contain colloquial language. However, we find a colloquialism in the word *naposledok* (l. 16) that
the poet uses when he describes how the mother powders her
cheeks and which suggests the mother's own language, which is
in contrast to such high-flown words as *pamjatnik* and *mramor*.

Attention has already been paid to figurative language in the
poem. Worthy of note is the concretizing of the abstract word
mysl' in the first line, which evokes a fragmentary image of the
mother in the son's memory. Very appropriate in connection with
the faint memory and the modest public position of the dead
mother is the comparison between melting snow and marble for
the poor. There is personification through verbal forms connected
with snow (*ssylaias*, l. 15), braincells (*nesposobnost' vspomnit*, l. 15–16)
and cities (*rvut*, l. 20), which indirectly enhances the emotional
involvement of the speaker.[15] The comparison in the last line of
the poem in its structure and especially in its sound aspect (a –
a – u // a – a – u) echoes the comparison in l. 1. This return of
the last line to the first is, in its circularity, primarily a return to
a negative image. The cities tear the retina apart and are noisy
with empty bottles. In this way they drive away the image of
the mother and make the memory 'empty' (a vacuum) as regards
her.

I have already remarked that in its construction of the lyric
plot 'Mysl' o tebe . . .' is a succession of statements, observations,
quotations in direct speech, exclamations etc. These rapidly changing forms of linguistic expression, which are accompanied by
different endings of lines (sometimes an exclamation mark, sometimes an enjambment) and sentences interrupted by interpola-
tions (ll. 7–8; 15–16) can be considered an iconic sign for the way

in which the speaker in flashes of memory remembers 'fragments' of the image of his mother. This fragmentariness is underscored by the irregular metre, in which at most an anapaestic impulse can be detected. The rhyme scheme is regular (abba), but does not result in a strophic arrangement in which the four-line stanzas form thematic unities. Only the last 'stanza', in which the lyrical plot is concerned with the future, can be considered a distinct unity. The emotion reaches its climax and the poem comes to an end in a minor key. The strong emotion in l. 18, indirectly expressed by the repeated *umerla*, is enhanced by the expressive repetition of a and u sounds (a – u – a – a – u). In l. 19 the negative image is 'illustrated' by the repetition of the consonants g, r, s and t.

Notes

1. See, for instance, Paul Ricoeur, *Interpretation Theory: Discourse and the Surplus of Meaning* (Fort Worth, 1976) pp. 25–37; *Hermeneutics and the Human Science* (Cambridge, 1981) pp. 147–9.
2. An example is the poem 'S grust'iu i s nezhnost'iu' (1964), in which the lyric 'I', addressing a fellow-patient, describes an evening in what is, to all appearances, a madhouse. Generally, the lyric subject addresses an absent addressee. In 'Liubov' (1971) the lyric 'I' awakes at night ('etoi noch'iu') in his bedroom; in 'Odissei Telemakhu' (1972) the speaker (Ulysses) is on an island far from home and addresses his son who is living at home and whom he has not seen for a long time.
3. The poem 'K Uranii' does not situate the speaker in his surrondings; in 'Na vystavke Karla Veilinka' there is no reference to a speaker at all and the spatial surroundings are only suggested by the title of the poem.
4. Tamara Sil'man, *Zametki o lirike* (Leningrad: Sov. pisatel' 1977) p. 9.
5. About the 'lyrical paradox' between the strictly personal and the universal see, for instance, Juryi Levin, 'Zametki o lirike', in *Novoe literaturnoe obozrenie*, vol. 8 (1994) pp. 62–72.
6. Joseph Brodsky, *Less than One: Selected Essays* (London: Penguin, 1987), hereafter *LTO*.
7. Brodsky's 'stoicism' is discussed by David Bethea, *Joseph Brodsky and the Creation of Exile* (Princeton: Princeton University Press, 1994) pp. 21–2. It is noteworthy that in the very autobiographical poem 'Mysl' o tebe . . .' Brodsky never uses the word 'I', probably as a deliberate counter-poise to a too direct personal and emotional involvement.
8. ' . . . s kazhdym stikhotvoreniem poet rasshiriaet sferu svoego videniia, pri etom proiskhodit effekt obratnoi sviazi – novye stikhotvoreniia

brosaiut svet na starye, vidoizmeniaiut i dopolniaiut ikh, delaia nevozmozhnye ranee tolkovaniia vozmozhnymi. Tak poet mozhet uluchshit' svoi starye stikhi, nichevo u nikh ne meniaia' (Mikhail Kreps, *O poezii Iosifa Brodskogo* [Ann Arbor: Ardis, 1984] p. 23).

9. Valentina Polukhina, *Joseph Brodsky: A Poet for Our Time* (Cambridge: Cambridge University Press, 1989).
10. See also Kreps, p. 23, who calls the poem 'forma bor'by poeta so vremenem'.
11. Joseph Brodsky, 'Beyond Consolation', *New York Review of Books*, 7 February 1974, p. 14.
12. This double way of opposing death of an in memoriam poem is probably the reason that Brodsky wrote so many of them.
13. The direct identification of time and cold we find for instance in the fifth part of 'Ekloga 4-ia (zimniaia)': 'Vremja est' cholod.'
14. In his discussion of these lines Bethea remarks: 'Life is full of holes, the chief one being death' (op. cit., p. 108).
15. Metaphor and simile in Brodsky's work is extensively discussed by Valentina Polukhina in her books and articles on Brodsky. See for instance 'Grammatika metafory i khudozhestvennyj smysl', in *Poetika Brodskogo: Sbornik statei*, ed. L.V. Loseff (Tenafly, NJ: Hermitage, 1986) pp. 38–62; *Joseph Brodsky*, pp. 102–45; 'Similarity in Disparity', in *Brodsky's Poetics and Aesthetics*, ed. L. Loseff and V. Polukhina (Basingstoke: Macmillan Press, 1990) pp. 152–79.

10

'Belfast Tune'

ROBERT REID

Here's a girl from a dangerous town.
　　She crops her dark hair short
so that less of her has to frown
　　when someone gets hurt.

She folds her memories like a parachute.
　　Dropped, she collects the peat
and cooks her veggies at home: they shoot
　　here where they eat.

Ah, there's more sky in these parts than, say,
　　ground. Hence her voice's pitch,
and her stare stains your retina like a gray
　　bulb when you switch

hemispheres, and her knee-length quilt
　　skirt's cut to catch the squall.
I dream of her either loved or killed
　　because the town's too small.

　　　　　　　　　　　　　　　　　1986

　　　　　　　　　　　　　　　　　　　(III: 386)

*　　　*　　　*

PUSHKIN IN BELFAST

The Troubles in Belfast have ensured for that city, whatever else,
a form of immortality. Cities build their renown or notoriety on
various foundations, but the disasters which befall them etch

191

themselves so deeply into historical consciousness that they become forever associated with their names and are sometimes, indeed, the principal association. The siege of Derry (or Londonderry), or of Stalingrad, the fall of Rome or of Constantinople or Jericho, all these attest to the compelling and enduring symbolic fascination exerted by cities in their moments of extreme peril or destruction, when, as microcosms of global desolation, they speak to the deepest and most universal fears of mankind. The twentieth century has added several more dreadful refinements to this ancient image: Coventry, Dresden, Hiroshima, though these, it may be argued, are merely more comprehensive and devastating versions of immemorial destructions which, like that of Carthage and Jerusalem 'leave not a stone upon a stone'.

More unique to our present age, perhaps, is the ulcerating urban conflict, which, unlike the sieges of old, is fuelled from within, rather than without; the city itself becomes a battlefield between the demotic armies of its different quarters. Both sides lay claim to its territory, which has deep emotional and symbolic significance for them and in order to live in it, they may, in time, come to maintain the violence at a tolerable level (though intolerable to the outside observer) and ritualize the manifestation of conflict in idiosyncratic ways which ensure a kind of stasis or equilibrium and also that the conflict will endure. In our own times Beirut and Belfast have become the exemplars of this situation and pre-unification Berlin, too, exhibited many of the characteristics.

Brodsky's 'Belfast Tune' (1986), his only poem about Northern Ireland, must be numbered among the corpus of poetry in English inspired by the city in its title. A good deal of this corpus is, of course, home grown: the prominence of Northern Irish poetry in contemporary English literature cannot be divorced from its raw origins in the seventies as a spontaneous reaction to the outbreak of violence. But in the now nearly 30 years of the Ulster Troubles Belfast has continually attracted the attention of international poets, Russians being no exception. During the seventies and eighties Belfast was visited by many of the famous names in modern Russian poetry: Yevtushenko, Voznesensky, Okudzhava and, in 1985, by Brodsky too. The reactions of these poets to Belfast and the effect of the city on their creative work (sometimes, indeed, there was none) were various and sometimes unpredictable. Yevtushenko, for instance, produced two substantial poems, 'Safari in Ulster' and 'Pushkin in Belfast', in which, with his characteristic brand of global humanism, he contemplates the Troubles as he encountered them on a visit in the mid-seventies. Brodsky's creative reaction is by comparison more sparing, again, perhaps, characteristically so, and shows an unorthodox insight into and approach to the city he visited in 1985. This is all the more striking since we know that Brodsky was quite capable of treating the theme of the strife-torn city in more extensive terms, incorporating symptomatic realia in a manner not wholly remote from that employed by Yevtushenko: in his 1980 'Berlin Wall Tune', for instance, where the physical presence of the wall and its surroundings is clearly conveyed.

It seems important that both these poems by Brodsky, as well as the thematically broader, though stylistically similar 'Martial Law Carol' (1980), were written in English. By addressing these politically charged subjects in English Brodsky internationalizes his voice on world issues. But it is also the case that Brodsky's English in these poems, as elsewhere, takes advantage of appropriate linguistic idiosyncrasies relevant to his theme, which would not have been available (or so forcefully available) in Russian. Thus the opening line of the 'Berlin Wall Tune' evokes a variation of the American idiom (first recorded by Mark Twain) 'passing the buck' ('This is the spot where the rumpled buck / stops'). But it equally resonates with the other pecuniary sense of the word 'buck' as well as recalling the fact that Kennedy (not mentioned by name in the poem, but indelibly associated with the wall) had its sententious derivative ('the buck stops here') displayed in prominent view in his office in the White House.[1] At the same time, however, the opening of the poem is structured around 'The House the Jack Built', an English nursery poem well known in Russian translation: 'This is the house destroyed by Jack . . . this is the wall that Ivan built'. Again, (Jack) Kennedy's celebrated hostility, to the wall, and the folk memory of his 'Ich bin ein Berliner' speech are evoked without explicit reference to the man himself. This ability to exploit the deep structure of English is striking in Brodsky (though occasionally this master of linguistic acclimatization strikes a wrong note in the adopted language[2]); 'Belfast Tune', in particular, even shows evidence of sensitivity to Irish speech cadences.

As I hope my subsequent analysis of 'Belfast Tune' shows, it in no way detracts from the poem's value to locate it firmly in the generic company to which it cannot fail to belong, that of a

lyric meditation by a foreign poet inspired by a short visit to
Belfast; *mutatis mutandis*, the work invites comparison with the
literary endeavours of other visiting poets who have undergone
a similar inspirational experience in the same place and for the
same short period of time. Indeed this is one of those cases where
the inspirational parameters for (very different) poets treating the
same theme can be established with a fair degree of common
ground. If we were to attempt to sketch out a typological poetics
for a visiting poet's Belfast poem, we would have to collocate
the immediate context of the poem, the concrete experiences, with
the much broader, yet less easily definable co-text of the author's
previous attitude to and preconceptions of the city. Taking the
matter further we might say that the entire creative process is
broadly fourfold: (1) the preconception; (2) the visit; (3) the reactions to the visit; (4) the creative evocation of the visit in the
form of poetry. Each of these four moments is characterized by
the interplay of constants and variables, in both the situational
and, creative context. A preliminary reading of 'Belfast Tune'
against its thematic predecessor, Yevtushenko's 'Pushkin in Belfast',
may prove instructive in this regard as well as providing an over-
ture to the more detailed analysis of Brodsky's poem to which
the rest of this essay is devoted.

Yevtushenko came to Belfast in October 1974 in the immediate
aftermath of the fall of the power-sharing Executive and the Ulster
Workers' Council Strike, during a period when random bombings,
particularly of pubs, were a frequent occurrence. The military
presence was ubiquitous and there was no feeling that the situation
might right itself politically, nor yet, as there was in the eighties,
a settling of the violence into the more predictable ritual of counting
coup on military targets. The Cold War still provided the crude
model by which east and west related to one another; the exiled
Solzhenitsyn was a thundering voice of criticism and focus for
dissent; Yevtushenko had managed to retain his reputation as a
gadfly on the Soviet body politic, but himself stopped short of
dissidence. His globalist humanism, though at times outspoken,
never really threatened his position as official poet, and, permitted to travel widely abroad, he produced poetry with a striking
variety of national settings and themes. The Soviet Union's view
of the Ulster conflict was by now well defined, simplistic and
inevitable for the time: the Ulster problem was one of late
colonialism or imperialism, the Irish of Ulster were an oppressed

people, held in check by the brutal force of the British army.[3] From this point of view the official Soviet line as articulated by *Pravda* and *Izvestya* was broadly in sympathy with Republican opposition to the Northern status quo, and there was little or no understanding of the political position occupied by Ulster protestants in the conflict: it was simply an international one. There is plenty of evidence of this attitude as a receptional given in 'Pushkin in Belfast'. The poem opens with Yevtushenko as tourist in Belfast where the poet was perhaps 'tactless . . . / thoughtlessly bringing my camera, / my tourist's substitute for vision, / for which I got an earful of English oaths / from a pimply little soldier / who waved his gun at me'.[4] However, Yevtushenko's unorthodox position (by official Soviet standards) is to see all as victims of the conflict: he understands 'the wretched boy . . . it is not his fault' that he is caught up in 'ancient Christian enmities'. Despite this, however, Yevtushenko subscribes to the conventional outsider's view of life in Belfast as one lived ' . . . among street killings, parcel bombs, / dynamite scented air / and fear for the future', an over-statement, even in the seventies.

Brodsky visits Belfast just over 10 years later on the very brink of the Gorbachev reforms. His status both as Russian and international poet is now well established. At the same time the Northern Ireland conflict and its images of violence have become a contemporary truism. Brodsky's readership will be English-speaking – Anglo-American – and will require no elucidation of this issue; nor is there any question of an 'official' line for this Anglo-American constituency (excepting a mild transatlantic bias towards one party for historical reasons). Any writer now daring to tackle this jaded subject must do so from a perspective of estrangement and by downplaying the harsher manifestations of political and military realia. By comparison with its predecessor by Yevtushenko, Brodsky's poem touches upon the Troubles only tangentially though, as will be seen, it is a remarkably sure and sensitive touch.

The visits of the two poets had a number of (perhaps it will be felt inevitable) points in common. Both gave readings to large audiences; both met members of the academic community and local poets in Belfast; both had organized for them the statutory tour of the city, and, in Yevtushenko's case (though not Brodsky's) of a number of places outside. The poems they produced, however, reflect aspects of the Belfast experience peculiar to each visit. Yevtushenko really did arrive early for his poetry reading in time to catch the end of a lecture on Pushkin, so that the apparently surrealistic fabula of his poem is fairly closely based on a real event. Brodsky's Belfast girl may very well be loosely based on one of his guides during his visit to the city. However, the choice of these two themes among the many available, as the basis for poetic inspiration, underscores the different approaches of the two poets. With a Russian audience in mind Yevtushenko appeals to a primal situation of alienation with which his readers could easily sympathize. Confused and uneasy in a dangerous city, the Russian lyric hero comes upon a most unlikely spectacle: a biographical lecture on Pushkin which concludes at a point just before the poet's death. Pushkin offers the ultimate reassurance to the visiting Russian both as man and poet; that which is best in Russia's cultural heritage has something to say to this strife-torn city; Pushkin's death in a duel will allow the poet's mythic fate to participate symbolically in the lethal violence of the city and like the real death in the streets it waits in ambush for the unsuspecting students who file out of the lecture hall. In this way, as, of course, its title suggests, 'Pushkin in Belfast' is a profoundly Russian poem with a nationalist tint: poetry can humanize, as Yevtushenko wishes to humanize, and Russia, through its national poet has something to say to those who suffer far beyond Russian borders.

Many would now claim for Brodsky in our own time some-thing analogous to Pushkin's status; but whereas Pushkin may be considered an unlikely candidate, chiefly through his untranslatability, for the kind of universal status which may be inferred from 'Pushkin in Belfast', Brodsky, as second Pushkin, uniquely for a Russian poet, writes and publishes in a language which all sides of the conflict in Belfast can understand without interpretation. And yet, by comparison, Brodsky's poem seems superficially detached, insouciant, unwilling to tackle the grand plot head on, concerned, apparently with the lineaments of a chance personal encounter such as could have taken place in any city. For a variety of reasons I will argue that this specious im-pression is flawed; that on closer examination the poem does engage with the reality of Belfast as fully as its predecessor, but, beyond that, via its minimalist structure and use of language it defines the position of the poet in a quite different and typically Brodskyan way.

'... A DANGEROUS TOWN'

Of course Brodsky, like Yevtushenko, is aware of this fact. But he throws it away in a description: 'Here's a girl from a dangerous town.' Danger has become an essential descriptive attribute of a personal encounter and a whimsical one too. It undoubtedly impinges on Brodsky's human subject at some level. The poet, presumably, has heard her talk about living alongside this danger and yet it stubbornly refuses to show itself in any describable way. This is not Yevtushenko's soldier 'waiting with shivering spine . . . for the bullet in the back'. Instead Brodsky allows the girl's hair to make light of the trauma: 'She crops her dark her short / so that less of her has to frown / when someone gets hurt'. So we have a girl described by means of her hair which the poet wittily transforms into an eccentric psychic talisman. Nevertheless, despite this joke, there is a grim truth: someone may well get hurt and she may well have to 'frown'. Why, however, simply frown? Brodsky, it seems, is not without his expectations. He may be light on the explicit humanistic baggage of his Russian predecessor in the city, but he is not without suppositions. The poem is throughout informed by a fascination with the Other's ordinariness, the absence of emotional turmoil which the visitor might expect from a dweller in dangerous places.

This juxtaposition of ordinariness and danger does not result in the impression that the former is capable of prevailing over the latter. Not only does the sympathetic magic of the cropped hair suggest the absurdity of trying to control unforeseen perils, but the metre and lexical arrangement of the poem make their subtle contribution to the same impression. The uneven distribution of stress, the unpredictability of the metrical units, the quantitative non-correspondence of the lines, combine to produce a situation which enhances the impact of the rhyme and of those features which find themselves foregrounded as fixed points in an insecure prosodic landscape.[5] Thus, though the first line is dominated by two dactyls (girl from a / dangerous) the impact of the female presence is weakened by the fact that *girl* is only the initial syllable of a foot which it shares with the syncategorematic 'from a', whereas *dangerous* enhances its impact by being commensurate with a whole foot. In similar vein, of the two substantives in l. 1, *town* is in the privileged terminal position enhanced both by stress and expectation of rhyme, whereas *girl* enjoys none of these privileges. The abrupt iambs of the following lines stress *crops* and *dark* but not the substantive *hair* and this leads paradoxically to the impression that the abbreviation of the hair is more important than the hair itself. Indeed, the whole line is made up of monosyllables (the quintessence of shortness) though these too, on closer inspection, suggest a spondaic or even syllabic alternative for reading this line. Interestingly if the latter readings of stress are adopted, thus allowing *hair* to be stressed equally with *short*, we have the curious emergence of 'hair shirt', a notion not out of keeping with the female penance of cropping the hair: there are ghostly evocations here of the ancient practice, resurrected during the early Troubles, of tarring and feathering, but also, more pertinently, of taking injury upon oneself, a sinister undercurrent beneath the ordinariness. Furthermore, we cannot rhyme *hurt* and *short* in anything other than an Irish accent. Ironically, then, the Irish ear will detect a closer correspondence between the two rhymes *short* and *hurt* than the English.

It is the rhymes, of course, which dominate as the co-ordinates of orientation in this chaos: *town, short, frown* and *hurt* seem sufficient to carry in embryo the tragic fabula of this city and its relation to the individual who inhabits it. Hurting and frowning, violence and trauma, these are the protasis and apodosis of all human conflict, and provide the paradigm which all instances follow. The metrical structure of the two last lines of this stanza serve to enhance this dynamic relationship. The third line begins with a docked dactyl and proceeds through another dactyl and anapaest, concluding with the stressed *frown*. Such a connection, between dactyl and anapaest inevitably leaves a pyrrhic void of unstressed syllables in the line, and into this *her* is tipped, leaving a privative and a metonym (*less* and *frown* to speak of individual disempowerment. And, though *someone* in the last line receives an initial stress, it is neutralized by the semantic vagueness of this word (who is this someone?). All we know is that they *hurt*.

The first stanza establishes a tension between the ordinary and the dangerous by means of a suppressed joke: 'Do you wear your hair short so that there is less of you to shoot at?'[6] Verse enables Brodsky to put this joke a good deal more discreetly than this; indeed this part of the poem has the feel of a thought tactfully unspoken. While the juxtaposition of the humdrum and the horrific is a truism of the Northern Irish conflict (and certainly was by the time Brodsky arrived in Belfast), his interpolation of motifs of curtailment produces, in the course of the poem, a quite novel perspective on this theme.

The second stanza reflects a remarkable mixture of opposites. The reader is inducted into the realia of everyday life of the female protagonist who has only been a metonymic presence in the first stanza. In the bald retelling it would appear that the ordinary prevails here: she is a vegetarian, she cooks using the traditional Irish fuel. True, 'they shoot here where they eat' (shoot up restaurants, that is) but then her private eating, like that of many in Belfast, protects her from this danger. The simile in the first line, however, hopelessly complicates this survivalist adaptation. Memory is like a parachute, we are told. Memory, therefore, can save us when we are in free fall, that is, keep us from hitting the ground of reality too hard. What, however, are we doing when we fold up these memories: storing them for future use, or as good paratroopers, protecting ourselves from detection? This is a wonderfully polyvalent image which plays with the mnemonic propensity of Irish culture.

Parachute, however, is a double modifier: *memories* is its first subject, via simile; *dropped* is the second subject via metaphor. This second metaphorical instance is, in a sense, an opportunistic appropriation of *parachute* which exploits connotations untapped by the simile. Yet the syllepsis of the metaphor enforces a kind of discretion in the introduction of this connotation which is very much in keeping with the whole poem's project of maintaining an inferential rather than explicit approach to the underlying violence. This modifier, then, introduces the inevitably martial dimension of the word *parachute*. What is now hinted at is a paratroop drop and the subsequent peat-gathering and cooking is transformed into the survivalist precautions of an attacking bridgehead. The basic binary of any occupying military situation is thus hopelessly confounded here: military and civilian are inextricably intertwined, enmeshed in a single state of perpetual *qui vive*. That we are meant to infer such a situation is emphasized by Brodsky's play on the (probably) international proverb 'You don't shit where you eat': it is a kind of anthropological fundamental that these two basic human functions, polar opposites, should be kept apart. The *shoot/shit* correspondence is sustained by the rhymes of stanza 2 which exploit the two relevant vowels (*oo/ea* [= *i*]). Brodsky's jocular substitution of *shoot* for *shit* changes the binary to that of life and death; however, this binary unlike the former proverbial one is constantly violated in Belfast's unnatural situation.[7]

It is at this point, too, that the principle of catachresis, present in a broad sense in the unexpected purpose of the haircut in the first stanza, becomes an explicit factor in the verbal structure. The conclusion of a line marks the end of a rational protasis (short hair, parachute, shoot) which, in the following line, is immediately succeeded by an unexpected apodosis ('so that less of her has to frown'; [she is] 'dropped like a parachute'; 'where they eat'). On one level, of course, this is pure play; at a deeper one it keeps the reader at a certain degree of alertness, much as Brodsky himself must have felt in that city of which he had heard so much (I do not know anyone who has not reacted to a first visit to Belfast in this way); and, as we shall see, there is more of this to come.

The correspondence between the four rhymes in stanza 2 is very strong: they are indeed two pairs of pararhymes. More than that, the second member of each full rhyme pair is an ancephalous derivative of the first: *parachute/chute*; *peat/eat*, with a common consonantal element (*p* sacrificed in each case). The effect, one of literally stripping away, is a kind of *ostranenie*, making strange. Beneath these two significant elements of Irish setting – the timeless peat and the intrusive military presence (parachute) – lies the truth of life – the eros and thanatos of eating and shooting. These are the formal core of that of which *parachute* and *peat* are the visible matter. This is an extraordinary penetration into the nature of the Northern Irish Troubles, all the more remarkable for its being effected via formal structure and poetic artifice. But there is more to the syllabic economy than this: it focuses on a privativeness and tendency to reduction which has been present in the poem from the very beginning. Brodsky's female figure has shortened her hair to shorten her emotions, and we may also assume that she is a vegetarian and so, in this vital matter of self-nourishment, has further reduced her options, presumably, since Brodsky does not tell us, for the usual ethical reasons, which, again, we might hazard, have to do with 'frowning less' when a living thing is hurt.

For Brodsky, then, the city and its inhabitants are marked by a sort of self-inflicted reduction amounting almost to agoraphobia,

and this restrictiveness will be explored in the rest of the poem.
It is not the most obvious feature of Belfast, or indeed of Northern Irish life in general, for a visiting poet to pick up (Yevtushenko
seems unaware of it among the armoured cars and check-points
of his Belfast); yet it is a not unrealistic view of this small geographical area with a population of less than two million where
the hostility is often sustained between small ghettos of tightly
knit communities.[8] Perhaps this tightness of the setting took
Brodsky by surprise, much as Walter Scott's visitors were said to
have been taken aback by the unremarkable flatness of the country
around Abbotsford which his writings had romanticized. More
likely, Brodsky was viewing matters from a special perspective
to which his own experience lent a peculiar breadth. This possibility only emerges, however, towards the end of the poem. In
stanza 3 a more explicit, but, again, jocular explanation is offered:
there is 'too much sky' and too little ground: 'more sky than,
say, ground'. That *say* is a kind of admission that this pithy aphor-
ism is flawed: with what, after all, we are to bring the sky into
quantitative comparison, if not the ground? It is a statement of
the obvious, yet it applies here. There is not enough room down
below. But, leaving that aside, Brodsky tells us, the true parameters
by which we should measure Belfast are sky and earth, up and
down. Why, however? Has anyone ever suggested that the key
to the Ulster problem lies in some sort of proper appreciation of
its *y*-axis? Nevertheless, it is the key to one kind of perspective
and a legitimate one at that; but we will resist unlocking it awhile
and turn to something else, of equal importance, in the third
stanza.

The girl is now an insistent entity. We have moved from
observed behaviour and description to arresting confrontation:
she is now a speaking and looking presence. The voice is unusual, the stare memorable. The voice, we infer, is high. This is
established by a catachresis similar to that which operated in stanza
1, only in reverse: there her salient feature, short hair, was presented as the *cause* (or guarantor) of limited emotional response;
here another striking feature, the voice, is the unexpected effect
of the quantitative mismatch between earth and sky. In this place
there is more up than down, therefore her voice is more up than
down. It is less preposterous as mere juxtaposition than as explanation; the poet knows that it is no kind of explanation; for there
will always be, everywhere, more sky than ground. Why is a

person's voice high pitched? This is a rhetorical question and like all rhetorical questions is really an exclamation, an affirmation of the remarkable, all the more remarkable for having no explanation. While this treatment of voice suggests a strong sense of presence, that of the eyes, the *stare*, has a strong sense of absence. The reader does not grasp the significance of this at once. Both subject and modifier of this, the second simile of the poem, are profoundly mnemonic: both a bulb and a stare stain the retina when they have been switched off. The after-image on the retina is a kind of primal somatic memory. The qualitative starkness of this on/off modifier is reinforced by the enjambment which separates adjective from noun: nothing in the words *stare* or *gray* prepare the reader for the *bulb* which is round the corner. The device not merely evokes, but actually creates in the reader the epistemic disorientation and uncertainty which the Belfast context motivates. Indeed the preceding enjambment *say/ground* represents the same effect, wryly, under the guise of a creative aporia. The final enjambment – *switch/hemispheres* – is as unguessable in advance as its predecessors but far more rhetorically and conceptually ambitious. The enjambment operates across two stanzas, but the paradoxical effect of the device is to disjoin thematically the two units which it formally unites.[9]

Hemispheres is the most dramatic of all the instances of catechresis in the poem and amounts to a bathos. This cheating of the reader is all the more dramatic for its complete destruction of the lectorial chronotope: '*Here's* a girl from a dangerous town . . . There's more sky in *these parts* . . .' (my emphasis). The deictics suggest presence and, beyond that, the convention of the travelling poet making his experiential *now* available to the reader. In fact, however, 'Belfast Tune' suddenly enforces an abrupt re-assessment of perspective from the present to the past, from immediacy to reminiscence. Brodsky has switched hemispheres: this may be a mid-Atlantic composition or an American one, but it is least likely to be an Irish one. Here, then, is the significance of the aerial dimension, the *y*-axis, which informs the poet's perspective on what he is describing. For Brodsky, indeed, there is more sky than ground. His experience of the city is framed by a coming out of and return into *sky*. It is a ruthlessly honest intentionality, a laying bare of the phenomenon of the visiting poet which both limits and subjectivizes what the latter can say. A reduction of his subject by so many tropological means is one way of restoring objectivity: it seems to tell us less, but is more experientially truthful. It is a *tune* because a tune is remembered; it is (penultimate line) a *dream* because a dream is both immediate and recollected. Yet it would be wrong to conclude that Brodsky's aerial perspective alone, his valedictory moment of creative self-reflection above a vanishing Irish landscape, is solely, or even principally, responsible for the reductive imagery which informs the entire work and which intensifies in the final stanza. His effective acknowledgement of his perspectival limitation does not invalidate the hard conclusion which he reaches regarding Belfast. As far as Brodsky is concerned, there is a real correlation between the Troubles and the circumscribed nature of the setting: his heroine will be 'either loved or killed / because the town's too small'. Belfast imposes small-town alternatives, which, though unique in their extremeness, are common to many communities elsewhere (it is this more generalized aphoristic connotation which enables such an idea to function as the poem's epilogue). Brodsky hints at a kind of murderous provinciality to which he has, presumably, been already sensitized by both his Russian and American experiences. But one must conclude that the fate of the girl in the provincial town (*town*, note, although Belfast is officially a city) concerns Brodsky as much for personal, emotional reasons as for ideological ones. The poem insists that, despite everything, its theme is one of personal encounter and memory, is therefore a profoundly lyrical one, and only ideological on a secondary level. Indeed, throughout the poem, profound, often uniquely socio-political reasons make themselves felt, figuratively, tropologically, even metrically and vocalically. With what level of conscious effort on the part of the poet it is impossible for the present author to say, but they are undoubtedly there: *pitch*, for instance, strangely completes the tar-and-feather image alluded to above in connection with cropped hair. The curious *quilt*, a deliberate pararhyme with *killed* will be felt by most readers to be inappropriate to the description of a garment. In an effort to rationalize it, the reader is tempted in one direction towards *guilt* or, more plausibly, to *kilt* which is then (indeed perhaps more so when pronounced with an Irish accent) almost indistinguishable from the second rhyme *killed*.[10] Either way the semantic 'wobbliness' of the word intensifies the grim impression conveyed by the rhymes of the final stanza: [*quilt/guilt/killed*] *squall*; *killed*; *small*.

On the other hand, it may be that *quilt* in this context correlates with *loved* so that, figuratively, at least, an erotically reassuring, even life-affirming symbol, hides beneath it this dark mass of sinister connotations: thanatos and eros again conjoined.

The poem is profoundly spondaic: out of the 101 words which comprise it, five are disyllabic, five trisyllabic and the rest monosyllabic. Since the number of syllables in each line is variable and there is resistance to any regular foot pattern, the rhymes, all masculine and relatively orthodox in their correspondence, receive particular semantic emphasis, which, it is hoped, this essay has sufficiently explored. It is not merely the rhymes which find themselves emphasized under these conditions. The trisyllabics are, by their semantics and their metrical position, calculated to carry maximum emphasis in the line. Each stanza is dominated by one (in one case two) trisyllabic which acts as the thematic determinant for the entire four-line unit: *dangerous* in stanza 1; *memories/parachute* in stanza 2; *retina* in stanza 3; *hemispheres* in stanza 4. Thus isolated, their thematic coherence is at once laid bare (the stress on the initial syllable is significant as is the strong assonant tendency towards *e*): the military (*dangerous/parachute*) and the mnemonic (*memories/retina*) connected by the polyvalent *parachute* with its ambivalent symbolism in the context of danger. *Hemispheres* lies outside this quaternity but encapsulates the inherent binariness which structures the whole theme: the essential duality of human existence caught between survival and danger, earth and sky; but also, as we have observed, the 'American' poet's orientation to the Northern Ireland troubles which play themselves out in a different *hemisphere*. This is a grand metaphysical implication but, typically for this poem, and perhaps for Brodsky, it still does not exhaust the connotational potential of the word. Brodsky's attitude to his Irish girl has been whimsical throughout: he is teasing us as readers but also her. It is not by chance that this word is punningly juxtaposed with a knee-length *kilt* suggesting, therefore, *hem*, leaving the rest to emerge as a droll predicate '-*ispheres* = *is fears*' which makes its emotive contribution to the general theme and more particularly to the relationship between curtailment and anxiety established in the first stanza. And finally, since this word, though related to the sense of stanza 3 with its more psychological content, has, for effect, been pushed down into 4 where there is more explicit description of the female form, it is hard not to read *hemispheres* as in part hinting at an obvious attribute of female physicality. Again, a tropological bifurcation: one qualifier serving two subjects, one abstract, one intensely personal and physical. Such is Brodsky's modest meditation on a city which has both produced and attracted talented poets. The poem, like its heroine, remains an enigma. And, though those of us who remember his visit to the city well, may even be able to conjecture the source of its inspiration, this little detracts from the sphinx-like quality of the work. In its soaring loftiness there is both sympathy and detachment, in its structure the rawness of a ballad and in its thematic the sophistication of metaphysical verse.

Notes

1. Apparently, however, he inherited this motto from one of his predecessors in office – President Truman.
2. In 'Belfast Tune' I would put 'veggies' (v. 2, l. 3) in this category.
3. Lenin's considerable interest in the Easter Rising as a paradigmatic anti-colonial struggle helped to perpetuate this view of modern Irish history in Soviet Russia. See, for instance, A. D. Kolpakov, *Irlandiia na puti k revoliutsii 1900–18* (Moscow, 1976).
4. This and subsequent translations from 'Pushkin v Belfaste' are my own and taken from Yevgeny Yevtushenko, *V polnyi rost: Novaia kniga stikhov i poem* (Moscow, 1977) pp. 50–2.
5. Daniel Weissbort conjectures the influence of Hopkins' rhythmic experimentalism in Brodsky's English prosody and there is indeed something of the Hopkinsian sprung rhythm in these lines. Daniel Weissbort, 'Pamiati Iosifa Brodskogo', *Bostonskoie vremia* [*Russian Weekly*] 2 January 1997, p. 2.
6. Humour based on making oneself more or less of a target in relation to gunfire must be as old as the hills. It is at best a black humour, born out of genuine fear of death. How serious, though, was Francis Galton when he claimed that successful military leaders were small because smaller men make smaller targets on the battlefield?
7. Of course, as Brodsky was no doubt aware, the implications of the close assonance of these two words is deeply structured in English, reinforced in popular culture by jokes linking defecation with fear under military fire.
8. In an interview with Noel Russell during his Belfast visit Brodsky was asked for his views on the Troubles. His reply is characteristically tongue in cheek, but nevertheless germane to this aspect of the poem: 'I think I know what should be done – you want to have better aerials to receive more television, to occupy that meaningless leisure time which has been provided by unemployment. What is

there to do in the evening, except having a drink and shooting people? It would be of course desirable for the North to have some external enemy against which it could unite. Something like a Libya or Argentina. I think that could help, some new foundation that would steal people's imagination or energies from internal fighting. Some new reality.' 'Interview: Noel Russell Talks to Joseph Brodsky', *The Literary Review* (January 1986) pp. 10–12 (12).

9. Donald Davie is quite hard on the enjambments in 'Belfast Tune', pronouncing Brodsky's use of them 'coarse', 'cavalier' and, more particularly, 'violent': '. . . in none of these cases does the whirl across the line-end, with the consequent jar or thud at the first pause in the next line, mirror a corresponding violence in feeling, in what is said'. However, even allowing for figurative jars and thuds as metaphors for the dynamics of enjambment, it is not at all self-evident (or even logical) that it is a formally 'violent' device and that it therefore demands a complementary violence of content. See Donald Davie, 'The Saturated Line' (review of Brodsky's 'To Urania'), *The Times Literary Supplement*, 25–9 December 1988, p. 1415.

10. Kilt would be deeply ambiguous in the Irish context. On one level it suggests a pan-Gaelic emblem of difference from the Anglo-Saxon. On another, via the gradual incorporation of that emblem into the British army during the last century, it carries connotations of a quite different order.

11

'Darling, Tonight I Went Out Late …'*

Dorogaia, ia vyshel segodnia iz domu pozdno vecherom

SERGEY KUZNETSOV

Дорогая, я вышел сегодня из дому поздно вечером
подышать свежим воздухом, веющим с океана.
Закат догорал в партере китайским веером,
и туча клубилась, как крышка концертного фортепьяно.

Четверть века назад, ты питала пристрастье к люля и
                                                    k финикам,
рисовала тушью в блокноте, немножко пела,
развлекалась со мной, но потом сошлась с инженером-
                                                    химиком
и, судя по письмам, чудовищно поглупела.

Теперь тебя видят в церквях в провинции и метрополии
на панихидах по общим друзьям, идущих теперь сплошною
чередой; и я рад, что на свете есть расстояния более
немыслимые, чем между тобой и мною.

Не пойми меня дурно. С твоим голосом, телом, именем
ничего уже больше не связано; никто их не уничтожил,
но забыть одну жизнь человеку нужна, как минимум,
еще одна жизнь. И я эту долю прожил.

Повезло и тебе: где еще, кроме разве что фотографии,
ты пребудешь всегда без морщин, молода, весела, глумлива?

* Translated from the Russian by Ryan deFord.

Ибо время, столкнувшись с памятью, узнает о своем бесправии.
Я курю в темноте и вдыхаю гнилье отлива.

(III: 184)

*   *   *

'Darling, Tonight I went Out Late...'

Darling, tonight I went out late / to breathe the fresh air coming from the ocean. / The sunset was dying in an amphitheatre like a Chinese fan / and a cloud billowed like the lid of a concert piano. / /

A quarter century ago you had a weakness for lyulya-kabob[†] and dates, / did ink drawings in your sketchbook, sang a little, / had fun with me, then began living with a chemical engineer / and, judging by your letters, grew awfully stupid. / /

Now they often see you in church, in the provinces and in the capital, / at memorial services for our mutual friends, which nowadays happen / one after another; and I'm happy that there are in the world distances more / inconceivable than the one between you and me. / /

Don't understand me wrong. Nothing is associated with your / voice, body, name any longer; nobody destroyed them / but in order to forget one life man needs, as a minimum, / one more life. And I have lived it. / /

You're also lucky: where else, save, perhaps, photographs, / will you stay forever without wrinkles, young, cheerful, arrogant? / For Time, when it collides with Memory, learns that it has no rights. / I smoke in darkness and inhale the rot of low tide.

*   *   *

[†] A Caucasian dish of grilled spicy ground lamb. [*Ed.*]

This poem by Joseph Brodsky was originally published almost simultaneously in the journals *Kontinent* (no. 61, 1989) and *Ogonek* and since then has been reprinted several times in various collections, including *Primechaniia paporotnika* (Hylaea, 1990) and volume IV of *Sochineniia Iosifa Brodskogo* (St Petersburg, 1994). In each edition, a dedication to 'M. B.' was included.

Previously[1] I have already had occasion to discuss how by the end of the 1980s Brodsky's poetry had condensed into a complicated thematic cluster from which, if desired, one might derive a certain conception of space and time. Although in the case of a poet as difficult to systematize as Brodsky any generalization must be tentative, I will permit myself to make a few comments on this earlier analysis.

Brodsky's lyric hero moves irreversibly through space–time: from the past towards the future, from East to West (as did Brodsky himself by emigrating), to the upper layers of the atmosphere, like the hawk from 'Osennii krik iastreba' [The Hawk's Cry in Autumn] (1975), to the poles ('Poliarnyi issledovatel' [A Polar Explorer], 1978) or to the bottom of the sea ('Novyi Zhiul' Vern' [The New Jules Verne], 1976). Each movement is irreversible: it is as impossible to turn back in a spatial sense as it is to travel back in time to one's own past. One ceaselessly moves forward, making an endless flight; Brodsky develops this idea in his autobiographical essay 'Less than One' (1976), in which the metaphysical flight appears in the form of leaving school, the abandonment of contacts with the political system, separation from a lover, and departure from one's native country. Another result of this ceaseless and irreversible movement appears to be the 'losses' which accompany Brodsky's hero along his path: 'the one who lost a limb, a girlfriend, a soul / is a product of evolution'.

The termination point of this movement appears as a boundary: a peninsula, the corner of a table, a dead-end, a cone, the horizon, and so on.

It is also necessary to point out that in Brodsky's poetry it is possible to conditionally delineate two forms of time: continuous time or time the destroyer, and pure time – unembellished duration, in which the past and the future are fused together, engulfing the present and the 'warm body' of the human who is located there. Brodsky associates this pure time, which is close to the traditional conception of eternity, with the ocean, emptiness, the Cosmos, cold, death, uniformity, absence of sensation,

and so forth.[2] It is precisely that time which begins beyond the
boundaries of space and 'normal' linear time:

> Consisting of love, filthy dreams, fear of death, and dead flesh,
> sensing the fragility of its bones and the vulnerability of its
> groin,
> a body, by the ocean, serves as space's semen-percolating
> foreskin; making his cheekbone silvery with a tear,
> man is his own end
> and he juts out into Time.
>
> ('Lullaby of Cape Cod', 1975)

By the beginning of the 1980s, Brodsky seems to falter at this
boundary between space and pure time, peering into it. In a certain sense for the poet, who is always gazing into the 'dozing
forest of eternity',[3] this is the only point at which he can exist.
The model described above was in many ways for Brodsky
not just poetical or ethical, but was also, if it is possible to make
such a generalization, a guide for existence, the framework of
which governed his perception of the events in his own life, and
which, possibly, he employed in decision-making. It is not by
chance that in numerous interviews given in 1987–9, in response
to the question of whether he planned to return to Russia, Brodsky
readily expounded upon his conception of irreversible movement
as it applied to his own life. Here is just one of an almost infinite number of similar examples:

> I am not a pendulum, Lyuba. To swing one's self back-and-
> forth . . . I don't think I would ever do that. It's just that a person
> moves in only one direction. And only AWAY. Away from a place,
> away from that thought which has occurred, away from one's
> self. It's impossible to enter the same river twice. And you can't
> step twice on the same pavement. It has changed with each new
> wave of cars. I've often joked that it still makes sense for a criminal
> to return to the scene of the crime, but to return to a place of
> love is completely senseless. Nothing is buried there except for the
> proverbial hatchet. [. . .] either through my physical motion, or
> just with the passage of time – you become more and more an
> autonomous body, you become a capsule, released towards an
> unknown destination. For a certain amount of time, the force of
> gravity is still active, but at some point you pass beyond a certain
> boundary and a different system of gravity arises – on the outside.[4]

Thus in 1989, when his poem 'Darling, Tonight I Went Out Late . . .' was written, Brodsky was in exactly the same position as an astronaut who has passed beyond a certain limit and feels a different system of gravity.

In a sense this poem exists, as does any, at the intersection of several lines or planes which form different texts for the author. It is exactly as such a junction of thought that this article attempts to examine 'Darling, Tonight I Went Out Late . . .'.

The first thematic line, which is immediately apparent to anyone who is familiar with Brodsky's works, is the cycle of poems dedicated to M.B., the poet's lover, and the mother of his son. It is known that Brodsky gathered the numerous poems dedicated to her in the collection *Novye stansy k Avguste* [New Stanzas to Augusta] placing the poems almost exactly in chronological order. Thanks to the organization of that collection, each additional poem dedicated to M.B. seems like a distinct 'continuation' of *Novye stansy k Avguste*.[5] One almost wants to clip it from the journal in order to include it with the others in the book. In this sense, 'Darling, Tonight I Went Out Late . . .' has a unique status – it is absolutely the *last* poem dedicated to M.B., completing the cycle, and in effect making its continuation impossible.

Admittedly, many of the previous verses dedicated to M.B. were also written as 'last poems':

This is the end of our
perspective. Pity it's not longer.
Further there are some amazing wonders
of time, of superfluous days,
of races toward the finish in blinkers
of cities, and so forth;
of superfluous words, none of which is about you.

('Strophes', 1978)

We part for good, my little friend.
Draw a simple circle on piece of paper.
It will be I: nothing inside.
Look at it – then erase.

('It Is Not that One's Muse Keeps Her
Mouth Shut . . .', 1980)

Note that *New Stanzas to Augusta* concludes pathetically with 'I was just that which you touched with your palm . . .', an obvious paraphrase of 'The Prophet', one of Brodsky's favorite works by Pushkin.[6] None the less, each of these poems was followed by more and more new ones – for which, in my opinion, isues of genre were primarily responsible.

In a similar way to many of the other poems dedicated to M.B., both the works cited above belong to the popular genre of 'a farewell to a far-away lover'. The classical text of this genre is John Donne's poem 'A Valediction: forbidding Mourning', which was more than familiar to Brodsky, who had translated it into Russian in 1970:

> But we by a love, so much refined,
>   That our selves know not what it is,
> Inter-assured of the mind,
>   Care less, eyes, lips, and hands to miss.

> Our two souls therefore, which are one,
>   Though I must go, endure not yet
> A breach, but an expansion,
>   Like gold to aery thinness beat.

Almost as if he were following Donne's metaphor proving the impossibility of separation, Brodsky stretched out his separation from M.B. over more than 10 years, as if he was trying, like Donne, to prove the inseparability of their souls. Physical separation became a proof of the powers of love – an idea, which Brodsky gave tribute to not just in *New Stanzas to Augusta* (see, for example, 'Singing without Music'). For a time, while the intonation remained that of a lover bidding farewell to his partner, the cycle had to continue. It could only be concluded by the death of one of the romance's heroes or of the emotion which connected them. 'Darling, Tonight I Went Out Late . . .' is dedicated to reflections on the realization of the latter.

When the topic is a poem which completes a cycle of works, one expects to find within it a 'summary' of the motifs which were developed by the author throughout the cycle. These expectations are even more natural because the 'network of motifs' within Brodsky's poetry is uncommonly dense. However, let us see whether or not that expectation holds here.

Note that the motifs previously developed by Brodsky (*shore, evening, separation, photographs, memory*, etc.) are concentrated in the odd stanzas of the poem, while the second and fourth stanzas practically withdraw from the network of motifs found in his preceding works. We will return to the even stanzas later but will first concentrate on the first, third and fifth stanzas, and examine the degree to which the motifs developed within them are characteristic of the cycle of poems dedicated to 'M.B.'

The very first word of the poem, 'darling', is Brodsky's frequent address for a girlfriend / lover (not just M.B.) and is found throughout his work, from his earliest poems ('Letter to A.D.', 1962) to other verses which were also written in 1989 ('The bees have not flown away and the rider has not galloped away . . .'). Of the poems included in *New Stanzas to Augusta* this address is found only in 'Strophes', if one disregards the masculine adjective in 'From Nowhere with Love Umpteenth of Marchember . . .': 'From nowhere with love umpteenth of marchember darling honorable dearest . . .'.[7]

The time and place (evening and the shore of the ocean) are linked to the history of the relationship between the author and his lover (their life in Kellomäki/Komarovo and the Crimea), but they are also a favorite topos of Brodsky, comprising as it were a dual border, between water and dry-land and between day and night. In this sense, the ocean is a visible symbol of time:

I was always adhered to the idea that God is time, or at least His spirit is. Perhaps this idea was even of my own manufacture, but now I don't remember. In any case, I always thought that if the Spirit of God moved upon the face of water, the water was bound to reflect it. Hence my sentiment for water, for its folds, wrinkles, and ripples, and – as I am a Northerner – for its grayness. I simply think that water is the image of time, and every New Year's Eve, in somewhat pagan fashion, I try to find myself near water, preferably near a sea or an ocean, to watch the emergence of a new helping, a new cupful of time from it. I am not looking for a naked maiden riding on a shell; I am looking for either a cloud or the crest of a wave hitting the shore at midnight. That, to me, is time coming out of water[.][8]

In addition, in Brodsky's love poems the ocean is often conceived
of as a barrier, separating the addressee from the author:

> three scores lands away, a body tossed
> with which for a long time
> there was nothing in common, save for
> the ocean's bottom and the habit
> of nakedness.

('Lullaby of Cape Cod')

or Russia from America:

> Like a wine glass
> leaving an imprint
> on the tablecloth of the ocean
> which is not to be outthundered,
> the luminary moved to another
> hemisphere where
> only a fish in water is left alone.

('Strophes', 1978)

Here, as is evident, the time coincides as well – late evening,
sunset, dusk.

One can see that all the motifs developed in the initial lines
are, in general, quite characteristic of Brodsky, and are not strictly
connected with *New Stanzas to Augusta*. This can also be said of
his characteristic linkage of the motifs of *separation* and *death*.

> Now they often see you in church, in the provinces and in
>   the capital,
> at memorial services for our mutual friends, which nowadays
>   happen
> one after another; and I'm happy that there are in the world
>   distances more
> inconceivable than the one between you and me.

Brodsky used similar constructions earlier, in which death stood
for the continuation of separation. However, unlike the cases listed
above, the poem which is being examined here introduces a third

party, as if in this way breaking the thread stretching from the poet to his lover. The death of another cannot be evenly shared between two people, it can only be divided among three. By comparing the lovers' separation to their death, Brodsky makes it absolute; through juxtaposition with the death of other people (common friends), he lessens its significance. In the face of separation from a lover it is possible to speak of her death or of one's own; but with the death of another, talk about one's own suffering becomes 'metaphysical swinishness'.[9]

The distance between the poet and his lover was always so incomprehensible for Brodsky that he was forced to flee to a third, cosmic entity (a UFO in 'Strophes', a star in 'Singing without Music', the sun in 'Lullaby of Cape Cod') in order to illustrate the scale of this distance. Now something even more incomprehensible has occurred – and separation stops being a prototype of death, and becomes the object of ironic estrangement. With this stanza, it is as though Brodsky excuses himself for the cosmic metaphor 'I was only that which you touched with your palm . . .'.

The theme of *photographs as memory* introduced in the last stanza was also employed by Brodsky many times before:

> There are places
> where nothing changes. These are
> substitutes for memory, the acid triumph of fixing solution.

Occasionally Brodsky himself is inclined to explain the link between the themes of the photograph and memory that develop from biographical factors:

> Maybe it's because you are a son of the photographer and your memory simply develops a film. Shot with your own two eyes almost forty years ago. That's why you couldn't wink back then [. . .][10]

Photography is also connected with Brodsky's perceptions of water:

> I love water more than anything in the whole world. My father was a professional photographer and the greater part of his life was connected with maritime journals, and I loved it so

much when water appeared in developed pictures [. . .] I saw
water not only with my own eyes, but also with his eyes, and
even through the eye of the camera.[11]

Once again, poetry is created in the form of something which is
sent out from the shoreline: 'I smoke in darkness and inhale the
rot of low tide'.
Vasily Telezhinsky once pointed out that this line seemed to
comprise two citations from Brodsky's own work – one from 'I
Always Kept Saying that Fate is a Gamble . . .' ('I sit in darkness . . .')
and one from 'Flight from Byzantium' ('[I]nhaling the smell of
rotting seaweed'). Along with the latter quotation one could cite
'and the strong smell of seaweed from East' ('Albert Frolov: From
the School Anthology').
To summarize, it could be said that really the only poem from
the 'to M.B.' cycle with a detectable connection to 'Darling, Tonight
I Went Out Late . . .' is 'Strophes' of 1978. This is not accidental:
it is precisely in 'Strophes' that a new level for contemplating
the relationship with M.B. became evident: there was a transition from love to recollections. Most revealing is the development of the metaphor which originally was sketched as early as
1967 in a previous poem with the same title, 'Strophes' (stanzas
4 and 5):

The closer the union
the darker the break-up.
Neither a long shot nor a close-up,
will prevent the fade-out.
There's no longer any point
to our firmness. What is appreciated –
is the shard's talent
for living the life of a vessel.

So fill yourself with wine.
Be emptied to the bottom.
We will share only the volume
but not the strength of the wine.
And I have not completely perished,
even if from now on
it will be impossible to see [in us] common features
except jagged scars.

Eleven years later, the 'jagged scars' have already been erased:
stanzas 4 and 5 of the 'new' 'Strophes':

> Everything that we used to call personal,
> that we tried to preserve, [even] sinning,
> time considers superfluous and
> grinds it away like surf
> grinds pebbles – now caressing,
> now chiselling –
> to come up finally with a Cycladic
> thing devoid of facial features.
>
> Ah, the smaller the surface
> the more modest the hope
> that it will arouse impeccable loyalty
> to itself.
> Perhaps, in general, the disapperance of
> a body from sight
> is the revenge of the landscape
> on farsightedness.

After eleven more years, this process had come to its conclusion:
the author's complete estrangement from his recollections had
occurred, they had lost their emotional significance:

> A quarter century ago you had a weakness for lyulya-kabob
> and dates,
> did ink drawings in your sketchbook, sang a little,
> had fun with me, then began living with a chemical
> engineer
> and, judging by your letters, grew awfully stupid.

The last line, of course, sounds almost insulting. This, however,
is not the first time that Brodsky has permitted himself to use
sharp expressions with his lover – it is sufficient to recall the
passage: 'you too were married to a whore. We have quite a few
things in common...' in 'The Bust of Tiberius'. Even so, the calm-
ness of tone and emphasis on distance ('judging by your letters')
clearly distinguish this line from the others. Recalling the juxtaposition of written texts with photography, which is especially
apparent in 'A Polar Explorer', one could say that the 'letters' of

the second stanza, as witnesses to the changes which the heroine has undergone, seem to create a contrasting pair to the 'photographs' of the fifth stanza, the faded memories.
    Irreversible movement has carried Brodsky far away: his past
life has already ceased to invoke suffering, sadness or nostalgia.
'Darling, Tonight I Went Out Late . . .' is a 'farewell' uttered by a
person who has nearly forgotten the woman to whom the words
of parting are addressed. It is for this reason that the poem contains almost none of the 'exclusive' motifs which characterize *New
Stanzas to Augusta*.
    The works of the period 1988–90 form another, 'horizontal',
plane for examining this poem. The number of thematic links is
not very large, yet they are even more essential for gaining an
understanding. The second to last line ('For Time, when it collides with Memory, learns that it has no rights') recalls the poem
'Elegy', which was published as part of the same selection as the
poem analysed here, and its theme of memory vanquishing reality. 'Elegy', in turn, corresponds to the 'Elegy' of 1978, which
was dedicated to M.B. ('Even now when I recall your voice . . .').[12]
    However, in this context the fourth stanza is the most important:

Don't understand me wrong. Nothing is associated with
                                                      your
voice, body, name any longer; nobody destroyed them
but in order to forget one life man needs, as a minimum,
one more life. And I have lived it.

A year earlier, the idea of 'one more life' had been elaborated in
a work with the symptomatic title 'New Life'; a poem which, at
first glance, presents a post-apocalyptic vision. Note that the cycle
of poems entitled 'Centaurs', which was published in the same
selection as 'New Life', was also dedicated to life after a catastrophe, and to the mutations which accompany it. However, similar
motifs are seen in Brodsky's earlier works; for example, in the
finale of 'The Bust of Tiberius'. Valentina Polukhina is correct in
writing that Brodsky's work exhibits a 'consistent theme of after
the end of love, after the end of life in Russia, after the end of
Christianity';[13] the theme of 'a new life after catastrophe' could
of course be added to this list. In a certain sense, all of these
'afters' are in some way equivalent: 'after Russia' is also 'after
love', and 'after love' is *post aetatem nostram*. In this sense, the

'war' which is 'finished', evokes the memory, not of 'Lines on the Winter Campaign' and not even 'Less than One' or 'The Spoils of War', but of 'The War in the Cypris' Refuge', one of the poems which chronologically border *New Stanzas to Augusta*, and also 'A Polar Explorer', written on M.B.'s birthday[14] (in both cases Brodsky, who often did not even place the year of composition beneath his poems, indicated the precise month and day). Let us recall that Cypris is one of the names of Aphrodite:

> Death appears in the form of a bullet from
> magnolia groves, in pairs.
> An explosion looks like a temporary palm tree
> swaying in the breeze.
>
> (II: 335)

Thus the 'catastrophe' turns out to be not just 'war' or even some sort of global 'end of the world', so much as an event in the personal life of the author: 'after all, a catastrophe is that after which it is difficult not to change' ('Centaurs').

Returning to the poem 'New Life', we should note several additional motifs that correspond to those of 'Darling, Tonight I Went Out Late . . .', such as *dusk* and *photographs*.

> Twilight in a new life. [. . .]
> And there is already enough gloss in your features to
> scribble 'greetings!' on their other side and affix a stamp.

Here photography and letters become fused in the form of the postcard, preserving at the same time all connotations of dying, characteristic of 'Polar Explorer'.

Paradoxically, it can be seen that despite attempts to find roots for the poem discussed here in texts of 1988 and 1989, we are confronted by the close ties of the poetry of this period to the poems dedicated to M.B. which were *not* included in *New Stanzas to Augusta* and in particular to 'The War in the Cypris' Refuge'.

Considering Brodsky's previously noted ability to conceptualize his own life, constantly reinterpreting it in fairly complex categories, it can be proposed that the 'new life' is simply a name for a new period in his own biography. Because of this, everything below is largely only a hypothesis, which is in some ways risky and possibly not ethically irreproachable. It is a hypothesis or an attempt to understand what the period 1987–9 meant for Brodsky. As everyone knows, in 1987 Brodsky received the Nobel Prize, which is considered to be the highest level of societal recognition for a literary figure. Although Brodsky seemingly experienced mostly irritation as a result of his fame, and especially due to the occurrences which accompanied it, perhaps at certain times he too was not indifferent to this aspect of a poet's life. In 1995 at a conference in St Petersburg dedicated to Brodsky, one of the poet's old friends related that, in his childhood, Brodsky, like many others, was impressed by a Soviet film of the Stalinist era about the turn-of-the-century geographer and explorer of Central Asia, Przhevalsky. In the film's culminating scene, Przhevalsky descends an enormous staircase while all the people below greet him. As Rein further related, in the 1990s, he and Brodsky happened to be in a museum where, among other things, a portait of Przhevalsky hung. 'Do you remember that staircase?' Brodsky asked, 'that's where it all began'.

Of course, the receiving of the Nobel Prize involved (at least for Brodsky's friends and admirers) that same staircase, along which the poet went accompanied by the grateful applause of future generations and the rustle of international fame. That same year, 1987, seemed to close a certain very long period in Brodsky's life, the more so because at that time the publication of his poems in Russia began and many old friends appeared in New York. It can be said that 1987–9 were the years of triumphant recognition of Brodsky as a poet, a recognition that assumed a mass nature and was for that reason especially unpleasant for Brodsky.

However, this is not all that was of importance. In the journal *Kontinent*, no. 62 (the issue immediately following the one which contained the poem analysed here), an interview was printed in which Brodsky answered a question about the line from 'Fin-de-siècle', 'The century will end soon but I sooner . . .':

Well, that's completely natural . . . It's not some sort of 'achievement' on my part, but . . . how to put it? . . . an 'achievement' of chronology itself. That's to say, of course, the century will end in eleven years, and I, it seems, will not survive those eleven years. That's it. I'm 49, I've had three heart attacks and two heart operations . . . That's why I've got certain reasons to suppose that I won't live that long.[15]

In the same way, the end of the 1980s became a transition period for Brodsky. It was if he had been recognized as the victor, but even so, he had been warned that he did not have much time left. Judging by his interviews and the quality of his essays, he understood this well.[16] The question of 'existence in the face of death', which so occupied Kierkegaard and Shestov, finally ceased being theoretical for Brodsky.

Similarly, the presence of Brodsky's lyrical subject at the border between existence and non-existence, at the termination point of irreversible movement, was perceived by Brodsky as the reality of his own life. The metaphor which he was working out over the duration of the last 10 years of his life materialized and at the same time demonstrated its exhaustion:

Having sampled
two oceans and two continents, I
feel almost the same as the globe does.
That is, it's the end. Beyond this only stretch
stars. And they shine.

('Lullaby of Cape Cod', 1975)

I propose that in 1988–9 Brodsky attempted to find a certain different 'beyond', and that these attempts can be traced in his poetry. And if in 'New Life' 'beyond' recalls Brodsky's 'pure time' (dusk, empty niches for statues, a steady voice, and so on), then in 'Darling, Tonight I Went Out Late ...' another way is identified.

That is, the conception of a life's journey, which was described at the beginning of this article, for all of its singularity, dates back to the old romantic scheme which was developed by Brodsky, beginning with his earliest works. It is only a slight exaggeration to say that Brodsky tried for 30 years to go beyond the bounds of this scheme (one of the most important steps was in fact the identification of eternity with monotonic and 'gray' pure time). None the less, the situation of a lonely poet, pining for his distant lover, flawlessly expressed in *New Stanzas to Augusta* was a logical continuation of this scheme.

In much the same way as in 'Darling, tonight I went out late ...' the parting occurs not so much with M.B. as with that posture of the romantic poet which Brodsky had perfected for a quarter of a century. It is the conclusion not just of an existence, but of a genre.

It's no coincidence that in a preface which was written a little later for a collection of verse by Evgeny Rein, Brodsky expresses the wish to visit Rein in the possible heaven of a shoreline, in order 'to place before him a pen and a sheet of paper and leave him for a while, preferably a long time, alone. For inspiration I would leave something nearby on the table [. . .] something *without ambition, and written, to all appearances, unhurriedly, over a long period of time*'[17] [my italics – S. K.]. Essentially, in many ways this is a retreat towards the circumstances of a 'private individual, who prefers privacy for his entire life to any societal role'.[18] The poet, as Brodsky said in his youth, must 'barge through like a tank', but the private individual should do none of this: he can write poems (in Brodsky's case in his own style, as before), fall in love, begin a new family and have children. Life's events have already ceased to be a stimulus for the writing of poetry: the private individual no longer imagines himself above all as the bearer of the poetic function or in the role of the romantic poet. In this sense 'Darling, Tonight I Went Out Late . . .' more than most of Brodsky's poems remains not only a 'linguistic event', but also a witness to the internal transitions which the author has experienced.

What is surprising is that the decision to conduct one's self 'unhurriedly, over a long period of time' came to Brodsky at the moment when he already understood well that he only had a short time left. This was not like Tolstoy, who renounced his creative work in favour of social activism, or Salinger, who chose seclusion, but more like Pushkin (with whom Brodsky has been so stubbornly compared), who broadened himself over his last years as a historian, playwright and prose writer. And so did Brodsky, gradually departing from that which he had been doing all his life, largely moving on to translations, prose and political and cultural projects (like his proposal for the establishment of a Russian–Italian academy).

The last few years of Brodsky's life are a lesson in dignity rare for a writer of his stature. It was as if, without informing anyone, he decided to cease being a 'great poet', although that was the posthumous mask which everyone, including his friends and the press, placed on him. Brodsky himself had enough taste to bring his life's strategy to its logical conclusion, to a solitary death at dusk, on a cape protuding into the sea.[19]

Notes

1. See also: S. Kuznetsov, 'Iosif Brodskii: popytka analiza' [Iosif Brodskii: An Attempt at Analysis], 1993, unpublished. Revised fragments of this work were published in the form of separate articles (S. Iu. Kuznetsov, 'Osip Mandel'shtam i Iosif Brodskii. Motivy pustoty i molchaniia' [Osip Mandelshtam and Iosif Brodskii: Motifs of Emptiness and Silence] in *Osip Mandel'shtam. K 100-letiiu so dnia rozhdeniia Poetika i tekstologiia* [Osip Mandelshtam: On the Occasion of His Centenary: Poetics and Textology], (Moscow: Sovet po istorii mirovoi kultury, Komissiia po kompleksnomu izucheniiu khudozhestvennogo tvorchestva, Mandelshtamovskoe obshchestvo, 1991) pp. 33–6; S. Kuznetsov, 'Iosif Brodskii. Poetika i estetika' [Iosif Brodskii: Poetics and Aesthetics], *Diapazon*, no. 1 (1994); S. Kuznetsov, 'Iosif Brodskii telo v prostranstve' [Iosif Brodskii: A Body in Space], *Nachalo* (IMLI, 1995) pp. 186–207; S. Iu. Kuznetsov 'Raspadaiushchaiasia amalgama' [Disintegrating Amalgam], *Voprosy literatury*, (1997) pp. 24–48; and also were presented as papers. The text of the first four chapters of this book can be found in their entirety on-line on the World Wide Web at: http://www.sharat.co.il/krok/brodsky
2. For a discussion and modification of this conception see V. Kulle, *Russian Literature*, vol. XXXVII (1995) nos 2–3, and also S. Kuznetsov's review of this special edition of *Russian Literature* in *Novoe literaturnoe obozrenie* (1997), no. 23, pp. 408–12.
3. I. Brodskii, 'O Marine Tsvetaevoi: Poet i proza' [On Marina Tsvetaeva: A Poet and Prose], *Brodskii o Tsvetaevoi* (Moscow: Nezavisimaia Gazeta, 1997) p. 56.
4. I. Brodskii, 'Interviu s Liubov'iu Arkus' [Interview with Liubov' Arkus], *Seans*, no. 1 (1988) pp. 44–7.
5. Here and later *New Stanzas to Augusta* refers to the collection of poems dedicated to M.B. and not to Brodsky's poem of 1964 which bears the same name.
6. For more information see S. Kuznetsov, 'Pushkinskie konteksty v poezii Iosifa Brodskogo', [Pushkinian Contexts in Iosif Brodskii's Poetry] in *Chetvertyi pushkinskii kollokvium. Materialy* [The Proceedings of the Fourth Pushkin Colloquium] (Budapest: in press).
7. By the way, 'dearest' (*milaia*) as a form of address had a distinctly ironic quality for Brodsky. Cf. Marianna Volkova's memoirs: 'They say that Joseph responded to a woman acquaintance, who had called after a long interval and who had gone into explanations and excuses for her long absence, like this: "Thank you, dearest!" That had the meaning of thank you for not bothering me.' M. Volkova, 'Photographing Brodsky' in M. Volkova and S. Volkov, *Brodskii v N'iu-Iorke* (New York: Word, 1990) p. 6.
8. Joseph Brodsky, *Watermark* (New York: Farrar, Straus & Giroux, 1992) pp. 42–3.
9. **I.B.**   When you are dealing with a drama and its hero, you always have to try to understand how it was for him, and not how it is for yourself. Often a poet writes verses about the death of someone

and sets forth his own *Weltschmertz*. He feels sorry for himself. He very quickly loses sight of the person who is no more, and if he sheds any tears, then usually these tears are due to his sense that he is doomed to the same fate.
It's all just in such bad taste, not even bad taste, but swineshness, in a, well . . .
P.V. . . . metaphysical sense.
I.B. Well, yes.
'Beseda Iosifa Brodskogo s Petrom Vailem', Iosif Brodskii, *Rozhdestvenskie stikhi* (Moskva: Nezavisimaia gazeta, 1996) p. 61.
10. Joseph Brodsky, 'In a Room and a Half', in *Less than One: Selected Essays* (London: Penguin, 1987) p. 465.
11. Joseph Brodsky, interview for *The Voice of America* (1987).
12. The first to notice the similarities between the two 'Elegies' (Brodsky wrote six poems with this title in all) was V. V. Ivanov at the 1991 Moscow Mandelshtam Conference.
13. V. Polukhina, *Brodskii glazami sovremennikov* (St Petersburg: Zvezda, 1997) p. 42.
14. Besides which, in *Uraniia* 'The War in the Cypris' Refuge' comes directly before 'Strophes', which, of course, could be a coincidence.
15. 'Nikakoi melodramy. Beseda s I. Brodskim' [No melodrama: A Conversation with I. Brodskii], *Iosif Brodskii razmerom podlinnika* (Tallin, 1990) p. 126.
16. For more information on the development in Brodsky's work of the theme of his own 'corporal feebleness', see S. Kuznetsov, 'Iosif Brodskii: telo v prostranstve' [Joseph Brodsky: A Body in Space], *Nachalo* (IMLI, 1995) p. 186.
17. I. Brodskii, 'Tragicheskii elegik. O poezii Evgeniia Reina' [A Tragic Elegiac Poet: On Evgeny Rein's Poetry], *Znamia*, no. 7 (1991) p. 182.
18. Joseph Brodsky, 'Nobel Prize Acceptance Speech'.
19. Brodsky also had enough taste to not leave 'Darling, Tonight I Went Out Late . . .' as the *last* poem dedicated to M.B.: four years later, on 25 December 1993, he placed her initials above one of his Christmas verses.

12

'On the Centenary of Anna Akhmatova'*

Na stoletie Anny Akhmatovoi

LEV LOSEFF

Страницу и огонь, зерно и жернова,
секиры острие и усеченный волос –
Бог сохраняет все; особенно – слова
прощенья и любви, как собственный свой голос.

В них бьется рваный пульс, в них слышен костный хруст,
и заступ в них стучит; ровны н глуховаты,
затем, что жизнь – одна, они из смертных уст
звучат отчетливей, чем из надмирной ваты.

Великая душа, поклон через моря
за то, что их нашла, – тебе и части тленной,
что спит в родной земле, тебе благодаря
обретшей речи дар в глухонемой вселенной.

1989
(III: 178)

* * *

'On the Centenary of Anna Akhmatova'

A page and fire, grain and millstones, / the cutting edge of a poleaxe and a cut-off hair – / God preserves everything; especially words / of forgiveness and love, / as his own voice. //

* Translated from the Russian by the author and Barry Scherr.

In them [the words] there beats a lacerated pulse, in them can be heard a crunch of bones, / and a [gravedigger's] spade in them pounds; flat and somewhat muffled, / since one has only one life, from mortal lips they / sound more clearly than from the cotton wool above this world. / /

Great soul, greetings [*literally*: a bow] from across the seas / for finding them, – to you and to the decayable part of you / which sleeps in [its] native land, [that] thanks to you / acquired the gift of speech amidst a deaf-mute universe.[1]

*   *   *

INTRODUCTION: ON THE CREATIVE HISTORY OF THE POEM

I once came across a rough drawing by Brodsky among my papers. It was sketched, I believe, in the late sixties, in any case before 1971, when I visited Akhmatova's grave in Komarovo for the first time. In fact it was done to give me an idea of how the grave site looked. The conversation was about replacing the temporary wooden cross with a permanent monument that included an iron cross made by Vsevolod Smirnov, a sculptor from Pskov. Brodsky did not like the monument at all: he found its allegory tasteless. The 'birdie', as he called the thing on the crossbar, struck him as especially vulgar. Presumably, it was an allusion to the 'prison dove' from the epilogue of 'Requiem', while a piece of masonry nearby, with a small fake window in it, was to illustrate lines from the same poem about the wall of 'The Crosses' prison in Leningrad. Brodsky found this sepulchral kitsch so insulting to Akhmatova's memory that the night after seeing the new monument he returned to the cemetery, knocked down the 'birdie', and threw it away. Thus, he committed a misdemeanor punishable by up to six months imprisonment or even more, considering his previous conviction.[2]

Brodsky erected a monument worthy of Akhmatova more than twenty years later, on the occasion of her centenary, not in the form of a 'cloud-thrusting stony object'[3] but a Horatian poem-monument. According to the poet's friend, Diana Myers, the poem was written in London in early July of 1989. Brodsky had been invited to the Akhmatova Centenary conference at the University of Nottingham; he could not attend, but a few days before the event he gave Dr Myers a new poem to be read at Nottingham.[4]

What follows is an attempt to analyse how Akhmatova's monument was made by Brodsky.

ON GENRE

In Brodsky's vast repertoire of genres, 'On the Centenary of Anna Akhmatova' is the only celebratory poem written for a particular anniversary. It should not be listed in the same genre category as the 'in memoriam' poems, of which Brodsky created about two dozen, including such masterpieces as 'To a Friend: In Memoriam' ('It's for you whose name's better omitted – since for them it's no arduous task . . .'),[5] 'The Thought of You Is Going Away Like a Maid-servant' (in memory of the poet's mother), 'In Memory of My Father: Australia', and 'Vertumnus'[6] (in memory of Italian writer Giovanni Buttafava). The gaping absence of poetic response to the death of his dear older friend and mentor, Akhmatova, is especially evident against the background of Brodsky's prolific contribution to the genre of mourning: besides elegies in which he mourned deaths of relatives and close friends, he has poems on the deaths of Robert Frost, T. S. Eliot, Boris Pasternak ('The Dialogue'), the Soviet Second World War military commander, Georgy Zhukov, and numerous others, including such historically distant deaths as those of Evgeny Baratynsky and John Donne. Six years after Akhmatova's death, Brodsky dedicates to her 'Nunc Dimmitis', a paraphrase of a New Testament scene, and after seventeen more years 'On the Centenary of Anna Akhmatova'. Both poems do not satisfy the requirements for the 'in memoriam' genre as established in Brodsky's canon: they contain no intimate recollections of the dead person and, in the case of the latter poem, no emotionally charged meditations on the subject of human mortality.[7] Some details in the centennial poem correspond to Akhmatova's personality and biography – the flat and somewhat muffled voice,[8] arrhythmic pulse, and the habit of burning manuscripts – but they are hardly as individualistic as those featured in the 'in memoriam' poems: here we are dealing with an entirely different level of generalization.

ON STRUCTURE

The epigrammatic brevity of the poem is enhanced by its structure. Each of the poem's three stanzas is one complete sentence: complex in stanza I, compound-complex in stanza II, and complex in stanza III. Despite the syntactic intricacy of each sentence, the main theme of the poem evolves logically and straightforwardly in the main clauses: '(I) God preserves everything, especially words of forgiveness and love, [but] (II) from mortal lips they sound more clearly; [therefore] (III) Great soul, *a bow* [expression of gratitude] for finding them [.]' The author posits a dialectic triad of sorts where thesis, 'Deus conservat omnia' (the Sheremetev family motto used by Akhmatova as the epigraph for 'The Poem Without a Hero'), is followed by antithesis (grammatically 'anti-' is expressed through the use of an adjective in its comparative form, отчетливей [more clearly]), that which is preserved by God is substantiated, or God Himself is transubstantiated, only in the creative act of a mortal, which leads to the synthesis: thus a mortal becomes a 'Great Soul' (Anima Magna) and deserves universal gratitude.

The basic semantic structure of the poem is also clear-cut. It begins and ends with easily visualizable images of the material world. In the beginning (ll. 1 and 2) we are presented with a series of fragmentary, syntactically and narratively unconnected icons of destruction: paired instruments and objects of destruction. There is, however, a pattern to detect: the instruments – fire, millstone, and poleaxe – are immeasurably bigger than what they destroy; the latter objects are either just small (a page) or minute, barely visible (a grain, a hair). The picture of the material world returns at the end (ll. 9–12) on a global and cosmic scale: the author's vision in the third stanza is continuously dynamic; horizontal movement from one hemisphere to another is followed by upward movement to the heights of the Universe. On the whole, the juxtaposition of 'close-ups' in the beginning to the immensely panoramic view in the finale creates the impression of a rapidly widening perspective. Let us recall that at the end of 'Nunc Dimittis' Simeon's transition from the physical to the metaphysical world, or the victory of the New Light over the 'deaf-mute realms of Death' (cf. 'deaf-mute universe' in this poem), were described in terms of 'widening': 'The old man's torch glowed and the pathway grew wider.' Similarly, in 'The Funeral of Bobo': 'Your image will not be [. . .] getting smaller but, on the contrary, [bigger] in Rossi's unbelievable perspective'. It has been observed that 'Nunc Dimittis' is an attempt at poetic icon-painting[9] and, perhaps, Brodsky consciously introduced into his 'icon' poems the icon-painters' device of reverse perspective.[10]

Generally speaking, the motif of 'widening' is but a variation of a philosophical motif central to Brodsky's works: one as a daily-life person is 'less than one', but through the act of poetry one becomes a 'part of speech', i.e. 'more than one' – this is Brodsky's paradoxical reinterpretation of Horace's 'Non omnis moriar, multiquae pars mei vitabit Libitinam . . .' (Odes 3, XXX, ll. 6–7). Among the numerous Russian translations of this ode, it was, probably, that by Derzhavin, one of Brodsky's favorite poets, which prompted the 'part of speech – less than one' imagery, because in that version the famous line sounds somewhat ambiguous. 'часть меня большая' can be understood traditionally, as 'a great part of me', but also as 'a part of me that is greater than I'. It is noteworthy that Akhmatova used the words by Horace that immediately precede the above-quoted statement, 'fuga temporum' (the flight of time), as the title for the last edition of her collected works.

The emphasis in the middle part of the poem, stanza II, is not on visible but on audible images. They are, at first, the sounds of tragedy: an arrhythmic heartbeat, the crunch of broken bones (presumably, in a torture chamber), and the thumping of a gravedigger's spade, and then the poet's voice. Senseless, erratic and terrifying sights and sounds (ll. 1–2 and 5–6) begin to acquire coherence and meaning through the poet's act of vocalization–verbalization (ll. 7–8). The transformation of a cruel and chaotic world into the benevolently animated cosmos of the concluding lines takes place precisely in the middle of the poem.

ON SOME ASPECTS OF VERSIFICATION

Although Brodsky had experience with almost all variations of Russian syllabo-tonic verse, except some of the most exotic,[11] by as early as the mid-1970s, poems written in iambic hexameter are extremely rare in his œuvre. Before the poem in question, only four poems had been written in this, or predominantly this, metre, and in each case the stanzaic form makes the poem sound quite different from Alexandrines, i.e. the iambic hexameter couplets common in Russian poetry.[12] True Alexandrines, I6:aabb . . ., Brodsky used only once, in his translation of Auden's 'Stop all the clocks, cut off the telephone' (1994). The metric pattern, chosen for the centennial poem, I6:aBaBcDcDeFeF, sometimes called the 'elegiac Alexandrine', had no precedent in Brodsky's practice and was repeated thereafter only once: in 'Letter to an Oasis' (1991), a poem connected with 'On the Centenary of Anna Akhmatova' in more than one way. Added to the fact that after the mid-1970s Brodsky rarely employed syllabo-tonic metres in general, the uniqueness of this poem's metric pattern becomes one of its important thematic components.

Ian Lilly discussed the metric context of the poem in his above-quoted article, which is specifically dedicated to that subject. In addition to his thorough discussion, I would propose that the iambic hexameter has here representational significance in creatng a verbal portrait of Akhmatova in accordance with a certain established tradition. Most obviously, it provides the poem-monument with an appropriately solemn tone. Its pronounced caesura divides lines symmetrically, thus underscoring antithetical pairs and isolated appositions, so important for the poem.[13] Brodsky also stresses two components of the Alexandrine's semantic aura: (1) its being the metre of Neo-Classical tragedy and (2) its echo of Hellenistic and the even more archaic, Egyptian, antiquity (reflected in the very term chosen for this metric pattern). The Neo-Classical component is rich in literary associations. First of all, it brings to mind Mandelshtam's widely known poetic view of Akhmatova as Phaedra in Racine's tragedy. Some of Brodsky's contemporaries were frequent users of the Alexandrine, notably Nikolai Zabolotskii and Aleksandr Kushner,[14] but incomparably more Alexandrine couplets were penned by Soviet translators of French and other European classics. Brodsky could listen to recitals of their new works *ad nauseam* when he attended meetings of the Translation Section at the Leningrad Writers Union. That might be one of the reasons why he avoided this hackneyed verse form most of the time. But when it came to portraying Akhmatova, this metre came in handy: by using it Brodsky could achieve great artistic economy and depict her as a regal and tragic heroine, a new Phaedra or Dido,[15] without using direct comparisons and epithets, which had become cliché.

While the poem's first line with its symmetrical weak second and fifth ictuses evokes the typical Russian Alexandrine of the 18th century,[16] the elegiac Alexandrine of the entire work reminds one of Mandelshtam's poem, 'The Egyptian. II', where, incidentally, a grain-grinding millstone is mentioned alongside other details of ancient daily life. This is hardly just a coincidence, because Brodsky himself said that poems from Mandelshtam's early collections, *Stone* and *Tristia*, which he first read when he was twenty years old, 'had stuck' in his memory.[17]

Why Brodsky decided to shape his Akhmatova monument as an '*Alexandrine* Pillar', the 'Egyptian' substratum of the poem, can be better understood by comparing it to 'A Letter to an Oasis', but here we should turn to some peculiarities of its rhythmic structure, which is unusual as far as the distribution of strong and weak ictuses is concerned (see Table 1).

The very distinct 'beat' of the poem is due to its unusual stress pattern. Let us compare the distribution of stressed and unstressed ictuses in 'On the Centenary of Anna Akhmatova' with Scherr's data on iambic hexameter in the 18th and 19th century and in the Soviet period (Table 2).[18] In the left hemistichs of the centenary poem the accentuation is higher than the norm for all periods, while in the right ones it is significantly lower because the long epithets – 'усеченный', 'из надмирной', and 'глухонемой' – all are shifted to the right.

TABLE 1

```
— ` —¶--¶-`-¶¶-`-¶--¶-`-
```
Стра ни цу и о гонь, зер но и жер но ва,
```
-`-¶--¶-`-¶¶--¶-`-¶-`-¶-
```
се ки ры ос три ё и у се чён ный во лос –
```
`--¶-`-¶-`-¶¶-`-¶--¶-`-
```
Бог со хра ня ет всё; о со бен но сло ва
```
-`-¶--¶-`-¶¶-`-¶--¶`-`-¶-
```
про ще нья и люб ви, как собс твен ный свой го лос.
```
`-`-¶-`-¶-`-¶¶-`-¶-`-¶-`-
```
В них бьёт ся рва ный пульс в них слы шен кост ный хруст,
```
-`-¶-`-¶-`-¶¶-`-¶--¶-`-¶-
```
и за ступ в них сту чнт; ров ны и глу хо ва ты,
```
-`-¶-`-¶-`-¶¶-`-¶-`-¶-`-
```
за тем что жизнь од на – о ни из смерт ных уст
```
-`-¶-`-¶--¶¶-- ¶-`-¶-`-
```
зву чат от чёт ли вей, чем из надмнр ной ва ты.

```
— ` —¶--¶-`-¶¶-`-¶--¶-`-
```
Ве ли ка я ду ша, пок лон че рез мо ря
```
-`-¶-`-¶-`-¶-`-¶¶-`-¶-`-¶-`-¶-
```
за то, что их наш ла, – те бе и час ти тлен ной,
```
— ` —¶-`-¶-`-¶¶-`-¶--¶-`-
```
что спит в род ной зем ле, те бе бла го да ря
```
-`-¶-`-¶-`-¶¶--¶-`-¶-`-¶-
```
об рет шей ре чи дар в глу хо не мой все лен ной.

TABLE 2 (*percentage*)

	I	II	III	IV	V	VI
18th C	91.8	64.4	73.1	95.1	44.1	100
19th C	90.7	64.7	75.5	94.1	39.8	100
Soviet period	84.5	53.5	93.5	90.5	44.0	100
'On Centenary...'	91.7	66.7	91.7	75.0	50.0	100

Four hypermetrical stresses in the poem (ll. 3–5) play a very important emphatic role: the first two enhance words 'Бог' [God] and the related possessive pronoun, 'Свой' [His], while the third and the fourth coincide with the repeated preposition+pronoun 'в них [in them], i.e. 'in the words of forgiveness and love'. Thus this rhythmic device underscores the idea of God's transubstantiation in the poet's words. At the same time, the two added stresses in l. 5 rhythmically 'illustrate' as it were the interruption of the heartbeat ('lacerated pulse') and the sudden 'crunch of bones'. By the same token, when 'в них' [in them] appears for the third time, it appears at a normally stressed ictus in the phrase depicting the regular pounding of the gravedigger's spade.

Brodsky begins l. 3 with a hypermetrical stress, 'Бог' [God], and ends it with enjambment that highlights the word 'слова' [words]. The second enjambment occurs in the penultimate line and it is even more expressive because it is combined with the inversion ('тебе благодаря' [to you thanks] instead of normal 'благодаря тебе' [thanks to you]), and because an enjambment which leaves a preposition or conjunction hanging at the end of a line is always especially arresting. Such enjambments are Brodsky's trademark but here we deal not with some 'и' [and] or 'на' [on] but with 'баагодаря' [thanks], i.e. a preposition which in Russian is homonymous with the adverbial form of the verb 'благодарить' [to thank; to be grateful]. Thus the line reverberates with a motif of gratitude.

When Lilly discusses euphonic features of the poem, he mentions one paronomastic pair in each stanza: (I) *zerno-zhernova*, (II) *zastup-stuchit*, and (III) *obretshii-rechi*.[19] To list all the alliterative-assonant groupings in the poem would require rewriting the whole text several times over: its sound structure is extremely systematic. Some of the more prominent sound repetitions include: *sekiru-usechennyi* (l. 2), *pul's-khrust* (l. 5)-*stuchit* (ll. 5–6), *stuchit* (l. 6)-*chto* (in Brodsky's Petersburgian pronunciation;[20] l. 7)-*zvuchat otchetlivei chem* (l. 8).

In stanza III five out of six hemistichs with masculine clausulae have *a* as a stressed vowel (*dusha, moria, nashla, blagodaria, dar*), while the two remaining, feminine, clausulae have **-nn-** in posttonic position (*tlennoi, vselennoi*). This forms a quite evident anagram of the addressee's name, **Anna**, 'sweetest of names on people's lips and to their ears'.[21] (An echo of Akhmatova's surname can be heard in the feminine rhyme of the preceding stanza: '*glukhovaty-nadmirnoi vaty*'.)

An analysis of the consonantal make-up of the poem reveals a definite strategy. Although the distribution of voiced and unvoiced consonants throughout ll. 1–10 is approximately even – there are a few more voiced than unvoiced ones in ll. 1, 4, 7, 8, 9 and vice versa in ll. 2, 3 (devocalization taken into account), 5, 6, 10 – the overall impression of a somewhat muffled sound prevails, prompted by the alliteration of *s*, which runs uninterruptedly through ll. 1–7 (cf. the evocation of Akhmatova's 'flat and some-what muffled' voice in l. 6). Against this whispering background the resounding vocalization of the two final lines, with 27 voiced consonants vs only eleven unvoiced, is all the more striking. While the sound structure of the poem and its rhythmic and intonational patterns are pronounced and refined, the six rhymes are common to the point of predictability, which is very uncharacteristic for the mature Brodsky.[22] This seems to be a consciously exercised restraint: more extravagant rhyming would destroy the reverential tone of the poem, and it would sound as an inappropriate challenge to Akhmatova's own poetics, which are characterized by undistinguished rhyming.[23] The final rhyme of the poem, *tlennoi–vselennoi*, echoes the 18th-century odes, where *-enn[oi]* rhymes were very common: in Derzhavin's 'Depiction of Felitsa [Catherine II]' alone it occurs sixteen times.

All in all, the heightened attention to the acoustics of the poem directly corresponds to its main theme: transformations of God's voice, which manifests itself in the voice of the poet, who, at the same time, speaks for his people and verbalizes the tragic experience of the nation. To the old proverb, 'vox populi–vox dei', Brodsky adds a stipulation: 'vox populi' must be articulated by the poet.[24] Voice was Akhmatova's own constant metaphor for poetry:[25] 'This is the voice of a mysterious lyre, dwelling on the nether world's meadow . . .' (about Mandelshtam); 'An inimitable voice fell silent yesterday . . .' (on Pasternak's death); 'There are still many things, which, I suppose, want to be praised by my voice . . .'; and, undoubtedly most important for Brodsky, *Requiem*, where in the Prologue she accepts the challenge to voice the suffering of her people and in the Epilogue asks her people to remember her, even if 'they will gag my tortured mouth through which a hundred million scream'.[26]

ON DICTION

'On the Centenary of Anna Akhmatova' serves as a perfect illustration for the 'Acmeist principle' of poetry writing, which Brodsky loved to quote:[27] use as many nouns as possible. The poem's diction is predominantly nominal: 26 nouns and seven personal pronouns (five of them stand for noun 'words' and two for the name of the addressee); eleven adjectives, two participles and one numeral function as epithets; and two adjectives (слышен [heard/audible] and отчетливей [clearer/more clearly]) appear in predicate position. There are only five verbs.

From the point of view of referentiality, nouns are used in such a way that the reader is aware of their possible concrete and abstract connotations simultaneously. At the start, by means of a two-line long inversion, Brodsky establishes an intricate interplay of the material and the abstract, the concrete and the figurative: he begins with three antithetical pairs of nouns and only in the middle of l. 3 do we learn that within the inverted syntactic structure of the first sentence they are specifying objects attached to 'everything', which is the direct object of God's action ('Deus conservat omnia'). Within each of the three antitheses one noun signifies an agent of destruction and the other the object being destroyed and, significantly, each of the six nouns can be read both in its concrete meaning and as a common trope: 'a page' is a sheet of paper carrying some text but also a metaphor for human experience (cf. the common expressions: 'a page of life', 'a page of history', and so forth). The order in which the three pairs are presented eschews moral judgement on the author's part: book burning and beheadings are violent acts, while grain grinding is a peaceful activity, but it is up to God to judge them. The word 'words' is especially polysemic in this context, for it represents both humanly articulated words and at the same time divine words of all-forgiving love and eternal memory, Gumilev's Word-Logos.

In addition to 'voice' and 'words', the same semantic iridescence characterizes two other key notions in the poem that are related to these – 'deafness' and 'muteness'. One instance is the correspondence between the definition of Akhmatova's voice in the middle of the poem as 'somewhat muffled' (in Russian literally: 'deaf-ish' [глуховатый]) and that of the universe as 'deaf-mute' at the end. This is another manifestation of the poem's harmonizing pathos: paradoxically, the silence ('deaf-muteness') of the universe *sounds* in Akhmatova's voice. The finales of two other memorable pieces of modern Russian poetry immediately come to mind in this regard. One is the ending of Vladimir Mayakovsky's long lyrical poem, 'A Cloud in Trousers' (1915):

Hey, you!
Heavens!
Take off your hat!
I'm coming!

Deafness.

The universe is sleeping,
its giant ear, with the ticks of stars stuck in it,
on its paw.[28]

The other is the final two lines of Boris Pasternak's 'Definition of Poetry' (1919):

Mirth would suit these stars
But *the universe* is a *deaf* place.[29]

The differences in their temperaments notwithstanding, both Mayakovsky and Pasternak romantically confront the world order, the universe, which is 'deaf' to their lyrical demands; Brodsky's heroine, though, is an inalienable part of the divine cosmos, its 'part of speech'.

Notes

1. This literal translation is borrowed from Ian Lilly, 'The Metrical Context of Brodsky's Centenary Poem for Axmatova', *Slavic and East European Journal*, vol. 37 (1993) no. 2, pp. 211–19. Several changes were made to make it more literal, albeit at the expense of smoothness.
2. See *Ugolovnyi kodeks RSFSR* [The Penal Code of the Russian Soviet Federative Socialist Republic] (Moscow: Gosudarstvennoe izdatel'stvo iuridicheskoi literatury, 1950) p. 111 (Article 175). Another account of the same episode exists: 'Once, a little while after the funeral, we – on that particular day it was Brodsky and I – came to the grave site and instead of the oak cross, which had stood there since March 10, saw the current one – huge, wrought-iron with a shapeless she-dove, made from some light-colored metal, attached close to the end of the crossbar. A small wall built of stone fenced the grave off from the solemn pines, which had cast their shadow on it so naturally; the soil was paved over with stones. The little earthy mound over the grave had disappeared, it was levelled with the stone pavement. It looked as if somebody was going to build a crypt

but ended up with the interior of something. Altogether it was in glaring contradiction to Akhmatova's own vision and prediction: "I will sleep quietly in a country churchyard beneath an oaken cross." Then the "birdie" disappeared: someone of the monument builders had taken it away.' A. G. Nayman, 'Chetyre stikhotvoreniia' [Four poems] in *Svoiu mezh vas eshche ostaviv ten'* . . . *Akhmatovskie chteniia* [Still leaving my shadow amidst you . . . Readings in Akhmatova], issue 3 (Moscow: Nasledie, 1992) p. 52. See also D. Bobyshev's poem 'The Mourning Octaves': 'The sandy mound was dusted with snow, / two pieces of wood made a cross; / then they were replaced by something stronger – iron. / A she-dove landed on the crossbar, / but then flitted away somewhere . . . Good riddance!' (ibid., pp. 55–6). All translations, if not otherwise attributed, are by the author and co-translator of the article.

3. From 'Roman Elegies'; Joseph Brodsky, *To Urania: Selected Poems, 1965–1985* (London: Viking 1988) p. 66.

4. This author's interview with Dr Myers in London, 26 and 27 May 1997. A copy of the original typescript in Dr Myers' archive contains only one significant variation from the published version: in l. 5, 'птичий крик' [bird's cry] instead of 'рваный пульс' [lacerated pulse]. The 'bird's cry' of the earlier version is, probably, a reflection of Akhmatova's famous line about her dead friends, Mandelshtam and Pasternak, 'Чудится мне на воздушных путях / Двух голосов перекличка' [It seems to me that I can hear two voices calling each other on aerial ways] ('Komarovo Sketches', 1961); the same line had been a likely original impulse for Brodsky's own poem in memory of Pasternak, 'The Dialogue' (1962).

5. *To Urania*, p. 4, translated by the author; the news of that friend's death later proved to be false.

6. *So Forth: Poems* (New York: Farrar, Straus & Giroux, 1996) p. 36.

7. This characterization of the 'in memoriam' genre only summarizes Brodsky's own thoughts: see the extensive passage on the subject at the beginning of his long interpretive essay dedicated to Marina Tsvetaeva's poem on Rilke's death (*Brodskii o Tsvetaevoi* [Moscow: Nezavisimaia Gazeta, 1997] pp. 78–9). I cannot agree with Mikhail Lotman who believes 'On the Centenary . . .' to be representative of the *in memoriam* genre (see p. 46 of this book). Similarly, Ian Lilly is wrong when he places it in the same genre as Lermontov's famous poem on the death of Pushkin, Pasternak's on the death of Maya-kovsky, and Akhmatova's on the death of Pasternak (Lilly, p. 213).

8. This is a commonplace of many poems dedicated to Akhmatova; see in *O, muza placha . . . Stikhotvoreniia, posviashchennye Anne Akhmatovoi* [O, Muse of Weeping . . .: Poems Dedicated to Anna Akhmatova] (Moscow: Pedagogika, 1991): 'And you sing in a measured, some-what muffled voice . . .' (Georgii Shengeli, 1943; p. 80), 'I could hear a somewhat muffled voice . . .' (Vsevolod Azarov, late 1960s; p. 127), 'your muffled words . . .' (Gleb Semenov, 1978; p. 136); E. P. Galperina-Osmerkina, a speech specialist, also described Akhmatova's voice as muffled (*Svoiu mezh vas ehche ostaviv ten'* . . ., p. 8).

9. See this author's 'Niotkuda s liubov'iu' [From Nowhere with Love], *Kontinent*, no. 14 (1977) pp. 307–31, and Kees Verheul, 'Tishina in Akhmatova' [Silence in Akhmatova] in *Tsarstvennoe slovo. Akhmatovskie chteniia* [The Regal Word. Readings in Akhmatova], issue 1 (Moscow: Nasledie, 1992) pp. 17–20.

10. See 'Obratnaia perspektiva' [Reverse Perspective] in Rev. Pavel Florenskii, *Izbrannye trudy po iskusstvu* [Selected Essays on Art] (Moscow: Izobrazitel'noe iskusstvo, 1996) pp. 9–71.

11. See Barry Scherr 'Strofika Brodskogo' [Brodsky's Stanzaic Forms], in *Poetika Brodskogo. Sbornik statei* [Brodsky's Poetics], ed. L. Loseff (Tenafly, NJ: Hermitage, 1986) pp. 112–18.

12. 'Peschanye kholmy, porosshie sosnoi . . .' [Sandy dunes, overgrown with pine . . .] (1974), '1867' (1975), 'Piataia godovshchina' [The Fifth Anniversary] (1977), and 'Chem bol'she chernykh glaz, tem bol'she perenosit . . .' [As the Number of Dark Eyes Grow, So Does the Number of Nose Bridges . . .] (1986); Lilly, p. 213; Lilly takes into account only the latter two poems, but the two earlier ones do not contradict his conclusions.

13. Cf. 'Whenever his subject is antiquity or a tragic situation, or a tragic feeling, Mandelshtam chooses heavily caesura-ed verse which clearly echoes the hexameter' (Iosif Brodskii, 'S mirom derzhavnym ia byl lish' rebiacheski sviazan . . .' [With the World of the Empire I Had Only a Childish Connection . . .] in *Materials from the Mandelshtam Centenary Conference, School of Slavonic Studies, London, 1991*, compiled and ed. Robin Aizlewood and Diana Myers [Tenafly, NJ: Hermitage, 1994] p. 15).

14. Lilly, p. 215.

15. Cf. Brodsky's poem, 'Didona i Enei' [Dido and Aeneas], in *Sochineniia Iosifa Brodskogo* [Works of Joseph Brodsky], vol. II (St Petersburg: Pushkinskii fond, 1992) p. 163); also Brodsky's comments on Akhmatova's cycle 'Shipovnik tsvetet' [Dogrose in Bloom], where she herself compares her fate to that of Dido: '"Romeo and Julia" as performed by the members of a royal family. Or rather "Dido and Aeneas" . . .' and 'there was something in her very appearance of a wandering, shelterless queen' in *Vspominaia Akhmatovu. Iosif Brodskii–Solomon Volkov. Dialogi* [Remembering Akhmatova: Joseph Brodsky and Solomon Volkov: Dialogues] (Moscow: Nezavisimaia Gazeta, 1992) pp. 38 and 47.

16. See Barry Scherr, *Russian Poetry: Meter, Rhythm, and Rhyme* (Berkeley: University of California Press, 1986) p. 63, Table 8.

17. *Vspominaia Akhmatovu*, p. 8.

18. Scherr, Table 8.

19. Lilly, p. 217.

20. A Muscovite would say 'shto'.

21. From Akhmatova's 'Epic Motifs'; translated by Judith Hemschemeyer, in *The Complete Poems of Anna Akhmatova*, vol. II, ed. Roberta Reeder (Sommerville, MA: Zephyr Press, 1990) p. 327.

22. Even *volos–golos*, a rhyme compromised by a popular scatological saying, found its way into the text (Brodsky had used it once before, in 'I Was Born and Grew Up in the Baltic Marshland . . .').

23. In our conversations Brodsky often referred to the 'poor rhymes' of Mandelshtam and Akhmatova.

24. On the other hand, he wrote: 'If [Akhmatova's] poems were not exactly *vox populi*, it's because a nation never speaks with one voice', *Less than One* (New York: Farrar, Straus & Giroux, 1986) pp. 42–3.

25. Cf. 'The voice is the most captivating and the most elusive thing about a person. The voice is the interior mold of one's soul', Maximilian Voloshin, 'Golosa poetov' [Poets' voices], *Rech'*, 4 June 1917 (quoted in Osip Mandelshtam, *Kamen'* [Stone] (Leningrad: Nauka, 1990) p. 236, and commentary, p. 356.

26. *The Complete Poems of Anna Akhmatova*, vol. II, p. 113 (edited for greater accuracy). Brodsky rated *Requiem* very highly: 'The degree of compassion with which the various voices of *Requiem* are rendered can be explained only by the author's Orthodox faith; the degree of understanding and forgiveness which accounts for this work's piercing, almost unbearable lyricism, only by the uniqueness of her heart', Joseph Brodsky, 'The Keening Muse', *Less than One*, p. 51; also: *Vspominaia Akhmatovu*, pp. 31–5.

27. See, for example an interview in *Russkaia mysl'*, no. 3450 (3 February 1983) p. 9.

28. Vladimir Maiakovskii, *Sobranie sochinenii* [Collected Works], vol. 1 (Moscow: Khudozhestvennaia literatura, 1955) p. 196. Italics added. The clumsy 'deafness' in our translation does not do justice to the original, where Maiakovskii capitalizes on the triple meaning of the Russian word 'glukho': (1) 'deaf', (2) 'remote/forsaken', and (3) as an idiomatic expression, 'no response'.

29. Boris Pasternak, *Stikhotvoreniia i poemy* [Poems and Narrative Poems], vol. 1 (Leningrad: Sovetskii pisatel', 1990) p. 134. Italics added. The wordplay with 'deaf' is the same as in Mayakovsky.

13

Joseph Brodsky's 'To My Daughter'

DAVID M. BETHEA

Joseph Brodsky is a bundle of contradictions. This statement might be problematic if he were a philosopher, but his consistent inconsistency makes perfect sense to those studying his primary status – that of poet. Stoic toward the arbitrariness of the world order (or disorder), deeply melancholic (if not corrosively sceptical) about 'human nature', yet passionately believing in language's ontological priority as the only *thing* (note this word) in human existence approaching a genuine God-term, Brodsky could be maddening in the sheer outrageousness, the 'demanding-the-maximum-and-the-hell-with-the-rest' quality, of his metaphorical thinking. But that is what poets, especially great poets, do – they challenge our cognitive, emotional, aesthetic and metaphysical constants with their sprung logic. And Brodsky could do this with the best of them, including his teachers Mandelshtam and Tsvetaeva, whose own metaphorical thinking and contrary, 'vertical' argumentation the younger poet extended not only into the texture of his verse but also into that of his prose essays.

As Lotman, following Jakobson, has suggested with his characteristic precision, there are only two ways to make meaning ('new information') out of language: either we can assert a similarity between two different things or we can assert a difference between two things taken to be similar.[1] In both cases, however, we are dealing with a process akin to rhyme – the *coexistence* of similarity within difference. But poets and poetry, roughly speaking, begin by scaling the metaphorical axis, which means that they are drawn to see the sameness in items or ideas that most of us would not choose to link up otherwise. This accounts for both the inspiring 'shock of recognition' (this is really bold and fasci-

240

nating) and the deflating 'realization of improbability' (this is more ingenious than it is real) that often go with our responses to poetic, that is, metaphoric logic. Along the so-called metonymic axis, on the other hand, the one we generally associate with novelistic thinking, there is 'contiguity', which is to say there exists an a priori attitude toward things and ideas which before now we might have seen as 'alike' by virtue of their proximity in time and space but which now we begin to distinguish among and to see as 'nuanced', as different. Operating in his primary mode (which is only a tendency), the novelist will give you five different names for a window when describing *how to see* a house ('meaning' is created by understanding the different nuances among windows – *that* is 'reality'); operating in his mode (which is also only a tendency), the poet will tell you that the window is an eye to the universe ('meaning' is created by understanding that there is a genuine parallel between inorganic glass and organic tissue – *that* is 'reality'). Neither of these viewpoints ever 'wins', but it is important to realize before turning to Brodsky's concrete practice as a poet that everything he believed in and dedicated his life to (and, while he often went on record as saying that he would prefer if we didn't mention it, *suffered for*) relates to the 'truth' of poetic thinking. Poets live in heroic simultaneity, since few people would be willing to stake their lives on the proposition that a window is an eye; it is simply too hard, too risk-laden, to believe in this as a way of being in the world. It is far easier to live in a world of prosaic distinction, where everything is both part of something else, either prior in time or adjacent in space, and a 'logical' extension of it.

But let us return to the 'matter' (Brodsky's pun, as we shall see) at hand. In order to understand a Brodsky poem, it is crucial to understand first something about his thinking, or, as he would have said it, 'vector'. He himself might have denied this or argued something to the effect that the poem 'speaks for itself', but here I think he is being as ever the contrarian: Brodsky, at least the Brodsky of his later years, is not very understandable 'on his own'. His metaphors have coalesced into a kind of 'system', but one whose verbal layering and retrieval, whose archaeology if you will, is consistently non-rational, paradoxicalist, fragmentary (both in image and method), and defiant of any explanation from origins. In this respect, his poems need his essays, his essays need his poems, and even then the reader needs to

come to his words with a certain amount of additional information in tow. His words always make us think, and that is good,
but it is even better if we have enough information so that our
thinking is at least on the right track. For example, here is a sentence from Brodsky's late essay 'A Cat's Meow': 'Now, matter, I
believe, comes to articulate itself through human science or
human art presumably only under some kind of duress'.[2] This
statement is, I would argue, completely incomprehensible to most
non-specialist readers. How can matter, which whether organic
or inorganic is as far as we know pre-conscious, come to articulate itself, i.e. to perform a conscious act? How can it experience
duress? In what sense does matter articulate itself through science or art? In short, these words seem intentionally riddling,
too clever by half, arch, and possibly insincere – i.e. made for
effect rather than for their truth value. However, as I will try to
demonstrate in the remainder of this essay, these words make
perfect sense in the context of Brodsky's 'voice zone', prior history, and the larger Russian lyric tradition that gave him his start.
They even make sense, albeit highly idiosyncratic, in terms of
the Anglo-American tradition (Auden, Lowell, Frost, Hardy, etc.)
that he eventually made his own. Not only are these words not
insincere, they are an article of faith, incredibly 'hot' while giving
every appearance of being maximally cool (metaphorical thinking, as we have been saying, forces powerful differences into
cohabitation), and the 'reason' (or Logos) underlying the belief
that allows the poet to keep his love alive in that most vulnerable of all positions – when the dying father has to say goodbye
to the baby daughter who will never know him outside of some
'wooden' words.

Let us begin with the poem itself, published by Brodsky in the
Times Literary Supplement on 2 December 1994:

To My Daughter[3]

Give me another life, and I'll be singing	1
in Cafe Rafaello. Or simply sitting	2
there. Or standing there, as furniture in the corner,	3
in case that life is a bit less generous than the former.	4
Yet partly because no century from now on will ever	
manage	5
without caffeine or jazz, I'll sustain this damage,	6

and through my cracks and pores, varnish and dust
all over,   7
observe you, in twenty years, in your full flower.   8

On the whole, bear in mind that I'll be around. Or
rather,   9
that an inanimate object might be your father,   10
especially if the objects are older than you, or larger.   11
So keep an eye on them always, for they will no doubt
judge you.   12

Love those things anyway, encounter or no encounter.   13
Besides, you may still remember a silhouette, a contour,   14
while I'll lose even that, along with the other luggage.   15
Hence, these somewhat wooden lines in our common
language.   16

There are certain skeletal 'facts' about this poem that one should
have in mind before taking the first step toward understanding
or 'interpreting' it. First of all, these verses are, as the title says,
written to the poet's daughter – Anna Maria Alexandra, who was
born on 9 June 1993, to Brodsky and his wife Maria Sozzani.
Thus at the time of this writing, the little girl, named in honor of
Anna Akhmatova and Brodsky's parents (Maria and Alexander),
was a year and a half old, while the father had little more than
a year to live (Brodsky would die of longstanding heart problems on 28 January 1996).

Second, the poem is, technically speaking, written in a cadence
that could be called a loose heroic hexameter, one which Brodsky
would be familiar with from both the Russian and the English:
most lines have six metrical stresses (exceptions: ll. 1, 2 and 10),
the anacrusis (the unstressed syllable[s] leading up to the first
stress) 'wanders' here (cf. the Russian hexameter should have zero
anacrusis), the intervals between metrical stresses are normally
one to two syllables (typical for the Russian), and the clausula
(the unstressed syllable[s] following the last stress) is constantly
one syllable (also typical for the Russian). While the Russian practice
of hexameter use avoids rhyming, Brodsky's English practice here
does not: instead of unrhymed feminine endings (the 'heroic' or
'Gnedich' expectation), we have rhymed ones, deployed in a symmetrical, 4-quatrain scheme of aabb (the exception being l. 12).

Brodsky's rhymes are often not 'pure' but slant and quite ingenious. His use of enjambment, especially in the poem's opening
lines, is striking, and begs to be 'semanticized' in the context of
slipped metrical stresses. Likewise, his use of intonational pauses
(the 'caesura') skips around in this poem, which is more typical
for English practice, while it would have remained in one place
(i.e. it would have been part of the metre) in Russian. We will
return to these formal issues, and most pointedly to that of English
versus Russian hexameter, in a moment.

And third, in terms of diction or stylistic register, this poem is
as 'matter-of-fact', as implicitly 'unlyrical', and as apparently
stripped bare of high culture (often Brodsky's trademark elsewhere), as is its primary theme of furniture and inorganic
'thingness'. The only factual curiosity in the poem, other than
the speaker's tendency to project himself into the future not only
as deceased but precisely as an 'inanimate object', is the reference to Cafe Rafaello. There is indeed such a place in Manhattan, on 7th Avenue South, near where Brodsky, himself clearly a
product of a century that could not manage without caffeine or
jazz, once lived in Greenwich Village. The Italian resonances in
its name would not be lost on a poet who had written so much
about and 'to' Venice, Rome, antiquity, classical poets, thinkers
and statesmen, and who was now contemplating his own demise
and entry into history from precisely this location.

These facts are what we need to get started on the poem. But
they don't yet 'mean'. And in this respect, it is the 'typical' critic's
move from the one to the other, from the inanimate/descriptive
(the 'form' of a hexameter or a chair) to the animate/conscious
(these things' inner illumination through an unexplained and
unexplainable use of language), that the poet in Brodsky always
resisted. Even when he spoke about others' verse, say Frost's or
Hardy's in *On Grief and Reason*, he always minimized the biographical element (all the while giving his students or his readers enough to ground his statements in something) and tried to
show how poetic language worked from the inside. So 'To My
Daughter' doesn't mean, doesn't *become a poem*, because the speaker
is soon to die and his daughter is starting life, or because the
Cafe Rafaello is near his old home in Greenwich Village. Nor
does the knowledge alone that his words are framed in hexameters make his poem mean either, although this is, technically
speaking, closer to the truth. Facts, and biographical facts *a for-*

tiori, do not 'cause' meaning (the – to Brodsky – much-detested explanation from origins); they merely give it a place to be born. How these facts become meaning is through language. Thus, such vintage Brodsky 'one-liners', already familiar to readers of *Less than One*, as 'to make a long story short, a poet shouldn't be viewed through any prism other than that of his poems'; or 'it is language that utilizes a human being, not the other way around'; or 'The last bastion of realism, biography is based on the breathtaking premise that art can be explained by life'; or, if 'what critics do' is to 'subordinat[e] literature . . . to history', what poets do is the opposite.[4]

In a word, Brodsky had a romantic view of the poet, but one that he tempered with large doses of adoptive democratic spirit, irony and humor (another paradox). He shared with Tsvetaeva her disdain for the critic as the *poète manqué*, the one whose definitions and terms inevitably fail because they can never get to the vantage of the other. The poet was special, but not because he was uniquely endowed in a way he could take personal credit for or enjoy or use in and as 'life'. Rather, he was nothing more or less than the site where language, in its mythical role as something older and greater than the State or History (note the explanation from origins doing flips over itself here), brought meaning to life. A poem that succeeds is, therefore, according to Brodskian sprung logic, literally an inanimate life form. By the same quirky token, poetic language is permanent, but not because it can be preserved on papyri or computer disks. It is so because it is the intersection of the finite and the animate, i.e. the human being, on the one hand, and the infinite and the inanimate, i.e. matter *per se*, on the other. Don't look for meaning in anyone's life, including the poet's; human history is hopelessly anthropomorphic and solipsistic; better, as the poet once told the graduating class at Dartmouth College, to learn 'the lesson of your total insignificance' *vis-à-vis* the universe, and so on.[5] 'Meaning', then, if not an illusion, is what the poetic soul experiences as it sees and feels, in a process it can't control or summon but none the less lives for, its life being tranformed into the matter of language. Note that the stress here is not language's vague anthropomorphic immortality (Yeatsian birds keeping drowsy emperors awake, etc.) but precisely its character as materiality, as something that has outgrown human pain but is able – indeed fated – to contain it. Rather than the miracle of Christian Logos, the word-become-flesh, it is, again quite literally and along a trajectory that Brodsky repeated obsessively in his mature verse, the flesh-become-word, or, to use another familiar metaphor, the poet become his own 'part of speech'.[6]

But where, finally, do Brodsky's views on poetic language, as opposed to the poetic locutions themselves, come from? And if language is the God-term, then what, if any, is its creed? The answers to these questions provide a segue back into 'To My Daughter' and its enigmatic meaning. Brodsky saw a poem's prosodic manifold as a virtual memory bank whose contents could be drawn upon to invoke an entire tradition. This was especially true of his work as a Russian lyric poet: in general, the Russians have been much more aware of the links between the history of a prosodic form and its semantic and thematic 'aureole' than have their English-speaking colleagues. For Brodsky, as for Mandelshtam before him, the Muse Mnemosyne and the 'memory' of prior forms being able to say certain things in certain ways are synonyms or at least collateral hypostases. Such is 'history' from a poet's point of view and such is the notion Brodsky has in mind when he writes of poetic language as 'restructured time' and as possessing, despite its indifference to human tragedy, the attributes of a 'personality' or a (Mandelshtamian) soul/psyche. In any event, when the poet once said goodbye to another child, his son Andrei, in a poem that was written on the eve of his exile to the West, the form that he invoked in 'Odissei Telemaku' [Odysseus to Telemachus] (1972) was blank verse (unrhymed iambic pentameter). The form had an interesting Russian genealogy that went back to various instances in Zhukovskii, Pushkin, Ogarev, Blok, Gumilev, Khodasevich, Knut, Akhmatova and Brodsky himself (e.g. 'Ostanovka v pustyne' [A Halt in the Wilderness] (1966).[7] Its thematics, established (as so much else) irrevocably when Pushkin rewrote Zhukovskii's 'Tlennost'' [Perishability] (1816), itself a rather pale translation from the German (Hebel), into the great 'Vnov' ia posetil' [Again I Have Visited] (1835), seemed to 'feel' the form by attaching itself to ruminations on death, generational passage, and a speaker's reactions as he returns to a place of prior activity. But it was with the startling fusion of the lyrical and the prosaic (the unrhymed quality, the simpler, more straightforward diction, etc.) that Pushkin set the semantic and thematic 'tone' for the form on Russian soil. Moreover, the longer 'breath' of the line, a concept dear to both Mandelshtam and Brodsky, had in this case not only the more obvious 'Shakespearean' associations (i.e. the source for blank verse models in Pushkin). In Brodsky's 'A Halt in the Wilderness', for example, the return motif had definite classical or 'antique' markings as well – what had once been a Greek Orthodox Church (with its potential links to both Hellenism and Christianity) had now become a modern 'concert hall'; thus Pushkin's affirmation of mortality and of the necessary ascendance of youth has turned in Brodsky into something ironic and sceptical – the ghastly Sovietism 'kontsertnyi zal'. And similarly, the application of a classically stylized biography in 'Odysseus to Telemachus' is meant both to show (not without a certain irony) the ancient in the modern and to foreground the poet's culture and sophistication in an otherwise barbarous state. The Greeks, Circe, Poseidon, Palamedes, Oedipus, etc. – these are the reference points out of which the poet constructs his tale of betrayal and exile, and his method has clear antecedents in the high modernist tendencies and neo-classicist display of such exemplars as Mandelshtam, Akhmatova and Tsvetaeva. But here the return to the scene of the action is not a homecoming but a pause before banishment.

The Brodsky who writes 'To My Daughter' is a very different creature, however. Or to be precise, he is the same Brodsky, but he has moved so far along his original 'self-estranging'[8] trajectory as to be virtually unrecognizable to all but his most persistent readers.[9] Thus, instead of a high modernist 'martyrological' biography (the poet – Mandelshtam and Akhmatova – as Christ or Mary figures) that once implicated him (the 'Christ child'[10]), the eschewal of biography altogether as a category of poetic understanding;[11] instead of the marked presence of Russian models (with a stray Auden or Montale) in *Less than One*, the defining role of adoptive 'others', in particular an Anglo-Saxon autodidact and sceptic (Hardy) and an American individualist (Frost), in *On Grief and Reason*; instead of busts, torsos, Ovidian candlesticks, and, in general, disfigured fragments/'ruins', with their ties to Mandelshtamiam *toska po mirovoi kul'ture* [nostalgia for world culture], the last frontier of furniture, particles of dust, and of decultured 'matter as such';[12] and instead of a Russian Mnemosyne as the mother of prosodic form (the blank verse of 'Odissei Telemaku'), an English-language understanding of hexameter, but one whose ears, significantly, were once Russian.[13] It is this Brodsky, then, who starts with the words,

Give me another life, and I'll be singing
in Cafe Rafaello. Or simply sitting
there. Or standing there, as furniture in the corner,
in case that life is a bit less generous than the former.

What, now that we have come this far, could they possibly mean?
To begin with, that the poet knows his days are numbered but
that were he to be granted a stay of execution ('another life'), he
would nevertheless choose to return to these familiar surroundings and to his role as singer.[14] Singing and returning, taken
together, imply the notion of rhyme, or poetic echo. The opening two lines are, for this reader, terribly poignant and already
storing up a lifetime of meaning because they implicate a return
as inanimate matter – language – even as they hint at, with the
'falling-off' of their repeated enjambments ('singing/in' and 'sitting/
there') and the insufficiency of their metrical stresses (5 instead
of the soon-to-be-established hexametric 6, with only 4 realized
in l. 2),[15] the arrival of death itself. So painful is it for this poet to
get a full 'breath', so weak is this heart that skips beats, that by
the time his language stabilizes into a pattern (l. 4),[16] 'he' will no
longer be there. He will, instead, with the help of the caesural
(i.e. temporally refining) 'or's, be turning into something, or some
thing: from 'singing' poet, to 'sitting' bystander, to furniture 'standing' in the corner. Thus, the 'another life', or life-after-death, may
not be in anything resembling human form – in this sense, it
may be 'less generous than the former'.
     The next stanza projects the poet's new status as 'dead-wood'
into the future:

Yet partly because no century from now on will ever manage
without caffeine or jazz, I'll sustain this damage,
and through my cracks and pores, varnish and dust all over,
observe you, in twenty years, in your full flower.

It is important that as Brodsky is saying goodbye to his daughter,
he is doing so in terms of a new-world urban culture that he has
made his own and that is hers by birthright – New York, a cafe
atmosphere, the stimulation of caffeine, the improvisation of jazz.
This is a culture that, for better or worse, does not look back ('no
century from now on') and seems to thrive on free and open
forms. What is left out of course is the dialogue between father

and daughter that will never take place. For what possible need could there be for poetry, for Mnemosyne and her prosodic memory bank, in this atmosphere? The 'damage' here is thus not only to the eventual petrification of the poet's memory as man and father, but to his language, which is not 'native', not completely 'fluent'. It, Brodsky's English-language verse, is in some crucial sense inorganic: it will have to strain through the wages of time and a palpable artificiality, 'through my cracks and pores, varnish and dust all over', with their fusion of human and inhuman wounds, in order to be present at the very organic blossoming of the daughter's young adulthood ('in your full flower'). Given all this, how is it then that the poet will not only not mind that he has died but that he has become furniture, and neglected, if not downright abused, furniture at that?

At this point, it might be helpful to recall that Brodsky completed several essays at the same time he wrote 'To My Daughter', all of which shed considerable light on this and the following quatrains.[17] Of these, perhaps the long Hardy piece, 'Wooing the Inanimate', is the most germane. Hardy turns out to be a remarkably congenial figure to Brodsky, and the fact that the latter was thinking about this 'pre-modern' near the time of his death is by no means coincidental. Hardy's status as autodidact, along with his compensatory passion for reading Greek and Roman classics, were definitely Brodsky's.[18] So too were the 'predominance [in Hardy] of the rational over emotional immediacy', the 'practiced self-deprecation', the 'abhorre[nce] [of] the smooth line' together with the 'crabby syntax', the interest in the formal qualities of verse,[19] the linking of a poem's 'length' with its 'breath', the notion 'that language flows into the human domain from the realm of nonhuman truths and dependencies, that it is ultimately the voice of inanimate matter', the 'general stylistic nonchalance' (definitely felt in 'To My Daughter') and love of paradox, and perhaps most of all the courageous insistence on 'a full look at the worst'.[20] Add to this the facts that Hardy married for a second time late in life and that his place in the tradition – as poet rather than as prose writer – has never been properly understood, and we begin to see why Brodsky, the Poet Laureate whose reputation in the anglophone world is at best mixed, was so taken with him precisely at this juncture.[21]

Interestingly, however, the parallels do not stop at this level of abstraction. The last Hardy poem that Brodsky discusses is

'Afterwards'. The teacher here has presumably saved the best for last: it is this poem, written near the end of Hardy's life, that serves as a kind of *'exegi monumentum'* – what will be left behind after the poet is gone. Hardy has mapped his absence onto the four seasons in their natural habitats (Hardy was as much a nature poet as Brodsky was urban), each presented in a quatrain that ends (both Hardy and Brodsky are famous for their 'punch lines') with an enigmatic statement about how this disappearance might be registered as either meaning or non-meaning. The 'overall sensation', as Brodsky says, is suffused with the 'future perfect tense'.[22] But it is Brodsky's comments on the interrelationship of form to meaning that is most apposite to our discussion of 'To My Daughter':

> These twenty hexametric lines are the glory of English poetry, and they owe all that they've got to hexameter.[23] The good question is to what does hexameter itself owe its appearance here, and the answer is so that the old man can breathe more easily. Hexameter is here not for its epic or by the same classical token elegiac connotations but for its trimeter-long, inhale-exhale properties. On the subconscious level, this comfort translates into the availability of time, into a generous margin. Hexameter, if you will, is a moment stretched, and with every next word Thomas Hardy in 'Afterwards' stretches it even further.[24]

This gloss on 'Afterwards', is, I submit, the point of departure for Brodsky's poem, or vice versa: either way, Brodsky was thinking about Hardy's death-defying hexameters set in nature as he devised his own set in a Manhattan coffee house. The 'generous margin' that the hexameters give is precisely what is needed *in case that life is a bit less generous than the former*. They are the breath the (prematurely) 'old man' in Brodsky is looking for. That Hardy's, and English-language verse's, hexameters rhyme, while their Russian counterparts do not, shows Brodsky making the bold (that is, self-estranging) gesture of immortalizing himself in a formal pattern that was not his to begin with.[25] Everything he says about the formal character of Hardy's 'autoelegy' could be said about his own: 'the stressed words here are two and three syllables long', 'the unstressed syllables play the rest of these words down with the air of a postscript or an afterthought', the caesuras are 'bravely shifted', etc.[26] In fact, 'Afterwards', with 'all its peregrination of stresses', its 'self-referential metaphor' of 'an interrupted yet resuming sound', and its 'thirst for the inanimate', could be called an extended rhyme partner to 'To My Daughter'.[27] And as strange as it may sound, 'Give me another life, and I'll be singing / in Cafe Rafaello' is a kind of translation, transposed into Brodsky's new world idiom, of the late Victorian 'When the Present has latched its postern behind my tremulous stay', the first line of 'Afterwards'.

With this lengthy aside, we are now ready for the third stanza of Brodsky's poem:

> On the whole, bear in mind that I'll be around. Or rather,
> that an inanimate object might be your father,
> especially if the objects are older than you, or larger.
> So keep an eye on them always, for they will no doubt
>   judge you.

One might not make so much of the formal aspects of Brodsky's verse here if he himself had not drawn attention to similar issues in Frost and Hardy. In the entire poem, there are only three lines (1, 2 and 10) in which the number of metrical stresses is fewer than 6 (the hexametric expectation). The line 'that an inanimate object might be your father' is one of them: _ _ _ * _ _ * _ _ * _ * _. Indeed, in this line not only are the metrical stresses fewer (5, with the first being omitted), but the actual number of fulfilled ictuses (4) is fewer still, making this, along with line 2, the least stressed, least 'hexametrically felt' section of the poem. Why? Because these are the parts of the poem where the theme of metamorphosis – man/father to furniture/inanimate object versus child/daughter to 'in full flower' – comes most palpably to the surface, where the father reaches out to the daughter first from 'this side' of the change, i.e. as he senses the 'petrification' coming on, then from the 'far side', after he has already become the inanimate object and is no longer recognizable, except in the 'wooden' language itself.[28] As Brodsky says at the end of the Hardy essay, in a statement repeated verbatim in 'A Cat's Meow': 'language is the inanimate's first line of information about itself, *released to the animate*.'[29] If the daughter would like to know who the father was and where 'he' is now, she should ponder these lines.[30] For he is passing on to her what might be termed the 'long view',

the sense that it is not we who judge and possess the world
('things'), but the other way around ('for they will no doubt judge
you'). 'To put it perhaps less polemically', concludes Brodsky in
'A Cat's Meow', 'language is a diluted aspect of matter. By mani-
pulating it into a harmony or, for that matter, disharmony, a poet
– by and large unwittingly – negotiates himself into the domain
of pure matter – or, if you will, of pure time – faster than can be
done in any other line of work.'[31] This is what the poet means
when he says, in his typical offhand way (e.g. 'on the whole'),
that he will 'be around'. Why 'judge you' is the only non-rhyme
in the poem is a tantalizing puzzle. My guess is that while inanimate matter, including the particles that were once her father,
will one day judge Anna Maria Alexandra, the speaker of these
lines cannot yet, while he is still alive, include her in this ontological echo-chamber, where birth inevitably leads to its rhyme
partner, physical dissolution and death. That is not yet think-
able, and thus she, so animate and vulnerable, is not yet part of
this process. The judgement that is literally in the phrase has
not been, as it were, poeticized – its clock has not begun ticking.

Brodsky ends his poem with the self-deprecating wit that has
always been his special signature as a poet. Hardy's 'Afterwards'
concluded with lines invoking one of Brodsky's favourites, John
Donne and his famous 'and therefore never send to know for
whom the bell tolls; it tolls for thee':

> And will any say when my bell of quittance is heard in the
>   gloom,
>   And a crossing breeze cuts a pause in its outrollings,
> Till they rise again, as they were a new bell's boom,
>   'He hears it not now, but used to notice such things'?

The question in Hardy shows his irony, his pessimism, his willingness to take, in his phrase, 'a full look at the worst'. The bell
is, to repeat, the 'self-referential metaphor', the notion of 'interrupted yet resuming sound', that is the poet's principal legacy –
his poetry itself. But will anyone notice the bells' tolling, and if
they do, will they link them with the consciousness that first
pondered them and gave them verbal form? Brodsky was clearly
a reader who heard the tolling of Hardy's bells, and so now he
looks for an analogous listener in his own posterity:

Love those things anyway, encounter or no encounter.
Besides, you may still remember a silhouette, a contour,
while I'll lose even that, along with the other luggage.
Hence, these somewhat wooden lines in our common
     language.

The Hardian irony is there, the sense that what the poet was as
a human being and what he lived for could possibly be lost entirely
– no one may notice the sounding bells that were his consciousness.[32] This inanimate-to-animate encounter with his beloved
offspring may, after all, not take place, since there may not be
enough left of 'him' – or the particles that were once him, the
'even that' – to register her animation on his total lack of it. But
despite all that, he urges gratitude and willing sacrifice: 'Love
those things *anyway*.' Her remembering, if she can manage it after
all the years, would be a return on the level of life (her domain):
the 'silhouette' or 'contour' of a small child's murky memories
of a departed father. His return, however, is the more heroic,
since he knows beforehand that he will have lost everything and
have joined ontological forces with his final rhyme pair: luggage/
language. Still, he celebrates. The 'hence' is the 'explanation' we
have been waiting for. His response to becoming 'luggage' is the
slightest shift of breath, and the last word – 'language'. The puns,
the ability of the words to say two or more things at once, in
'these somewhat *wooden* lines' and 'in our *common* language' give
the reader parsing them after the poet's death the feeling that
he is still with us. For these lines *are* wooden, in the sense that
they are intentionally flat (unlyrical) and at the same time they
are not: their lack is full of love, pain, feeling. The joke at his
own expense makes the wood almost organic, as though it were
the tree, altogether innocent, before it has been converted into
the rood of time.[33] By the same token, the language is common,
as in shared, and also common, as in maximally 'undistinguished'
(Brodsky may have put these feelings differently in Russian), but
all the same it is highly *uncommon* – this willingness to shed oneself
in order to (in various senses) 'become' oneself. It is on this note
that the last line of the poem returns to the first ('I'll be singing'),
and the tolling bell-cum-woodwind is heard by posterity, and the
'contrary to fact' quality of Brodsky's metaphorical thinking may
be, in the end, a 'matter of fact', may be, for all we know, right.

254 Joseph Brodsky# Notes

1. See Yurii M. Lotman, *The Structure of the Artistic Text* (Ann Arbor: Michigan Slavic Contributions, 1977) p. 45.
2. Joseph Brodsky, *On Grief and Reason: Essays* (New York: Farrar, Straus & Giroux, 1995) p. 310.
3. After its initial appearance in *TLS*, 'To My Daughter' was then collected in Brodsky's book of verse *So Forth: Poems*, published posthumously in 1996 by Farrar, Straus & Giroux (New York).
4. *On Grief and Reason*, pp. 315, 333, 85, 313. Cf. similar remarks by Brodsky in his first book of essays *Less than One: Selected Essays* (New York: Farrar, Straus & Giroux, 1986): 'This is also why her [Akhmatova's] verses are to survive whether published or not: because of the prosody, because they are charged with time in both these senses. They will survive because language is older than the state and because prosody always survives history' (p. 52); 'Writing is literally an existential process; it uses thinking for its own ends, it consumes notions, themes, and the like, not vice versa. What dictates a poem is the language, and this is the voice of the language, which we know under the nicknames of Muse and Inspiration' (p. 125).
5. *On Grief and Reason*, p. 109.
6. Again, these thoughts are by no means new for Brodsky and have been repeated often in *Less than One*, *On Grief and Reason*, and in numerous uncollected essays, reviews, and interviews. See, e.g., *Less than One*, p. 123: '[Poetry] is spirit seeking flesh but finding words. In the case of Mandelshtam, the words happened to be those of the Russian language.'
7. My comments here owe much to the discussion in chapter two of Michael Wachtel, *The Sense of Meter: A Pragmatic Approach to the Evolution of Russian Verse* (Cambridge University Press, forthcoming).
8. Cf. Brodsky's statement that as an artist he has set himself the goal of 'trying to see how inhuman [he] can become and still remain a human being' ('The Acceleration of the Poet', with Peter Forbes, *Poetry Review*, vol. 78 [1988] no. 1, p. 4).
9. In this respect, he has, as it were, turned his life into a metaphor for metaphorical thinking, by which I mean nothing postmodern, but simply that he has, by his own example, personalized and heroicized the very impersonality of language. Here too he has remained a kind of 'Old Testament' son: cf. the Isaac of his great early long poem *Isaak i Avraam*. The poet is tested by a Yahweh, the Yahweh of language, who is not a loving parent and has not made man in his own image, but has given him, in the wilderness of an arbitrary world order, speech.
10. See 'Sreten'e' [Nunc Dimittis] (1972) and discussion in David Bethea, *Joseph Brodsky and the Creation of Exile* (Princeton University Press, 1994) pp. 166–73.
11. This does not mean, by the way, that Brodsky denies his heroes (Mandelshtam, Akhmatova, Tsvetaeva, Auden, etc.) the possibility of inspiring lives; always the contrarian, he simply does not want that criterion (an uplifting biography that is read together with one's

works) applied to himself. See, for example, his comments in his Nobel speech: 'It is precisely their [the "heroes" mentioned above] lives, no matter how tragic and bitter they were, that make me often – evidently, more than I ought – regret the passage of time' (Lev Loseff and Valentina Polukhina (eds), *Brodsky's Poetics and Aesthetics* [Basingstoke: Macmillan, 1990] p. 1).

12. One almost imagines Brodsky, an inveterate punster, reprising the Biblical 'flesh-become-word' as 'flesh-become-wood'.
13. Cf. the marvellous hexameters in such well-known Mandelshtam lyrics as 'Sestry – tiazhest' i nezhnost' – odinakovy vashi primety' (Sisters, heaviness and tenderness, identical are your tokens).
14. And he would do so, as we know from other works, out of gratitude. See, for example, the lines concluding the poem Brodsky wrote on the occasion of his 40th birthday: 'Chto skazat' mne o zhizni? Chto okazalas' dlinnoi. / Tol'ko s gorem ia chuvstvuiu solidarnost'. / No poka mne rot ne zabili glinoi, / iz nego razdavat'sia budet lish' blagodarnost' (*Uraniia* [Ann Arbor: Ardis, 1987] p. 177); translated by the poet as 'What should I say about life? That it's long and abhors transparence. / Broken eggs make me grieve; the omelette, though, makes me vomit. / Yet until brown clay has been crammed down my larynx, / only gratitude will be gushing from it' (*To Urania* [New York: Farrar, Straus & Giroux, 1988] p. 3).
15. Line 1:* _ _ * _ * _ * _ * _; line 2: _ _ * _ _ * _ _ * _ * _.
16. Line 3 has 6 metrical stresses, but the 5th is omitted: * _ * _ * _ * _ _ _ * _ . Thus, l. 4 is the first line with all 6 stresses fulfilled: _ * _ * _ * _ * * _ * _ * _.
17. For example, 'Wooing the Inanimate: Four Poems by Thomas Hardy' (*On Grief and Reason*, pp. 312–75) is based on a series of lectures delivered to students in a poetry course ('Subject Matter in Modern Lyric Poetry') at Mount Holyoke in fall 1994; 'On Grief and Reason' (*On Grief and Reason*, pp. 223–66), the Frost essay, was also written in 1994; 'A Cat's Meow' (*On Grief and Reason*, pp. 299–311), Brodsky's talk on the sources of creativity, was delivered at a symposium organized by the Foundation for Creativity and Leadership and held in Zermatt, Switzerland, in January 1995. 'To My Daughter', to repeat, was published in *TLS* on 2 December 1994.
18. *On Grief and Reason*, p. 321. On the autodidact's interest in 'essences' over 'actual data', with what I take to be self-reference, see *On Grief and Reason*, pp. 362–3.
19. For example, Brodsky would have felt great affinity for what he calls Hardy's 'eye/ear/mind-boggling stanzaic designs unprecedented in their never-repeating patterns' (*On Grief and Reason*, pp. 319–20).
20. Brodsky, *On Grief and Reason*, pp. 319, 322, 331, 332, 333, 348, 361.
21. The connection between 'birdlike' and 'bardlike' (Brodsky's pun) in Hardy's self-portrait gave him something in common with Mandelshtam, one of Brodsky's heroes. See, for example, ' "An aged thrush, frail, gaunt, and small, / In blast-beruffled plume" [a line from Hardy's poem 'The Darkling Thrush'] is, of course, Hardy's self-portrait. Famous for his aquiline profile, with a tuft of hair hovering above a

bald pate, he had indeed a birdlike appearance – in his old age especially, judging by the available photographs' (*On Grief and Reason*, p. 330). Cf. similar bird/bard ruminations in the Frost essay (*On Grief and Reason*, pp. 227–32). On Mandelshtam's birdlike appearance and Brodsky's use of it in his own work, see Bethea, *Joseph Brodsky*, pp. 68–70.
22. *On Grief and Reason*, pp. 367–8.
23. Calling Hardy's lines '*the* glory of English poetry' demonstrates once again how willing Brodsky was to go against critical commonplace (i.e. Hardy's stature as an interesting but not 'great' pre-modern) if the latter did not correspond to what he, as a poet, *heard and felt* (whether Hardy sounded better in English to Brodsky's russophone ears is a fascinating imponderable).
24. *On Grief and Reason*, p. 366.
25. Note that Brodsky changes Hardy's rhyme scheme (from abab to aabb) – this is his way of answering his hero's 'challenge'.
26. *On Grief and Reason*, pp. 367, 370.
27. *On Grief and Reason*, p. 373.
28. Note that Brodsky returns to the same caesural use of 'or' ('Or rather') in the preceding line (9) that he had used in the opening lines (2 and 3) of the poem.
29. *On Grief and Reason*, pp. 311, 374; my emphasis.
30. Cf. the following excerpts from 'A Cat's Meow': 'what human inquiry indeed boils down to is the animate interrogating the inanimate'; 'Ideally, perhaps, the animate and the inanimate should swap places'; 'For the only opportunity available for the animate to swap places with the inanimate is the former's physical end: when man joins, as it were, matter'; 'Why would the infinite keep an eye on the finite? Perhaps out of the infinite's nostalgia for its own finite past, if it ever had one? In order to see how the poor old finite is still faring against overwhelming odds?' (*On Grief and Reason*, pp. 304–5). 'A Cat's Meow', to repeat, was delivered as a talk in January 1995, approximately a month after the appearance of 'To My Daughter' in *TLS* (2 December 1994).
31. *On Grief and Reason*, p. 311.
32. Another potentially self-referential passage from the Hardy essay comes to mind here: 'The real seat of poetry for him [Hardy] was in his mind. . . . With Hardy, the main adventure of a poem is always toward the end. By and large, he gives you the impression that verse for him is but a means of transportation, justified and even hallowed only by the poem's destination. His ear is seldom better than his eye, but both are inferior to his mind, which subordinates them to its purposes, at times harshly' (*On Grief and Reason*, pp. 321, 329). Similar statements could easily be made about Brodsky's own English-language poetry, and he knew it. Whether the same could be said about his Russian-language poetry is more debatable, however.
33. Cf. this passage describing an American poet's attitude to time and space (as opposed to a European's) in the Frost essay ('On Grief

and Reason'): 'When an American walks out of his house and encounters a tree it is a meeting of equals. Man and tree face each other in their respective primal power, free of references: neither has a past, and as to whose future is greater, it is a toss-up. Basically, it's epidermis meeting bark' (*On Grief and Reason*, pp. 225–6). One wonders whether Brodsky could be recalling Frost and his voice as 'American' poet when he describes 'epidermis meeting bark' in the 'somewhat wooden lines' of this farewell poem.